JUDITH E. BARLOW is an Assistant Professor of English at the State University of New York at Albany, where she teaches courses in American women playwrights, modern drama, and American drama. She received her B.A. from Cornell University and her Ph.D. from the University of Pennsylvania. Dr. Barlow's publications include essays on Eugene O'Neill and Ruth Wolff, and she serves as Associate Editor of *Theatre Survey*.

PLAYS BY AMERICAN WOMEN: THE EARLY YEARS

Edited and with an introduction by
JUDITH E. BARLOW

 A BARD BOOK/PUBLISHED BY AVON BOOKS

PLAYS BY AMERICAN WOMEN: THE EARLY
YEARS is an original publication of Avon Books. This
work has never before appeared in book form.

TRIFLES is reprinted by permission of Dodd, Mead & Com-
pany, Inc. from PLAYS by Susan Glaspell. Copyright 1920 by
Dodd, Mead & Company, Inc. Copyright renewed 1948 by
Susan Glaspell.

MISS LULU BETT by Zona Gale, Copyright 1921, is reprinted
by permission of Hawthorn Books, a Division of Elsevier-
Dutton Publishing Company, Inc.

MACHINAL by Sophie Treadwell, Copyright 1928, is reprinted by permission of the copyright holder.

AVON BOOKS
A division of
The Hearst Corporation
959 Eighth Avenue
New York, New York 10019

First Bard Printing, January, 1981

Printed in the U.S.A.

CONTENTS

INTRODUCTION

SHORTLY BEFORE Anna Cora Mowatt's *Fashion* opened in New York in 1845, a local newspaper announced: "A Native American Comedy, by a Mrs. Mowatt, is rumored to be in rehearsal at the Park. We have little confidence in female dramatic productions, of the present time, but we wish the lady a happy debut although it may be in five long acts." The "lady" did indeed have a "happy debut"—*Fashion* was a critical and box office success—but the notion that women were incapable of dramatic creation lingered on. In a country that has long worshipped British and European plays at the expense of its native drama, and that has consistently relegated fine women novelists and poets to the lesser ranks of the literary pantheon, it is not surprising to find the American woman playwright viewed as a curious aberration. In fact, women have made a significant contribution to the American theater. Women writing for the stage in this country today are the heirs of a neglected but not negligible tradition.

Drama had a difficult birth in the United States. The late eighteenth and early nineteenth centuries were bad times for the theater in western Europe and England, and America was no exception. The situation here was exacerbated by a number of factors: strong Puritan and Quaker opposition to the theater, which was considered immoral and frivolous; dependence on the mother country for all forms of art; a scarcity of theaters, urban audiences and native actors; a concern with building a nation rather than a national literature. Women were particularly affected by the Puritan-Quaker attitude toward the theater. As the supposed moral guardians of society, women could scarcely be allowed to participate—on any level—in so unacceptable an activity. Mowatt, for example, read all of Shakespeare's plays when she was a child and loved presenting family theatricals, but she refused to attend the professional theater for years because a minister convinced her that the stage was the home of the devil.

Understandably, few women wrote plays during this country's early years. The first American woman playwright was probably Mercy Otis Warren, also a poet and celebrated historian. It is doubtful that her satires and tragedies were produced, but they were published and widely discussed. Her most famous plays—*The Adulateur* (1772)* and *The Group* (1775)—are clever and penetrating if heavy-handed satires of Americans with Tory leanings. Like many propaganda writers, Warren published her work anonymously, but she seems to have been particularly worried about her role as a woman writer. She wrote to her friend John Adams, "Though from the particular circumstances of our unhappy time, a little personal acrimony might be justifiable in your sex, must not the female character suffer . . . if she indulges her pen to paint in the darkest shades even those whom vice and venality have rendered contemptible?" Happily, Adams replied that such was not the case. Shortly before she died, Warren asked Adams to contradict erroneous claims that *The Group* was written by another (male) writer. He did so, and her work became an inspiration for younger women authors.

A few native actresses emerged after the Revolution, but women playwrights remained scarce. One exception was Susanna Rowson, known today for her novel *Charlotte Temple.* Rowson herself acted in her only extant play, *Slaves in Algiers,* performed in Philadelphia in 1794. Despite numerous coincidences and reunions of long-lost relatives, dramatic staples of this period, *Slaves in Algiers* is an amusing, lively, and surprisingly readable comedy. The clever heroine, Fetnah, helps instigate a slave escape and refuses to be left out of the action just because she is female. Although in her epilogue Rowson

---

* Here and following, the date in parenthesis is that of first publication or production—whichever came first.

urges women to use gentle means to control "the lordly tyrant man," she also suggests that "Women were born for universal sway,/Men to adore, be silent, and obey"— surely an advanced view for the eighteenth century.

The woman who had the greatest impact on early American drama and theater was Anna Cora Mowatt (Ritchie). Truly a Renaissance woman, Mowatt published poetry while still in her teens, then went on to write short stories, novels, plays, and magazine articles. To support herself and her bankrupt husband, she also produced what she modestly called "compilations" on such subjects as knitting, housekeeping, and etiquette. While her work is often conventional—cautionary tales about the dangers of selfishness and the virtue of sacrifice, melodramatic romances doused in tears—it is frequently original and important. From her own experience, Mowatt was keenly aware of the problems of the working woman, especially in the theater. She was also sensitive to the cultural differences between America and Europe, where she spent her early years. *Fashion* (1845) is generally considered the best nineteenth century American comedy, and her invaluable *Autobiography of an Actress* provides humorous and penetrating insights into the nineteenth century theater.

Mowatt's influence on the theater extended far beyond her writing. In June of 1845 she became a professional actress, an unprecedented move in her day. Actors and actresses were social outcasts, drawn either from the lowest classes or from the sons and daughters of those already in the profession. The magnitude of Mowatt's step can be measured by her own attitude; several years earlier she had considered a position on the stage, but she felt then that "the idea of becoming a professional actress was revolting." Instead, Mowatt gave a series of public poetry readings. After her experiences as the author of *Fashion*, however, her prejudices against the theater were gone. She became one of the very first "gentlewomen" to appear on the stage, enjoyed a successful acting career for nearly nine years, and helped modify cultural attitudes toward actresses. Mowatt even improved the quality of audiences by attracting people who had formerly scorned the theater.

Mowatt was already an experienced writer—most of her early works were published under pseudonyms—when her friend Epes Sargent suggested that she try stage comedy. Mowatt admitted that *Fashion* was not intended to be a literary masterpiece: "There were no attempts in *Fashion* at fine writing. I designed the play wholly as an *acting* comedy." She judged her audience well. The play ran to acclaim for twenty performances in New York (a long run at the time), was well received in other cities, and even found favor in England. Edgar Allan Poe, one of the few American critics who had serious reservations about the comedy, was intrigued enough to see it every night for a week and conceded that "in many respects (and those of a *telling* character) it is superior to any American play." *Fashion* has been revived throughout the nineteenth and twentieth centuries, most notably in a very successful production by the Provincetown Players in 1924. Unfortunately, revivals in this century have often used inane songs and stage tricks to make fun *of* the play instead of asking audiences to laugh *with* the play.

Fashion incorporates many conventions of the period: paper-thin stereotyped characters, including a bumbling black servant; a predictable plot replete with melodramatic curtain scenes; heavy-handed asides; and a neat moral to conclude the tale. In the nineteenth century, comedy was obliged to be what television is today—popular entertainment. Mowatt handles the required plot elements deftly, keeps the action moving at a sprightly clip, and uses her genuine, sometimes biting wit to make *Fashion* an amusing social farce. Mowatt was one of our first playwrights to deal knowledgeably with Americans' mindless worship of foreign fashion, and she is alert as well to city-dwellers' emphasis on money and appearance as status symbols. The aged hero Adam Trueman's little homilies are annoyingly condescending (especially to women), but this variation on the stock "Yankee character" of earlier drama is close to the American mythic hero. He is not only rough, rural, wise, and as honest as George Washington; he is also rich. Mowatt knew her American dream well.

Fashion's female characters are obviously stereotypes. Prudence is the man-hungry gossip; Mrs. Tiffany is the extravagant wife who nearly ruins her patient husband; Seraphina is the frivolous young belle; and Gertrude—first glimpsed in white surrounded by flowers—is the standard pure heroine. On one level, Mowatt was clearly giving her audience what they wanted and expected. She was fully aware of the insipidness of her heroine; when later asked to act the role of Gertrude, Mowatt protested that the part was dull. On another level, Mowatt was expending her caustic wit against useless high-society women who did no productive work. Her fiction shows her sympathy for women who worked hard, as she herself did. Her comedy shows her disdain for those who wasted their lives gossiping and spending money—a group Clare Boothe would satirize more acidly a century later in *The Women. Fashion* succeeds as an engaging comedy, a significant indicator of the tastes of the time, and an example of the very best the nineteenth century theater had to offer. It was liberally copied by later authors, but even Mrs. Sidney Bateman's *Self* (1856), the most competent imitation, is markedly inferior.

The second half of the nineteenth century brought little improvement in the general run of American drama. Few women chose, or had the opportunity, to write for the theater. The most popular play of the nineteenth century, and probably the most popular drama ever produced in America, was based on the work of a woman: Harriet Beecher Stowe's *Uncle Tom's Cabin*. Stowe, however, neither wrote nor authorized the dramatic adaptations of her novel, and received no royalties from the hundreds of "Tom shows" that flourished for decades.

The growing agitation for women's rights began to affect the novel at the turn of the century, but touched the theater only slightly with a small spate of pro-suffrage plays acted mainly by amateur groups. While Kate Chopin wrote *The Awakening*, the drama remained largely asleep. In both content and form, drama tends to be a conservative medium. Readers and critics are more willing to accept new ideas and daring innovations when they are safely hidden between the covers of books, to be consumed in private, than when they are presented on the public stage. American drama has tended to be particularly cautious. Although Ibsen, Shaw, and Chekhov were bringing a new seriousness to the dramas of Europe and England, few American playwrights followed their lead with socially significant plays. Feminist dramas would scarcely have appealed to the powerful male producers and conventional audiences. Possibly some women wrote plays that, privately performed or unproduced and unpublished, have been lost to future generations. It is clear, however, that most talented American women of letters wisely confined their attention to fiction and poetry.

When Virginia Frame in 1906 published an article on "Women Who Have Written Successful Plays," she came up with more than a dozen names, none familiar today. Several of the women were also novelists who adapted their own or others' fiction for the stage or composed plays rapidly "to order" for specific stars. Many playwrights listed by Frame, and by Lucy France Pierce in a similar article, wrote light domestic comedies that celebrated the virtues of family life. Typical of these is Martha Morton's *A Bachelor's Romance* (1896), which ends with more romantic pairings than an audience can easily count. Morton churned out roughly thirty plays, mostly what Pierce considers "clean" comedies. In 1906 Morton, who may well have been the first American woman to make a career of playwriting, helped found the Society of Dramatic Authors. Started by women but open to men, this group was formed because women were excluded from the American Dramatists Club, which was organized in the late nineteenth century to encourage and protect playwrights.

Significant plays, comic or otherwise, were and are the exception rather than the rule. It is not surprising that conventional comedies dominated the work of women during the first decades of this century; most plays by men were similarly shallow. Women who wanted their work accepted by producers, virtually all of whom were male, understood they must hew to the predominating cultural myths. Critics (also nearly all men) and audiences encouraged such plays as Anne Crawford Flexner's *The Marriage Game* (1913), which blamed women for all marital problems and argued that American wives were the luckiest people in the world. Clare Kummer was very adept at composing frothy social farces like *Good Gracious, Annabelle* (1916). As her successful career testifies, her fast-paced comedies found producers and appreciative audiences.

A few women playwrights dared to be different. Josephine Preston Peabody's verse drama *The Piper* (1909), an imaginative retelling of the Pied Piper story that emphasizes the joylessness of the Hamlin townspeople, won a play competition in Stratford, England. Alice Brown wrote plays in addition to novels and a biography of Mercy Otis Warren. Brown's *Joint Owners in Spain* (1913) depicts the plight of two old women fighting for their privacy and pride in a nursing home. Her *Children of Earth* beat out nearly 1700 competing scripts to win a $10,000 prize offered by producer Winthrop Ames in 1913. Although unconvincing and sentimental at times, *Children of Earth* focuses on a strong-minded woman, Mary Ellen, who resents the years she spent enslaved to her selfish father. She refuses to be used again by her greedy brother and her former suitor. Tempted to run away with a married man she loves, Mary Ellen discovers that her attachment to the man's wife is stronger than her desire for some nebulous romantic escape. In short plays like *Overtones* (1913), *The Buffer* (1916), and *Beyond* (1917), Alice Gerstenberg used imaginative techniques to portray mismatched couples yoked together by false pride, concern for the children, and economic necessity. Despite the preponderance of plays bathed in sweetness and light, a few dramas by women were beginning to treat female characters seriously and to suggest that life on the homefront might not be ideal. Predictably, none of these plays reached the stage through the usual commercial route: they were either selected as winners in contests or performed by noncommercial "little theaters."

By far the most successful American woman playwright in the early part of this century was Rachel Crothers. Crothers, a teacher of acting and herself briefly an actress, wrote dozens of plays during a career that spanned three decades. Although women have very rarely been accepted as directors in this country, Crothers directed and cast most of her own plays, often designing the sets as well. In her last creative years she had an arrangement with producer John Golden that spared her the necessity of finding a new backer for each work. Her plays were consistently popular with audiences and appeared frequently in the Burns Mantle *Best Plays* volumes.

Crothers has often been dismissed as a writer of "conventional" comedies and problem plays. To a large extent this label is justified. Her works, although filled with convincing characters and clever dialogue, are rarely technically innovative. More disappointing is her approach to her subject matter. Particularly in her later plays, written in the twenties and thirties, most difficulties are solved by the standard marital reconciliation. In her popular comedy *Nice People* (1921), flapper Teddy Gloucester's restless desire for adventure is cured by three months in the country and the love of an ex-farm boy. Lucile Lingard of *As Husbands Go* (1931) tries a flirtation in Europe and has some hopes of a singing career, but ends tearfully repentant in the arms of her stolid yet adoring husband. *Susan and God* (1937) presents a thoroughly unpleasant woman who returns from England determined to proselytize for the new religion she's found. She discovers, of course, that she doesn't want to change the world—only to reclaim the affection of her teenage daughter and alcoholic husband. "All the things I've been running away from—are the only ones I want now," she declares, and the curtain falls on the expected embrace.

Yet there is far more to Crothers than these plays suggest. Crothers once said in an interview: "With few exceptions, every one of my plays has been a social attitude toward women at the moment I wrote it. . . . I [do not] go out stalking the footsteps of woman's progress. It is something that comes to me subconsciously. I may say that I sense the trend even before I have hearsay or direct knowledge of it." However conscious her motives, Crothers did put women at the center of nearly all her plays. She also dramatized many of the problems facing women: the conflict between marriage and career; motherhood and career; the unfairness of the double standard; the loneliness of the single career woman; the hollowness of many marriages; the opposition faced by strong, successful women. *Mary the Third* (1923) debunks the marriage myth through a bitter fight between a couple whose love has turned to disappointment and resentment. Their daughter, Mary the third, is horrified by the battle she accidentally witnesses. As the play concludes Mary prepares to make the same mistake her mother did—marry an unimaginative, dull suitor. What some critics took to be a conventionally happy ending is actually a heavily ironic one. In *He and She* (1911; revised version 1920) sculptor Ann Herford gives up a commission (won in a highly competitive contest) to tend to her obnoxious teenage daughter. Contemporary audiences will agree with critic Heywood Broun, who deplored Crothers's inability to acknowledge that someone other than a mother could care for the child. But Crothers does show, particularly in the revised version, that Ann will in the future deeply resent the choice she has made. Further, through the secondary character of Ruth Creel, Crothers suggests that career rather than marriage is the better option for some women. Although like many of her generation Crothers apparently could not envision women having both successful careers and marriages, she was sensitive enough to portray the painful decisions involved.

A Man's World (1909) is one of Crothers's earliest and most daring dramas. Frank Ware is an accomplished writer, loving adoptive mother, and generous friend. A hard-working woman of talent and courage, Frank is almost the only successful artist in a house full of struggling painters, musicians, and writers. Some of these so-called friends jealously denigrate her work and presume that a man provides either her material or her inspiration. Malcolm Gaskell, whom Frank rather inexplicably loves, observes that her book is not about "social evil in the real sense" because it concerns the problems of women and "this is a man's world." His familiar comments echo criticism that Crothers herself and nearly every other woman writer has faced. The main focus of *A Man's World*, however, is not the question of women's talent but the double standard. In most previous American drama, the "fallen woman" was thoroughly punished. At best, the reward for her repentance was a swift and comforting death. Err-

ing men, on the other hand, easily won forgiveness from
their understanding mates. Crothers reverses the usual
pattern by having Frank Ware reject the excuses of her
irresponsible suitor. In the last scenes of *A Man's World*—
reminiscent of the didactic conclusions of Ibsen's problem plays—Frank repudiates Gaskell's claim that biology
determines the double standard, and condemns him for
refusing to admit that men and women share equal responsibility for their sexual activity.

Clara Oakes lacks her friend Frank's strength and ability. With compassionate understanding, Crothers drama-
tizes the plight of a woman who is not trained to do func-
tional work, not talented enough to succeed in the
competitive art world, and not attractive enough to win
a husband. Clara laments, "If I were a man—the most
insignificant little runt of a man—I could persuade some
woman to marry me—and could have a home and children and hustle for my living—and life would mean
something." According to several critics, Clara's com-
plaint struck a responsive chord in the opening-night audience.

A Man's World was not one of Crothers's most popular
plays, but it had a respectable run of seventy-one performances in New York and was generally well-received in
other cities. Some viewers, however, were upset by
Crothers's stance in this drama. A year later Augustus
Thomas's *As a Man Thinks* appeared. Obviously a response to *A Man's World* (which is specifically mentioned by a character), Thomas's play is an extended defense of the double standard. Dr. Seelig, Thomas's
raisonneur, argues that "there is a double standard of
morality because upon the golden basis of woman's virtue
rests the welfare of the world." What this means is that
women must lead spotless lives lest men fear they are not
the fathers of their children. At the end of *As a Man
Thinks* Frank Clayton, who has had at least two affairs,
forgives his wife Elinor for her sole indiscretion—that of
going alone to a man's room. Critic and theater historian
Arthur Hobson Quinn praised Thomas's play because it
"gave the answer to the sentimental discussion of the
double standard of morality which is rampant in litera-

ture." Clearly, Rachel Crothers's *A Man's World* touched a sensitive nerve in the American male.

Few women playwrights were able, as Crothers was, to arrange a profitable partnership with a commercial producer. Around the time of World War I, however, so-called "little theaters" began to spring up, providing new outlets for women's talents. Little theaters—such as the Toy Theatre in Boston, the Little Theatre in Chicago, the Washington Square Playhouse, the Provincetown Playhouse, and the Neighborhood Playhouse in New York—rejected the pallid Broadway offerings. They favored either controversial European playwrights or unknown American authors. Since women often helped found these groups, artistic decisions were not solely in the hands of powerful men whose main interest was box-office receipts. Further, because participants and playwrights were unsalaried or minimally paid, these little theaters could scarcely afford to exclude women. The most important of these theaters was the Provincetown Playhouse. During the heyday of the Provincetown, 1916–1922, roughly one-third of the plays produced were by women. Women were also actively involved in play selection and direction, as well as in the business end of the theater. Interestingly, when in later years a reorganized Provincetown seemed more concerned with commercial success than artistic experimentation, participation by women dropped sharply.

The Provincetown is primarily famous today for giving Eugene O'Neill his start, but it also gave impetus to several woman authors. Some of these went on to successful writing careers in other genres, perhaps because they realized the obstacles involved in finding sympathetic commercial producers and wider audiences for their theatrical works. Edna St. Vincent Millay acted with the group and contributed *The Princess Marries the Page* (1918) in addition to her powerful anti-war drama *Aria da Capo* (1919). Plays by Djuna Barnes and Edna Ferber shared the Provincetown stage with pieces by such now-forgotten women as Neith Boyce, Louise Bryant, and Rita Wellman.

The most important woman playwright nurtured by the

Provincetown was Susan Glaspell. She was considered,
along with O'Neill, one of the group's two major
"discoveries." Born and raised in Iowa, Glaspell was a
reporter and published novelist before she and her husband George Cram Cook helped start the Provincetown
Players. Glaspell wrote or co-authored nearly a dozen
plays for the group, sometimes directing and acting in her
own work. Her first play, written with Cook in 1914, is
a mildly amusing spoof of Freudianism entitled *Sup-
pressed Desires*. Perhaps because Glaspell was not obli-
gated to please Broadway patrons, her plays are more innovative than Crothers's. Once she broke with the Provincetown Players, however, she turned mainly to fiction
writing. One exception is *Alison's House* (1930), a
competent but sentimental drama loosely based on the
family of Emily Dickinson. It won Glaspell a Pulitzer
Prize, possibly because of its conventionality.

Glaspell is not a consistently feminist playwright, but
her most provocative works investigate issues crucial to
women. *Women's Honor* (1918) tells the old story of a
man accused of murder who refuses to exonerate himself
by naming the married woman who could give him an
alibi. He is visited in jail by a variety of women—such as
"The Cheated One" and "The Motherly One"—who vol-
unteer to pose as the unnamed mistress. Despite jarring
bits of pointless humor, the play becomes a penetrating
discussion of women's honor: "The Cheated One" claims
that her life was ruined by a man who insisted on marrying her to protect her reputation; "The Scornful One"
points out that "women's honor" is a meaningless term
devised by men for their own benefit and glorification.
Inheritors (1921) is an insightful look at the decline of
liberalism through several generations of two families.
While her friends and relatives compromise their beliefs,
Madeline Morton risks jail rather than renounce the
ideals she has inherited from her grandfather. Claire
Archer in *The Verge* (1921) focuses her attention on a
collection of plants she is trying to coax into radically new
forms, plants that symbolize her own aspirations to escape from her biological and cultural heritage. *The Verge*
is at times muddled—Claire's confused desperation spills
over into the play as a whole—but it is an ambitious

drama, a compelling portrait of a woman driven to madness in her efforts to escape the socially-prescribed female roles of wife, mother, and mistress.

Trifles (1916) is Glaspell's most famous play, a splendid drama that has been widely translated. It has become a classic example of near-perfect short play construction. Glaspell records in *The Road to the Temple,* her biography of her husband George Cram Cook, that the play was written when Cook (without her knowledge) announced a new play of hers for the next Provincetown bill. Glaspell vainly protested that she had never studied dramatic writing, then sat herself down in front of their tiny wharf stage. She recalls:

> After a time the stage became a kitchen—a kitchen there all by itself. I saw just where the stove was, the table, and the steps going upstairs. Then the door at the back opened, and people all bundled up came in—two or three men, I wasn't sure which, but sure enough about the two women, who hung back, reluctant to enter that kitchen. When I was a newspaper reporter out in Iowa, I was sent down-state to do a murder trial, and I never forgot going into the kitchen of a woman locked up in town. I had meant to do it as a short story, but the stage took it for its own, so I hurried in from the wharf to write down what I had seen.

In a mere ten days *Trifles,* which Glaspell later turned into the short story "A Jury of Her Peers," was finished. It was performed by the Provincetown Players that summer, then moved to the Washington Square Playhouse in the fall.

In *Trifles* Glaspell introduced a technique she was to use again in *Bernice* (1919) and *Alison's House*: leaving the main female character off stage. Both Bernice and Alison are dead when the plays open so that Glaspell can explore their influence on surviving relatives and friends. In *Trifles* Minnie Wright remains unseen both to prevent giving her particularity (she is all women trapped in loveless marriages to harsh men) and to focus attention on

Mrs. Hale's and Mrs. Peters's growing empathy for the woman accused of killing her husband. Although the prevailing cultural myth speaks of men being "trapped in marriage," plays and novels by women consistently portray the wife as the imprisoned partner. Minnie was a bird trapped in a bleak farmhouse cage, even her singing stifled by her taciturn and brutal husband. With wit, economy, and convincingly understated dialogue, Glaspell deftly contrasts male and female perspectives. The men look for some overt, shocking evidence of motive; the women notice Minnie's despair in the uneven stitching on a quilt. Finally, Mrs. Peters and Mrs. Hale develop a sense of community with the imprisoned wife. They realize both the similarities in their situations and their own crime: refusal to help a fellow-prisoner in need.

Susan Glaspell continued writing plays at the Provincetown for six years after *Trifles,* but women who sought commercial outlets for their work fared less well. With the passage of women's suffrage in 1920, demand for equal rights diminished and the stage became, if possible, even more conservative. Women became increasingly the target of men's wrath. Sidney Howard's *The Silver Cord* (1926) brought to the stage America's favorite literary caricature: the destructively possessive mother. The dangerous wife who cares more for home than husband appeared in full flower in George Kelly's *Craig's Wife* (1925). While both authors show some understanding of the female characters' plight, the plays are primarily indictments of women who, in Walter Craig's words, dare to try controlling "the very destiny of a man." Some women playwrights also capitalized on female stereotypes, most notably Anne Nichols in *Abie's Irish Rose* (1922). Aptly characterized by a critic as a "masterpiece of mediocrity," this comedy features one overbearing female hypochondriac (Mrs. Cohen) and one helpless young wife (Rose Mary), as well as a stage Jew and a stage Irishman. Adoring audiences kept *Abie's Irish Rose* running for years.

Despite the prevailing mood in the country, a few new women playwrights emerged in the twenties to counter, or at least modify, the reigning stage clichés about women. Zoë Akins, Maurine Watkins, and Zona Gale were among the most successful. Akins's works—including *Déclassée* (1919) and *Daddy's Gone A-Hunting* (1921)—tend to be melodramas that focus on the sufferings of women who veer from the straight-and-narrow, although Akins presents the victims' plight with sensitivity. In the next decade she won a Pulitzer Prize for her adaptation of Edith Wharton's *The Old Maid* (1935), a depressing tale of a ruined life in which the chief villain is the old maid's jealous cousin Delia. As Clare Boothe discovered with *The Women* (1936), plays that show women harming each other can do well at the box office. Maurine Watkins took a different tack in her hilarious *Chicago* (1926), later turned into a popular musical and a film entitled *Roxie Hart*. Watkins's comedy about *"the prettiest woman ever charged with murder in Chicago"* includes Roxie Hart, who has callously shot her lover, and an array of similar female killers. Watkins, however, is not only accurately and wittily spoofing reporters who turn murderers into madonnas; she is also poking fun at all people who insist on seeing women through the gauze of their own fantasies. The cold-blooded Roxie easily convinces the gentlemen of the jury that she is a poor abandoned mother-to-be who wanted nothing more out of life than to stay home and raise a family. Roxie wins acquittal, of course, as well as a ten-week contract on the vaudeville circuit.

Zona Gale, like Susan Glaspell, was a midwesterner who began as a newspaper reporter and fiction writer before turning to drama. Most of Gale's few plays were adapted from her novels, which she continued to write throughout her career. Unlike Glaspell, Gale returned to the midwest after a brief sojourn in New York, becoming a prominent force in Wisconsin politics. Despite her mother's advice to "let that mess of women alone," Gale was an active champion of women's suffrage, a participant in the Women's Peace Party, a drafter of and campaigner for the 1923 Wisconsin Equal Rights Law, and a frequent speaker on women's issues.

Gale first gained fame with her "Friendship Village" stories, a series of tales and novels set (like most of her work) in the middle west. As the name "Friendship Village" implies, these charming but superficial stories painted the small town as a place where neighborliness overrides the occasional problems of prejudice and provincialism. Her best works, however, including *Birth* (novel, 1918; adapted into the play *Mister Pitt* in 1925) and *Faint Perfume* (novel, 1923; play, 1934), strip off the facade of small town geniality to show the underlying dullness and petty tyrannies. In company with Sherwood Anderson, Sinclair Lewis, and Edgar Lee Masters, Gale exposed the dreary core of the middle America so many idealized.

Gale's short novel *Miss Lulu Bett* was immediately successful when it appeared in 1920. Encouraged by producer Brock Pemberton, Gale spent less than two weeks turning out the dramatic version, which eventually made her the first of the small group of women to win a Pulitzer Prize for drama. Gale told an interviewer that even while writing the novel *Miss Lulu Bett*, she felt the material was more suitable for the stage.

Ironically, *Miss Lulu Bett* was presented at Sing Sing Prison the night before its Broadway opening. A performance of the play inaugurated a portable stage given to Sing Sing by impresario David Belasco. One wonders whether the inmates empathized with Lulu, a woman imprisoned in the home of her despotic brother-in-law. Unskilled and penniless, Lulu is also victim of the common myth that women are too weak to work—although she does the arduous chores for her sister Ina's demanding family. Ina adapts to her situation by selfishly enjoying her few wifely prerogatives and siding with her husband against her sister. At once a caricature and a realistic figure, Dwight Deacon is a smug bundle of clichés who effectively spoils what little pleasure the women have. He is condescending to everyone, including the sardonic Mrs. Bett, a widow who grudgingly accepts her dependence on her son-in-law but retaliates with caustic comments about the "cockroach" her daughter married. Lulu and Mrs. Bett are women without husbands or money, hence valueless in the eyes of the world. Lulu shares this low estimation of herself, gratefully accepting the first man who cares more for her than for her meat pies.

Miss Lulu Bett was greeted with mixed reviews by New York critics, several of whom complained that the play was "undramatic." Gale's deviation from traditional dramatic structure is, in fact, one of the play's virtues. The repetitive dialogue ·and action—including Gale's masterful stroke of beginning two successive scenes with almost identical arguments—make this satirical comedy surprisingly modern. The unhappy reviewers were apparently not prepared in 1920 for the banal conversations that would later become the hallmark of much European and British drama. On tour the play received almost unanimous raves, partly because out-of-town critics are less demanding than those in New York, but also because many tour reviewers immediately recognized Gale's accurate portrait of small town family life.

At the conclusion of the novel version of *Miss Lulu Bett*, Lulu discovers that her marriage to Ninian Deacon is invalid. She then weds another suitor, Neil Cornish. Gale rejected this ending for the play, believing that two marriages in two hours was more than an audience would accept. She composed instead an open ending, which several critics compared to the conclusion of Ibsen's *A Doll's House*. Shortly after *Miss Lulu Bett* premiered, however, Gale substituted still another, far more conventional, denouement. While there are dramatic virtues in the new last act (unity of place, for example, is preserved), it is clear that Gale capitulated to popular tastes and betrayed her original intentions by inserting a more easily acceptable conclusion. According to newspaper reports, reports so similar one suspects they are based on a single press release, Gale rewrote the play because numerous viewers complained that the original open ending was unsatisfying. Audiences were apparently pleased with the new last act; ticket sales increased and the play was assured a long run. More sensitive critics, however, condemned the watered-down version. Ludwig Lewisohn complained that "the significance and strength of the dramatic action [were] sacrificed at one blow." Heywood Broun, who wisely pointed out that the new conclusion was not as "happy" as audiences supposed, argued that placing conventional endings on plays like *Miss Lulu Bett* "seems about as wise as demanding feathers on the tail of everything, from a tomtit to a mountain lion." Gale herself jumped into the fray, insisting that the revised ending was less "artistic" but did not do violence to the characters she had created. To a certain extent she is right, but the revised ending does present Lulu in a substantially different light. Gale, obviously uneasy with her revision, included both versions of the conclusion when the play was published. Both endings are published in the present volume as well; readers may see how box-office pressures affected even so determined and outspoken a woman as Zona Gale.

The vast majority of women playwrights in the early part of this century, like most of their male counterparts, used basically realistic dramatic forms. The more adventurous, however, chose experimental modes. Sophie Treadwell was one of them. Born and raised in California, she had even more extensive reporting experience than Glaspell and Gale. Treadwell, who ignored the limitations usually imposed on women journalists, interviewed Pancho Villa in Mexico and went to Europe to cover World War I. Her dramatic canon includes *Gringo* (1922), partly based on her Mexican experiences, and a play about Edgar Allan Poe entitled *Plumes in the Dust* (1936). Treadwell's last Broadway production was the largely autobiographical *Hope for a Harvest* (1941), a compelling study of cultural change set in her native California. The central character, Carlotta Thatcher, refuses to capitulate to the prejudices of her family and friends, and succeeds in imbuing some of them with her own courageous determination. In an interview Treadwell admitted that she "felt awfully bitter" about the lukewarm critical reception of *Hope for a Harvest.* "It's easier to do novels," she added, and continued writing fiction long after she had given up creating for the professional stage.

When *Machinal* (the title is French for "mechanical") appeared in 1928, nearly everyone assumed that it was a dramatization of the famous Ruth Snyder–Judd Gray case in which the two were convicted of murdering her husband. Treadwell was unquestionably familiar with the celebrated trial; it dominated the headlines in 1927, and there are several similarities (the method of murder, for example) between the case and Treadwell's play. However, Treadwell's work, only tangentially inspired by the Snyder–Gray case, is neither a docudrama nor a melodrama. Treadwell has instead used expressionistic techniques like those in Elmer Rice's *The Adding Machine* (1923) to create a modern parable. "An ordinary young woman," not unusually intelligent or attractive, Helen Jones lives in a mechanized, money-oriented world. Treadwell takes her through the stages of Everywoman: work in a boring office, marriage to a boss she despises but who can offer her and her mother financial security ("he's a Vice-President—of course he's decent," her mother insists), a motherhood that oppresses her, and a lover who uses and abandons her. In her desperate attempt to be free, Helen succeeds only in destroying herself. The expressionistic form—flat characters, repetitive dialogue and action, numerous short scenes, harsh audio effects, confusion of inner and outer reality—is the perfect medium for presenting the life of a young woman who asks an impersonal society "Is nothing mine?"

The villain of the piece is not Helen's materialistic husband, whose smugness, selfishness, and banal jokes remind one of Gale's Dwight Deacon. Nor is it the cavalier lover (played in the original production by Clark Gable) who considers her just another conquest while she sees him as a romantic escape. Rather, the villain is a rigid society that has no room for human feelings and dreams, especially those of women. Like Ninian Deacon, Treadwell's Young Man has the freedom to travel, to find adventure, a freedom the women never know. George Jones has adapted well to his soulless existence, and he has the money and position to enforce his wishes within the system—a system created by men like him. Throughout the play, Treadwell portrays Helen facing a phalanx of male characters with the power to determine her life. Helen's only alternative, as she herself recognizes, is constantly to "submit."

Sophie Treadwell gained almost instant fame with the production of *Machinal*, a drama widely praised by critics who compared it favorably to Theodore Dreiser's *An American Tragedy* in theme and Elmer Rice's *The Adding Machine* in technique. Brooks Atkinson called it "an illuminating, measured drama such as we are not likely to see again," and other reviewers concurred. Yet despite its initial success, numerous European performances, revivals and a television production, both the play and its author are largely unknown today. One looks long and hard in histories of American drama for more than passing references to them. *The Adding Machine* is regularly taught in American drama classes; *Machinal* is forgotten.

Sophie Treadwell has company in anonymity. Rachel Crothers's plays are only beginning to be resurrected, and Susan Glaspell is still best known as a discoverer of Eugene O'Neill. Every undergraduate has heard of Sinclair Lewis and Sherwood Anderson, but how many know of Zona Gale, can name one of her novels or dramas? Even more than authors like Kate Chopin and Mary Wilkins Freeman—women ignored by literary historians who traced America's major fiction heritage through an all-male line from Cooper to Mailer—female playwrights have been disregarded and dismissed. One reason for this anthology is to bring together works that (with the exception of *Trifles*) have either been long out of print or are available only in large expensive anthologies. The five plays included here share the limitations of their eras, but surely *Trifles*, *Machinal*, and even *Miss Lulu Bett* are among the best plays written in this country. *Fashion* is our finest nineteenth century comedy, and all are important cultural documents that deserve preservation. All five were well received by audiences and many critics when first produced. Their authors' gender and dramatic emphases, rather than the quality of the writing, have unfairly consigned these plays to obscurity.

Despite changes in theatrical tastes, productions of *Trifles*, *Miss Lulu Bett*, and *Machinal* would most likely find receptive audiences today. There is little in technique or theme to date *Trifles*, and Gale's picture of domestic tyranny in *Miss Lulu Bett* is current in substance if not in minor details. Expressionism may have gone out of style, but the mechanistic world Treadwell vividly portrayed is indeed our own. The virtues of Crothers's solid problem plays are slowly being rediscovered, as evidenced in recent revivals of *He and She*. The bolder *A Man's World* merits equal attention. *Fashion*, shorn of the stage gimmicks and musical trappings imposed by recent adaptors, is a stage-worthy period comedy.

Why have plays by male authors survived while those of women have been relegated to theatrical footnotes? What distinguishes the work of American women playwrights from that of men? The differences have little to do with mastery of stage technique or choice of dramatic styles, as the wide range of plays included here testifies. When Walter Prichard Eaton complains that *A Man's World* "just misses the masculinity of structure," one blinks in astonishment. The structural problems of *A Man's World* have nothing to do with gender. The plays by women are very similar in form to those composed by men at the same time. It is true that women rarely set their plays on battlefields or baseball diamonds, as men sometimes do; most plays by women are set in homes. Interestingly, American men playwrights—including Eugene O'Neill, Clifford Odets, Arthur Miller, Tennessee Williams, and Edward Albee—have, to a greater extent than their European counterparts, also focused their attention on the family. Women writers are not unique in taking this building block of American society as their primary subject matter.

In a particularly condescending essay written in 1937, entitled "When Ladies Write Plays," Joseph Mersand asserts that women playwrights "rarely philosophize, their social consciousness is rarely apparent; they don't preach sermons; they don't raise you to the heights of aesthetic emotions." He concludes, "If it is the privilege or the weakness of the daughters of Eve to write faithfully of simple things, our women have availed themselves zealously of that privilege." Mersand's attitude, which directly echoes the scornful view Malcolm Gaskell takes of Frank Ware's work in *A Man's World,* is unfortunately common in much literary criticism. Men's blind dismissal of women's work as "trifles" is wonderfully dramatized in Glaspell's play of that name. Women do approach the subject matter of their plays differently than men do. Women almost invariably put female characters at the heart of their dramas, with the male characters less fully realized. Female dramatists emphasize the concerns and experiences of women: the oppressiveness of husbands and household duties, women's economic dependence, the difficulties of working women. Whether or not they write about the family, the playwrights represented here are sensitive to how society affects women. When Elmer Rice depicted the consequences of a mechanized society, he chose as his protagonist a male office worker; when Sophie Treadwell portrayed a similar world, she formed her drama around a young woman. When Rachel Crothers attacked the double standard, Augustus Thomas rushed to its defense. The plays in this volume reflect women's perspectives on such wide-ranging issues as the unfairness of moral codes, the inequalities of capitalism, and the stifling nature of many marriages. These are scarcely "simple things"; the critic, not the women's dramas, lacks "social consciousness."

With the exception of *Fashion* (a play deliberately tailored to nineteenth century tastes), the works included here all, in one way or another, protest against the positions women are forced to occupy. Yet most plays by women in the early years of this century are tame comedies that support the status quo. Indeed, none of the playwrights represented in this anthology could be called consistently feminist in her writings. It is difficult to believe that women so unconventional in their lives (and surely being a dramatist is unconventional for a woman) could be quite so conservative in their views. In an essay on Lorraine Hansberry, poet Adrienne Rich notes that "censors are interior when we are writing in the face of that judgment and culture of white males, that cultural jury which presumes to set standards, to determine whose experience counts, which themes are 'universal' and which 'parochial,' to define the literary canon, to define 'greatness' itself." Even before the women took their plays to the men who dominated production, direction, and criticism in the theater, they surely faced such internal censorship.

There are other reasons why women in this country have never had the impact on drama that they have had on the novel, poetry, and nonfiction. In 1973, forty-five years after the last play in this volume was written, the *New York Times* interviewed several women dramatists for an article entitled "Where Are the Women Playwrights?" Gretchen Cryer spoke of the guilt she felt in neglecting her children while attending rehearsals of her new play. Unlike a novel, a drama cannot be "completed" at home. A playwright must attend rehearsals to insure that the play on the stage accurately reflects the play on the page. Women, not men, have been brought up to feel guilty about shirking familial responsibilities. Mowatt, Crothers, Glaspell, Gale, Treadwell (not to mention Lillian Hellman, America's most outstanding woman dramatist)—is it coincidental that none of these women bore children? Rochelle Owens told the *Times* interviewer that a woman can be accepted as an actress or costume designer, but "God help her if she dares to *write* the play." Owens added that the woman dramatist "must have guts of steel and great forebearance to transcend the devious undermining, the negative expectations, and a mountain of other assaults on her sensibilities." All women writers face such "negative expectations," but the playwright—who must deal with producers, directors, and actors, and whose efforts can be destroyed in one night by hostile critics—is particularly vulnerable. It is no wonder that four of the five women represented in this anthology (Crothers is the sole exception) wrote primarily fiction in their later years.

Rosalyn Drexler, also interviewed by the *Times*, took a lighter approach. When asked "Where are the women playwrights?" she replied:

> They are deployed about the city waiting to make their move. They have already learned how to take apart and put together their typewriters in a matter of minutes, and how to keep them clean and well lubricated. At a signal, which may be the clapping of one hand, all women playwrights will shoot the vapids and proceed to a secret rendezvous where a hidden store of explosive topics is waiting to be used. With proper handling, each sentence will find its mark.

The recent works of such playwrights as Megan Terry, Tina Howe, Ntozake Shange, Marsha Norman, Adrienne

Kennedy, Corinne Jacker and Ruth Wolff indicate that many contemporary women are finding that hidden store. Anna Cora Mowatt, Rachel Crothers, Susan Glaspell, Zona Gale, and Sophie Treadwell drew them the map.

Judith E. Barlow

FASHION;
OR, LIFE IN NEW YORK.
A Comedy in Five Acts

ANNA CORA MOWATT

First performed 1845

CHARACTERS

ADAM TRUEMAN: a farmer from Catteraugus
COUNT JOLIMAITRE: a fashionable European importation
COLONEL HOWARD: an officer in the United States Army
MR. TIFFANY: a New York merchant
T. TENNYSON TWINKLE: a modern poet
AUGUSTUS FOGG: a drawing room appendage
SNOBSON: a rare species of confidential clerk
ZEKE: a colored servant
MRS. TIFFANY: a lady who imagines herself fashionable
PRUDENCE: a maiden lady of a certain age
MILLINETTE: a French lady's maid
GERTRUDE: a governess
SERAPHINA TIFFANY: a belle
LADIES and GENTLEMEN of the Ball-room

This text follows the 1854 edition; in a few cases,
punctuation and stage direction style have been
modernized.

ACT ONE

A splendid Drawing Room in the House of MRS. TIFFANY.

ACT TWO

SCENE 1: Inner apartment of MR. TIFFANY's Counting House.

SCENE 2: The interior of a beautiful conservatory.

ACT THREE

SCENE 1: MRS. TIFFANY's Parlor.

SCENE 2: Housekeeper's room.

ACT FOUR

SCENE 1: Ball-room, splendidly illuminated.

SCENE 2: Housekeeper's room.

ACT FIVE

MRS. TIFFANY's Drawing Room—same Scene as Act One.

PROLOGUE
by Epes Sargent

[*Enter a Gentleman, reading a newspaper.*]

" *'Fashion, A Comedy.'* I'll go; but stay—
Now I read farther, 'tis a *native* play!
Bah! homemade calicoes are well enough,
But homemade dramas must be stupid stuff.
Had it the *London* stamp, 'twould do—but then,
For plays, we lack the manners and the men!"

Thus speaks *one* critic. Hear *another's* creed:—
" *'Fashion!'* What's here? (*Reads*) It never can succeed!
What! from a *woman's* pen? It takes a *man*
To write a comedy—no woman can."

Well, sir, and what say *you?* And why that frown?
His eyes uprolled, he lays the paper down:—
"Here! take," he says, "the unclean thing away!
'Tis tainted with a notice of a *play!*"

But, sir!—but, gentlemen!—you, sir, who think
No comedy can flow from *native* ink,—
Are we such *perfect* monsters, or such *dull,*
That Wit no traits for ridicule can cull?
Have we no follies here to be redressed?
No vices gibbeted? no crimes confessed?

"But then, a female hand can't lay the lash on!"
"How know you *that,* sir, when the theme is 'Fashion'?"

And now, come forth, thou man of sanctity!
How shall I venture a reply to thee?
The *Stage*—what is it, though beneath *thy* ban,

5

But a *Daguerreotype* of life and man?
Arraign poor human nature, if you will,
But let the *Drama* have her mission still!
Let her, with honest purpose, still reflect
The faults which keen-eyed Satire may detect.
For there *be* men, who fear not an hereafter,
Yet tremble at the Hell of public laughter!

Friends, from these scoffers we appeal to you!
Condemn the *false*, but O! applaud the *true*.
Grant that *some* wit may grow on native soil,
And Art's fair fabric rise from woman's toil
While we exhibit but to reprehend
The social voices, 'tis for *you* to mend!

ACT I

A splendid Drawing Room in the House of MRS. TIF-
FANY. *Open folding doors, discovering a Conservatory.
On either side glass windows down to the ground.
Doors on right and left. Mirror, couches, ottomans, a
table with albums, beside it an arm chair.* MILLINETTE
dusting furniture. ZEKE *in a dashing livery, scarlet coat.*

ZEKE: Dere's a coat to take de eyes ob all Broadway! Ah!
Missy, it am de fixin's dat make de natural *born* gemman. A libery for ever! Dere's a pair ob insuppressibles
to 'stonish de colored population.

MILLINETTE: [*Very politely*] Oh, *oui*, Monsieur Zeke.
[*Aside*] I not *comprend* one word he say!

ZEKE: I tell 'ee what, Missy, I'm 'stordinary glad to find
dis a bery 'spectabul like situation! Now as you've
made de acquaintance ob dis here family, and dere
you've had a supernumerary advantage ob me—seeing
dat I only receibed my appointment dis morning. What
I wants to know is your publicated opinion, privately
expressed, ob de domestic circle.

MILLINETTE: You mean vat *espèce*, vat kind of *personnes*
are Monsieur and Madame Tiffany? Ah! Monsieur is
not de same ting as Madame—not at all.

ZEKE: Well, I s'pose he ain't altogether.

MILLINETTE: Monsieur is man of business—Madame is
lady of fashion. Monsieur make de money—Madame
spend it. Monsieur nobody at all—Madame everybody
altogether. Ah! Monsieur Zeke, de money is all dat is
necessaire in dis country to make one lady of fashion.
Oh! it is quite anoder ting in *la belle France!*

7

ZEKE: A bery lucifer explanation. Well, now we've disposed ob de heads ob de family, who come next?

MILLINETTE: First, dere is Mademoiselle Seraphina Tiffany. Mademoiselle is not at all one proper *personne*. Mademoiselle Seraphina is one coquette. Dat is not de mode in *la belle France*; de ladies, dere, never learn *la coquetrie* until dey do get one husband.

ZEKE: I tell 'ee what, Missy, I disreprobate dat proceeding altogeder!

MILLINETTE: Vait! I have not tell you all *la famille* yet. Dere is Ma'mselle Prudence—Madame's sister, one very *bizarre personne*. Den dere is Ma'mselle Gertrude, but she not anybody at all; she only teach Mademoiselle Seraphina *la musique*.

ZEKE: Well, now, Missy, what's your own special defunctions?

MILLINETTE: I not understand, Monsieur Zeke.

ZEKE: Den I'll amplify. What's de nature ob your exclusive services?

MILLINETTE: *Ah, oui! je comprend.* I am Madame's *femme de chambre*—her lady's maid, Monsieur Zeke. I teach Madame *les modes de Paris*, and Madame set de fashion for all New York. You see, Monsieur Zeke, dat it is me, *moi-même*, dat do lead de fashion for all de American *beau monde!*

ZEKE: Yah! yah! yah! I hab de idea by de heel. Well now, p'raps you can 'lustrify my officials?

MILLINETTE: Vat you will have to do? Oh! much tings, much tings. You vait on de table—you tend de door—you clean de boots—you run de errands—you drive de carriage—you rub de horses—you take care of de flowers—you carry de water—you help cook de dinner—you wash de dishes—and den you always remember to do everting I tell you to!

ZEKE: Wheugh, am dat *all?*

MILLINETTE: All I can tink of now. Today is Madame's day of reception, and all her grand friends do make her one *petite* visit. You mind run fast ven de bell do ring.

ZEKE: Run? If it wasn't for dese superfluminous trimmings, I tell 'ee what, Missy, I'd run—

MRS. TIFFANY: [*Outside*] Millinette!

MILLINETTE: Here comes Madame! You better go, Monsieur Zeke.

ZEKE: [*Aside*] Look ahea, Massa Zeke, doesn't dis open rich! [*Exit* ZEKE.]

[*Enter* MRS. TIFFANY, *dressed in the most extravagant height of fashion.*]

MRS. TIFFANY: Is everything in order, Millinette? Ah! very elegant, very elegant indeed! There is a *jenny-says-quoi* look about this furniture—an air of fashion and gentility perfectly bewitching. Is there not, Millinette?

MILLINETTE: Oh, *oui*, Madame!

MRS. TIFFANY: But where is Miss Seraphina? It is twelve o'clock; our visitors will be pouring in, and she has not made her appearance. But I hear that nothing is more fashionable than to keep people waiting—None but vulgar persons pay any attention to punctuality. Is it not so, Millinette?

MILLINETTE: Quite *comme il faut*—Great *personnes* always do make little *personnes* wait, Madame.

MRS. TIFFANY: This mode of receiving visitors only upon one specified day of the week is a most convenient custom! It saves the trouble of keeping the house continually in order and of being always dressed. I flatter myself that *I* was the first to introduce it amongst the New York *ee-light*. You are quite sure that it is strictly a Parisian mode, Millinette?

MILLINETTE: Oh, *oui*, Madame; entirely *mode de Paris*.

MRS. TIFFANY: [*Aside*] This girl is worth her weight in gold. Millinette, how do you say *arm-chair* in French?

MILLINETTE: *Fauteuil*, Madame.

MRS. TIFFANY: *Fo-tool!* That has a foreign—an out-of-the-wayish sound that is perfectly charming—and so genteel! There is something about our American words decidedly vulgar. *Fowtool!* how refined. *Fowtool!* *Arm-chair!* what a difference!

MILLINETTE: Madame have one *charmante* pronunciation. [*Mimicking aside*] *Fowtool! Charmante*, Madame!

MRS. TIFFANY: Do you think so, Millinette? Well, I believe I have. But a woman of refinement and of fashion can always accommodate herself to everything foreign! And a week's study of that invaluable work—*French Without a Master*, has made me quite at home in the court language of Europe! But where is the new valet? I'm rather sorry that he is black, but to obtain a white American for a domestic is almost impossible; and they call this a free country! What did you say was the name of this new servant, Millinette?

MILLINETTE: He do say his name is Monsieur Zeke.

MRS. TIFFANY: Ezekiel, I suppose. Zeke! Dear me, such a vulgar name will compromise the dignity of the whole family. Can you not suggest something more aristocratic, Millinette? Something *French!*

MILLINETTE: *Oh, oui,* Madame; *Adolph* is one very fine name.

MRS. TIFFANY: A-dolph! Charming! Ring the bell, Millinette! [MILLINETTE *rings the bell.*] I will change his name immediately, besides giving him a few directions. [*Enter* ZEKE. MRS. TIFFANY *addresses him with great dignity.*] Your name, I hear, is *Ezekiel*—I consider it too plebeian an appellation to be uttered in my presence. In future you are called A-dolph. Don't reply—never interrupt me when I am speaking. A-dolph, as my guests arrive, I desire that you will inquire the name of every person, and then announce it in a loud, clear tone. *That* is the fashion in Paris.

[MILLINETTE *retires up the stage.*]

ZEKE: [*Speaking very loudly*] Consider de office discharged, Missus.

MRS. TIFFANY: Silence! Your business is to obey and not to talk.

ZEKE: I'm dumb, Missus!

MRS. TIFFANY: [*Pointing up stage*] A-dolph, place that *fowtool* behind me.

ZEKE: [*Looking about him*] I habn't got dat far in de dictionary yet. No matter, a genus gets his learning by nature. [*Takes up the table and places it behind* MRS. TIFFANY, *then expresses in dumb show great satisfaction.* MRS. TIFFANY, *as she goes to sit, discovers the mistake.*]

MRS. TIFFANY: You dolt! Where have you lived not to

know that *fow-tool* is the French for *arm-chair?* What ignorance! Leave the room this instant.

[MRS. TIFFANY *draws forward an arm-chair and sits.* MILLINETTE *comes forward suppressing her merriment at* ZEKE's *mistake and removes the table.*]

ZEKE: Dem's de defects ob not having a libery education. [*Exit*]

[PRUDENCE *peeps in.*]

PRUDENCE: I wonder if any of the fine folks have come yet. Not a soul—I knew they hadn't. There's Betsy all alone. [*Walks in*] Sister Betsy!

MRS. TIFFANY: Prudence! how many times have I desired you to call me *Elizabeth? Betsy* is the height of vulgarity.

PRUDENCE: Oh! I forgot. Dear me, how spruce we do look here, to be sure—everything in first rate style now, Betsy. [MRS. TIFFANY *looks at her angrily.*] *Elizabeth,* I mean. Who would have thought, when you and I were sitting behind that little mahogany-colored counter, in Canal Street, making up flashy hats and caps—

MRS. TIFFANY: Prudence, what *do* you mean? Millinette, leave the room.

MILLINETTE: *Oui,* Madame. [MILLINETTE *pretends to arrange the books upon a side table, but lingers to listen.*]

PRUDENCE: But I always predicted it—I always told you so, Betsy—I always said you were destined to rise above your station!

MRS. TIFFANY: Prudence! Prudence! have I not told you that—

PRUDENCE: No, Betsy, it was *I* that told *you,* when we used to buy our silks and ribbons of Mr. Anthony Tiffany—*"talking Tony,"* you know we used to call him, and when you always put on the finest bonnet in our shop to go to his—and when you stayed so long smiling and chattering with him, I always told you that *something* would grow out of it—and didn't it?

MRS. TIFFANY: Millinette, send Seraphina here instantly. Leave the room.

MILLINETTE: *Oui,* Madame. [*Aside*] So dis Americaine ladi of fashion vas one *milliner?* Oh, vat a fine country for *les marchandes des modes!* I shall send for all my relation by de next packet!

[*Exit* MILLINETTE.]

MRS. TIFFANY: Prudence! never let me hear you mention this subject again. Forget what we *have* been, it is enough to remember that we *are* of the *upper ten thousand!* [PRUDENCE *goes up and sits down.*]

[*Enter* SERAPHINA, *very extravagantly dressed.*]

MRS. TIFFANY: How bewitchingly you look, my dear! Does Millinette say that that head dress is strictly Parisian?

SERAPHINA: Oh yes, Mamma, all the rage! They call it a *lady's tarpaulin,* and it is the exact pattern of one worn by the Princess Clementina at the last court ball.

MRS. TIFFANY: Now, Seraphina my dear, don't be too particular in your attentions to gentlemen not eligible. There is Count Jolimaitre, decidedly the most fashionable foreigner in town—and so refined—so much accustomed to associate with the first nobility in his own country that he can hardly tolerate the vulgarity of Americans in general. You may devote yourself to him. Mrs. Proudacre is dying to become acquainted with him. By the by, if she or her daughters should happen to drop in, be sure you don't introduce them to the Count. It is not the fashion in Paris to introduce—Millinette told me so.

[*Enter* ZEKE.]

ZEKE: [*In a very loud voice*] Mister T. Tennyson Twinkle!

MRS. TIFFANY: Show him up.

[*Exit* ZEKE.]

PRUDENCE: I must be running away! [*Going*]

MRS. TIFFANY: Mr. T. Tennyson Twinkle—a very literary young man and a sweet poet! It is all the rage to patronize poets! Quick, Seraphina, hand me that magazine—Mr. Twinkle writes for it.

[SERAPHINA *hands the magazine,* MRS. TIFFANY *seats herself in an arm-chair and opens the book.*]

PRUDENCE: [*Returning*] There's Betsy trying to make out that reading without her spectacles. [*Takes a pair of spectacles out of her pocket and hands them to* MRS. TIFFANY] There, Betsy, I knew you were going to ask for them. Ah! they're a blessing when one is growing old!

MRS. TIFFANY: What do you mean, Prudence? A woman of fashion *never* grows old! Age is always out of fashion.

PRUDENCE: Oh, dear! what a delightful thing it is to be fashionable. [*Exit* PRUDENCE. MRS. TIFFANY *resumes her seat.*]

[*Enter* TWINKLE. *He salutes* SERAPHINA.]

TWINKLE: Fair Seraphina! the sun itself grows dim, Unless you aid his light and shine on him!

SERAPHINA: Ah! Mr. Twinkle, there is no such thing as answering you.

TWINKLE: [*Looks around and perceives* MRS. TIFFANY] [*Aside*] The *New Monthly Vernal Galaxy*. Reading my verses by all that's charming! Sensible woman! I won't interrupt her.

MRS. TIFFANY: [*Rising and coming forward*] Ah! Mr. Twinkle, is that you? I was perfectly *abimé* at the perusal of your very *distingué* verses.

TWINKLE: I am overwhelmed, Madam. Permit me. [*Taking the magazine*] Yes, they do read tolerably. And you must take into consideration, ladies, the rapidity with which they were written. Four minutes and a half by the stop watch! The true test of a poet is the *velocity* with which he composes. Really they do look very prettily, and they read tolerably—*quite* tolerably—*very* tolerably—especially the first verse. [*Reads*] "To Seraphina T——."

SERAPHINA: Oh! Mr. Twinkle!

TWINKLE: [*Reads*] "Around my heart"—

MRS. TIFFANY: How touching! Really, Mr. Twinkle, quite tender!

TWINKLE: [*Recommencing*] "Around my heart"—

MRS. TIFFANY: Oh, I must tell you, Mr. Twinkle! I heard the other day that poets were the aristocrats of literature. That's one reason I like them, for I do dote on all aristocracy!

TWINKLE: Oh, Madam, how flattering! Now pray lend me your ears! [*Reads*] "Around my heart thou weavest"—

SERAPHINA: That is such a *sweet* commencement, Mr. Twinkle!

TWINKLE: [*Aside*] I wish she wouldn't interrupt me!

[*Reads*] "Around my heart thou weavest a spell"—

MRS. TIFFANY: Beautiful! But excuse me one moment, while I say a word to Seraphina! [*Aside to* SERAPHINA] Don't be too affable, my dear! Poets are very ornamental appendages to the drawing room, but they are always as poor as their own verses. They don't make eligible husbands!

TWINKLE: [*Aside*] Confound their interruptions! My dear Madam, unless you pay the utmost attention you cannot catch the ideas. Are you ready? Well, now you shall hear it to the end! [*Reads*]

"Around my heart thou weavest a spell
"Whose"—

[*Enter* ZEKE.]

ZEKE: Mister Augustus Fogg! [*Aside*] A bery misty lookin young gemman.

MRS. TIFFANY: Show him up, A-dolph!

[*Exit* ZEKE.]

TWINKLE: This is too much!

SERAPHINA: Exquisite verses, Mr. Twinkle—exquisite!

TWINKLE: Ah, lovely Seraphina! your smile of approval transports me to the summit of Olympus.

SERAPHINA: Then I must frown, for I would not send you so far away.

TWINKLE: Enchantress! [*Aside*] It's all over with her.

[*Retire up and converse*]

MRS. TIFFANY: Mr. Fogg belongs to one of our oldest families—to be sure, he is the most difficult person in the world to entertain, for he never takes the trouble to talk, and never notices anything or anybody—but then I hear that nothing is considered so vulgar as to betray any emotion, or to attempt to render oneself agreeable!

[*Enter* MR. FOGG, *fashionably attired but in very dark clothes.*]

FOGG: [*Bowing stiffly*] Mrs. Tiffany, your most obedient. Miss Seraphina, yours. How d'ye do, Twinkle?

MRS. TIFFANY: Mr. Fogg, how do you do? Fine weather—delightful, isn't it?

FOGG: I am indifferent to weather, Madam.

MRS. TIFFANY: Been to the opera, Mr. Fogg? I hear that the *bow monde* make their *debutt* there every evening.

FOGG: I consider operas a bore, Madam.

SERAPHINA: [*Advancing*] You must hear Mr. Twinkle's verses, Mr. Fogg!

FOGG: I am indifferent to verses, Miss Seraphina.

SERAPHINA: But Mr. Twinkle's verses are addressed to me!

TWINKLE: Now pay attention, Fogg! [*Reads*]—
   "Around my heart thou weavest a spell
   "Whose magic I"—
   [*Enter* ZEKE.]

ZEKE: Mister—No, he say he ain't no Mister—

TWINKLE: "Around my heart thou weavest a spell
   "Whose magic I can never tell!"

MRS. TIFFANY: Speak in a loud, clear tone, A-dolph!

TWINKLE: This is terrible!

ZEKE: Mister Count Jolly-made-her!

MRS. TIFFANY: Count Jolimaitre! Good gracious! Zeke, Zeke—A-dolph I mean. [*Aside*] Dear me, what a mistake! Set that chair out of the way—put that table back. Seraphina, my dear, are you all in order? Dear me! dear me! Your dress is so tumbled! [*Arranges her dress*] What are you grinning at? [*To* ZEKE] Beg the Count to *honor* us by walking up!
   [*Exit* ZEKE.]
   Seraphina, my dear [*aside to her*], remember now what I told you about the Count. He is a man of the highest— good gracious! I am so flurried; and nothing is so ungenteel as agitation! what will the Count think! Mr. Twinkle, pray stand out of the way! Seraphina, my dear, place yourself on my right! Mr. Fogg, the conservatory—beautiful flowers—pray amuse yourself in the conservatory.

FOGG: I am indifferent to flowers, Madam.

MRS. TIFFANY: [*Aside*] Dear me! the man stands right in the way—just where the Count must make his *entray!* Mr. Fogg—pray—
   [*Enter* COUNT JOLIMAITRE, *very dashingly dressed, wearing a moustache.*]

MRS. TIFFANY: Oh, Count, this unexpected honor—

SERAPHINA: Count, this inexpressible pleasure—

COUNT: Beg you won't mention it, Madam! Miss Seraphina, your most devoted! [*Crosses*]

MRS. TIFFANY: [*Aside*] What condescension! Count, may I take the liberty to introduce—[*Aside*] Good gracious! I forgot. Count, I was about to remark that we never introduce in America. All our fashions are foreign, Count.

[TWINKLE, *who has stepped forward to be introduced, shows great indignation.*]

COUNT: Excuse me, Madam, our fashions have grown antediluvian before you Americans discover their existence. You are lamentably behind the age—lamentably! 'Pon my honor, a foreigner of refinement finds great difficulty in existing in this provincial atmosphere.

MRS. TIFFANY: How dreadful, Count! I am very much concerned. If there is anything which I can do, Count—

SERAPHINA: Or I, Count, to render your situation less deplorable—

COUNT: Ah! I find but one redeeming charm in America—the superlative loveliness of the feminine portion of creation. [*Aside*] And the wealth of their obliging papas.

MRS. TIFFANY: How flattering! Ah! Count, I am afraid you will turn the head of my simple girl here. She is a perfect child of nature, Count.

COUNT: Very possibly, for though you American women are quite charming, yet, demme, there's a deal of native rust to rub off!

MRS. TIFFANY: *Rust?* Good gracious, Count! where do you find any rust? [*Looking about the room*]

COUNT: How very unsophisticated!

MRS. TIFFANY: Count, I am so much ashamed—pray excuse me! Although a lady of large fortune, and one, Count, who can boast of the highest connections, I blush to confess that I have never travelled—while you, Count, I presume are at home in all the courts of Europe.

COUNT: *Courts?* Eh? Oh, yes, Madam, very true. I believe I am pretty well known in some of the courts of Europe—[*Aside, crossing*]—police courts. In a word, Madam, I had seen enough of civilized life—wanted to refresh myself by a sight of barbarous countries and customs—had my choice between the Sandwich Islands and New York—chose New York!

MRS. TIFFANY: How complimentary to our country! And, Count, I have no doubt you speak every conceivable language? You talk English like a native.

COUNT: Eh, what? Like a native? Oh, ah, demme, yes, I am something of an Englishman. Passed one year and eight months with the Duke of Wellington, six months with Lord Brougham, two and a half with Count d'Orsay—knew them all more intimately than their best friends—no heroes to me—hadn't a secret from me, I assure you. [*Aside*] *Especially of the toilet.*

MRS. TIFFANY: [*Aside to* SERAPHINA] Think of that, my dear! Lord Wellington and Duke Broom!

SERAPHINA: [*Aside to* MRS. TIFFANY] And only think of Count d'Orsay, Mamma! I am so wild to see Count d'Orsay!

COUNT: Oh! a mere man milliner. Very little refinement out of Paris! Why, at the very last dinner given at Lord—Lord Knowswho, would you believe it, Madam, there was an individual present who wore a *black* cravat and took *soup twice!*

MRS. TIFFANY: How shocking! the sight of him would have spoilt my appetite! [*Aside to* SERAPHINA] Think what a great man he must be, my dear, to despise lords and counts in that way. [*Aside*] I must leave them together. Mr. Twinkle, your arm. I have some really very *foreign exotics* to show you.

TWINKLE: I fly at your command. [*Aside, and glancing at the* COUNT] I wish all her exotics were blooming in their native soil!

MRS. TIFFANY: Mr. Fogg, will you accompany us? My conservatory is well worthy a visit. It cost an immense sum of money.

FOGG: I am indifferent to conservatories, Madam; flowers are such a bore!

MRS. TIFFANY: I shall take no refusal. Conservatories are all the rage—I could not exist without mine! Let me show you—let me show you.

[*Places her arm through* MR. FOGG's, *without his consent. Exeunt* MRS. TIFFANY, FOGG, *and* TWINKLE *into the conservatory, where they are seen walking about.*]

SERAPHINA: America, then, has no charms for you, Count?

COUNT: Excuse me—some exceptions. I find you, for instance, particularly charming! Can't say I admire your country. Ah! if you had ever breathed the exhilarating air of Paris, ate creams at Tortoni's, dined at the Café Royale, or if you had lived in London—felt at home at St. James's, and every afternoon driven a couple of Lords and a Duchess through Hyde Park, you would find America—where you have no kings, queens, lords, nor ladies—insupportable!

SERAPHINA: Not while there was a Count in it?

[*Enter* ZEKE, *very indignant.*]

ZEKE: Where's de Missus?

[*Enter* MRS. TIFFANY, FOGG, *and* TWINKLE, *from the conservatory.*]

MRS. TIFFANY: Whom do you come to announce, A-dolph?

ZEKE: He said he wouldn't trust me—no, not eben wid so much as his name; so I wouldn't trust him up stairs, den he ups wid *his stick* and I *cuts mine.*

MRS. TIFFANY: [*Aside*] Some of Mr. Tiffany's vulgar acquaintances. I shall die with shame. A-dolph, inform him that I am *not at home.*

[*Exit* ZEKE.]

My nerves are so shattered, I am ready to sink. Mr. Twinkle, that *fow tool,* if you please!

TWINKLE: What? What do you wish, Madam?

MRS. TIFFANY: [*Aside*] The ignorance of these Americans! Count, may I trouble you? That *fow tool,* if you please!

COUNT: [*Aside*] She's not talking English, nor French, but I suppose it's American.

TRUEMAN: [*Outside*] Not at home!

ZEKE: No, Sar—Missus say she's not at home.

TRUEMAN: Out of the way, you grinning nigger!

[*Enter* ADAM TRUEMAN, *dressed as a farmer, a stout cane in his hand, his boots covered with dust.* ZEKE *jumps out of his way as he enters.*]

[*Exit* ZEKE.]

TRUEMAN: Where's this woman that's not *at home* in her own house? May I be shot if I wonder at it! I shouldn't think she'd ever feel *at home* in such a show-box as this! [*Looking round*]

MRS. TIFFANY: [*Aside*] What a plebeian looking old farmer! I wonder who he is? Sir— [*Advancing very agitatedly*] what do you mean, Sir, by this *ow*dacious conduct? How dare you intrude yourself into my parlor? Do you know who I am, Sir? [*With great dignity*] You are in the presence of Mrs. Tiffany, Sir!

TRUEMAN: Antony's wife, eh? Well now, I might have guessed that—ha! ha! ha! for I see you make it a point to carry half your husband's shop upon your back! No matter; that's being a good helpmate—for he carried the whole of it once in a pack on his own shoulders—now you bear a share!

MRS. TIFFANY: How dare you, you impertinent, *ow*dacious, ignorant old man! It's all an invention. You're talking of somebody else. [*Aside*] What will the Count think!

TRUEMAN: Why, I thought folks had better manners in the city! This is a civil welcome for your husband's old friend, and after my coming all the way from Catter-augus to see you and yours! First a grinning nigger tricked out in scarlet regimentals—

MRS. TIFFANY: Let me tell you, Sir, that liveries are all the fashion!

TRUEMAN: The fashion, are they? To make men wear the *badge of servitude* in a free land—that's the fashion, is it? Hurrah for republican simplicity! I will venture to say now that you have your coat of arms too!

MRS. TIFFANY: Certainly, Sir; you can see it on the panels of my *voyture.*

TRUEMAN: Oh! no need of that. I know what your escutch-eon must be! A bandbox *rampant* with a bonnet *cou-chant*, and a peddlar's pack *passant!* Ha, ha, ha! that shows both houses united!

MRS. TIFFANY: Sir! you are most profoundly ignorant— what do you mean by this insolence, Sir? [*Aside*] How shall I get rid of him?

TRUEMAN: [*Looking at* SERAPHINA. *Aside*] I hope that is not Gertrude!

MRS. TIFFANY: Sir, I'd have you know that—Seraphina,

my child, walk with the gentlemen into the conservatory.

[*Exeunt* SERAPHINA, TWINKLE, FOGG *into conservatory.*]

Count Jolimaitre, pray make due allowances for the errors of this rustic! I do assure you, Count—[*Whispers to him*]

TRUEMAN: [*Aside*] "Count!" She calls that critter with a shoe brush over his mouth "Count!" To look at him, I should have thought he was a tailor's walking advertisement!

COUNT: [*Addressing* TRUEMAN *whom he has been inspecting through his eyeglass*] Where did you say you belonged, my friend? Dug out of the ruins of Pompeii, eh?

TRUEMAN: I belong to a land in which I rejoice to find that you are a foreigner.

COUNT: What a barbarian! He doesn't see the honor I'm doing his country! Pray, Madam, is it one of the aboriginal inhabitants of the soil? To what tribe of Indians does he belong—the Pawnee or Choctaw? Does he carry a tomahawk?

TRUEMAN: Something quite as useful—do you see that? [*Shaking his stick*]

[COUNT *runs behind* MRS. TIFFANY.]

MRS. TIFFANY: Oh, dear! I shall faint! Millinette! [*Approaching*] Millinette!

[*Enter* MILLINETTE, *without advancing into the room.*]

MILLINETTE: *Oui*, Madame.

MRS. TIFFANY: A glass of water!

[*Exit* MILLINETTE.]

Sir, [*Crossing to* TRUEMAN] I am shocked at your plebeian conduct! This is a gentleman of the highest standing, Sir! He is a *Count*, Sir!

[*Enter* MILLINETTE, *bearing a salver with a glass of water. In advancing towards* MRS. TIFFANY, *she passes in front of the* COUNT, *starts and screams. The* COUNT, *after a start of surprise, regains his composure, plays with his eyeglass, and looks perfectly unconcerned.*]

MRS. TIFFANY: What is the matter? What *is* the matter?

MILLINETTE: Noting, noting—only— [*Looks at* COUNT *and turns away her eyes again*] only—noting at all!

TRUEMAN: Don't be afraid, girl! Why, did you never see a live Count before? He's tame—I dare say your mistress there leads him about by the ears.

MRS. TIFFANY: This is too much! Millinette, send for Mr. Tiffany instantly!

[*Crosses to* MILLINETTE, *who is going*]

MILLINETTE: He just come in, Madame!

TRUEMAN: My old friend! Where is he? Take me to him— I long to have one more hearty shake of the hand!

MRS. TIFFANY: [*Crosses to him*] Count, honor me by joining my daughter in the conservatory; I will return immediately.

[COUNT *bows and walks towards conservatory,* MRS. TIFFANY *following part of the way and then returning to* TRUEMAN.]

TRUEMAN: What a Jezebel! These women always play the very devil with a man, and yet I don't believe such a damaged bale of goods as *that* [*Looking at* MRS. TIFFANY] has smothered the heart of little Antony!

MRS. TIFFANY: This way, Sir, *sal vous plait.*

[*Exit with great dignity*]

TRUEMAN: *Sal vous plait.* Ha, ha, ha! We'll see what Fashion has done for him. [*Exit*]

ACT II

Scene 1

Inner apartment of MR. TIFFANY's *Counting House.* MR. TIFFANY, *seated at a desk looking over papers.* MR. SNOBSON, *on a high stool at another desk, with a pen behind his ear.*

SNOBSON: [*Rising, advances to the front of the stage, regards* TIFFANY *and shrugs his shoulders. Aside*] How the old boy frets and fumes over those papers, to be sure! He's working himself into a perfect fever—exactly—therefore *bleeding's* the prescription! So here goes! Mr. Tiffany, a word with you, if you please, Sir?

TIFFANY: [*Sitting still*] Speak on, Mr. Snobson, I attend.

SNOBSON: What I have to say, Sir, is a matter of the first importance to the credit of the concern—the *credit* of the concern, Mr. Tiffany!

TIFFANY: Proceed, Mr. Snobson.

SNOBSON: Sir, you've a handsome house—fine carriage—nigger in livery—feed on the fat of the land—everything first rate—

TIFFANY: Well, Sir?

SNOBSON: My salary, Mr. Tiffany!

TIFFANY: It has been raised three times within the last year.

SNOBSON: Still it is insufficient for the necessities of an honest man—mark me, an *honest* man, Mr. Tiffany.

TIFFANY: [*Crossing. Aside*] What a weapon he has made of that word! Enough—another hundred shall be added. Does that content you?

SNOBSON: There is one other subject which I have before mentioned, Mr. Tiffany—your daughter—what's the

22

reason you can't let the folks at home know at once that I'm to be *the man?*

TIFFANY: [*Aside*] Villain! And must the only seal upon this scoundrel's lips be placed there by the hand of my daughter? Well, Sir, it shall be as you desire.

SNOBSON: And Mrs. Tiffany shall be informed of your resolution?

TIFFANY: Yes.

SNOBSON: Enough said! That's the ticket! The CREDIT of the concern's safe, Sir! [*Returns to his seat*]

TIFFANY: [*Aside*] How low have I bowed to this insolent rascal! To rise himself he mounts upon my shoulders, and unless I can shake him off he must crush me! [*Enter* TRUEMAN.]

TRUEMAN: Here I am, Antony, man! I told you I'd pay you a visit in your money-making quarters. [*Looks around*] But it looks as dismal here as a cell in the States' prison!

TIFFANY: [*Forcing a laugh*] Ha, ha, ha! States' prison! You are so facetious! Ha, ha, ha!

TRUEMAN: Well, for the life of me I can't see anything so amusing in that! I should think the States' prison plaguy uncomfortable lodgings. And you laugh, man, as though you fancied yourself there already.

TIFFANY: Ha, ha, ha!

TRUEMAN: [*Imitating him*] Ha, ha, ha! What on earth do you mean by that ill-sounding laugh, that has nothing of a laugh about it! This *fashion*-worship has made heathens and hypocrites of you all! *Deception* is your household God! A man laughs as if he were crying, and cries as if he were laughing in his sleeve. Everything is something else from what it seems to be. I have lived in your house only three days, and I've heard more lies than were ever invented during a Presidential election! First your fine lady of a wife sends me word that she's not at home—I walk up stairs, and she takes good care that *I* shall not be *at home*—wants to turn me out of doors. Then *you* come in—take your old friend by the hand—whisper, the deuce knows what, in your wife's ear, and the tables are turned in a tangent! Madam curtsies—says she's enchanted to see me—and orders her grinning nigger to show me a room.

TIFFANY: We were exceedingly happy to welcome you as our guest!

TRUEMAN: Happy? *You* happy? Ah, Antony! Antony! that hatchet face of yours and those criss-cross furrows tell quite another story! It's many a long day since you were *happy* at anything! You look as if you'd melted down your flesh into dollars, and mortgaged your soul in the bargain! Your warm heart has grown cold over your ledger—your light spirits heavy with calculation! You have traded away your youth—your hopes—your tastes, for wealth! and now you *have* the wealth you coveted, what does it profit you? Pleasure it cannot buy, for you have lost your *capacity* for enjoyment. Ease it will not bring, for the love of gain is never satisfied! It has made your counting-house a penitentiary, and your home a fashionable *museum* where there is no niche for you! You have spent so much time *ciphering* in the one, that you find yourself at last a very *cipher* in the other! See me, man! Seventy-two last August!—Strong as a hickory and every whit as sound!

TIFFANY: I take the greatest pleasure in remarking your superiority, Sir.

TRUEMAN: Bah! no man takes pleasure in remarking the superiority of another! Why the deuce can't you speak the truth, man? But it's not the *fashion*, I suppose! I have not seen one frank, open face since—no, no, I can't say that either, though lying *is* catching! There's that girl, Gertrude, who is trying to teach your daughter music—but Gertrude was bred in the country!

TIFFANY: A good girl; my wife and daughter find her very useful.

TRUEMAN: Useful? Well, I must say you have queer notions of *use!*—But come, cheer up, man! I'd rather see one of your old smiles than know you'd realized another thousand! I hear you are making money on the true, American, high pressure system—better go slow and sure—the more steam, the greater danger of the boiler's bursting! All sound, I hope? Nothing rotten at the core?

TIFFANY: Oh, sound—quite sound!

TRUEMAN: Well, that's pleasant—though I must say you don't look very pleasant about it!

TIFFANY: My good friend, although I am solvent, I may say, perfectly solvent—yet you—the fact is, you can be of some assistance to me!

TRUEMAN: That's the *fact* is it? I'm glad we've hit upon one *fact* at last! Well—

[SNOBSON, *who during this conversation has been employed in writing, but stops occasionally to listen, now gives vent to a dry chuckling laugh.*]

TRUEMAN: Hey? What's that? Another of those deuced ill-sounding city laughs! [*Sees* SNOBSON] Who's that perched up on the stool of repentance—eh, Antony?

SNOBSON: [*Aside and looking at* TIFFANY'*s seat*] The old boy has missed his text there—*that's* the stool of repentance!

TIFFANY: One of my clerks—my confidential clerk!

TRUEMAN: Confidential? Why he looks for all the world like a spy—the most inquisitorial, hang-dog face—ugh! the sight of it makes my blood run cold! Come, [*Crosses*] let us talk over matters where this critter can't give us the benefit of his opinion! Antony, the next time you choose a confidential clerk, take one that carries his credentials in his face—those in his pocket are not worth much without!

[*Exeunt* TRUEMAN *and* TIFFANY.]

SNOBSON: [*Jumping from his stool and advancing*] The old prig has got the tin, or Tiff would never be so civil! All right—Tiff will work every shiner into the concern—all the better for me! Now I'll go and make love to Seraphina. The old woman needn't try to knock me down with any of her French lingo! Six months from today if I ain't driving my two footmen tandem, down Broadway—and as fashionable as Mrs. Tiffany herself—then I ain't the trump I thought I was, that's all. [*Looks at his watch*] Bless me! eleven o'clock and I haven't had my julep yet? Snobson, I'm ashamed of you! [*Exit*]

Scene 2

The interior of a beautiful conservatory; walk through the center; stands of flower pots in bloom; a couple of rustic seats. GERTRUDE, *attired in white, with a white rose in her hair, watering the flowers.* COLONEL HOWARD *regarding her.*

HOWARD: I am afraid you lead a sad life here, Miss Gertrude?

GERTRUDE: [*Turning round gaily*] What! amongst the flowers? [*Continues her occupation*]

HOWARD: No, amongst the thistles, with which Mrs. Tiffany surrounds you; the tempests, which her temper raises!

GERTRUDE: They never harm me. Flowers and herbs are excellent tutors. I learn prudence from the reed, and bend until the storm has swept over me!

HOWARD: Admirable philosophy! But still this frigid atmosphere of fashion must be uncongenial to you? Accustomed to the pleasant companionship of your kind friends in Geneva,* surely you must regret this cold exchange?

GERTRUDE: Do you think so? Can you suppose that I could possibly prefer a ramble in the woods to a promenade in Broadway? A wreath of scented wild flowers to a bouquet of these sickly exotics? The odor of new-mown hay to the heated air of this crowded conservatory? Or can you imagine that I could enjoy the quiet conversation of my Geneva friends more than the edifying chit-chat of a fashionable drawing room? But I see you think me totally destitute of taste?

HOWARD: You have a merry spirit to jest thus at your grievances!

GERTRUDE: I have my *mania*—as some wise person declares that all mankind have—and mine is a love of independence! In Geneva, my wants were supplied by

*Geneva, New York.

two kind old maiden ladies, upon whom I know not that I have any claim. I had abilities, and desired to use them. I came here at my own request; for here I am no longer *dependent! Voilà tout,* as Mrs. Tiffany would say.

HOWARD: Believe me, I appreciate the confidence you repose in me!

GERTRUDE: Confidence! Truly, Colonel Howard, the *confidence* is entirely on your part, in supposing that I confide that which I have no reason to conceal! I think I informed you that Mrs. Tiffany only received visitors on her reception day—she is therefore not prepared to see you. Zeke—Oh! I beg his pardon—Adolph, made some mistake in admitting you.

HOWARD: Nay, Gertrude, it was not Mrs. Tiffany, nor Miss Tiffany, whom I came to see; it—it was—

GERTRUDE: The conservatory perhaps? I will leave you to examine the flowers at leisure! [*Crosses*]

HOWARD: Gertrude—listen to me. [*Aside*] If I only dared to give utterance to what is hovering upon my lips! Gertrude!

GERTRUDE: Colonel Howard!

HOWARD: Gertrude, I must—must—

GERTRUDE: Yes, indeed you *must,* must leave me! I think I hear somebody coming—Mrs. Tiffany would not be well pleased to find you here—pray, pray leave me— that door will lead you into the street. [*Hurries him out through door; takes up her watering pot, and commences watering flowers, tying up branches, etc.*] What a strange being is man! Why should he hesitate to say— nay, why should I prevent his saying, what I would most delight to hear? Truly man *is* strange—but woman is quite as incomprehensible! [*Walks about gathering flowers*]

[*Enter* COUNT JOLIMAITRE.]

COUNT: There she is—the bewitching little creature! Mrs. Tiffany and her daughter are out of earshot. I caught a glimpse of their feathers floating down Broadway, not ten minutes ago. Just the opportunity I have been looking for! Now for an engagement with this captivating little piece of prudery! 'Pon my honor, I am almost afraid she will not resist a *Count* long enough to give

value to the conquest. [*Approaches her*] *Ma belle petite*, were you gathering roses for me?

GERTRUDE: [*Starts on first perceiving him, but instantly
regains her self-possession*] The roses here, Sir, are
carefully guarded with thorns—if you have the right to
gather, pluck for yourself!

COUNT: Sharp as ever, little Gertrude! But now that
we are alone, throw off this frigidity, and be at your
ease.

GERTRUDE: Permit me to *be alone*, Sir, that I *may* be at
my ease!

COUNT: Very good, *ma belle*, well said! [*Applauding her
with his hands*] Never yield too soon, even to a *title!*
But as the old girl may find her way back before long,
we may as well come to particulars at once. I love you;
but that you know already. [*Rubbing his eyeglass un-
concernedly with his handkerchief*] Before long I shall
make Mademoiselle Seraphina my wife, and, of course,
you shall remain in the family!

GERTRUDE: [*Indignantly*] Sir—

COUNT: 'Pon my honor you shall! In France we arrange
these little matters without difficulty!

GERTRUDE: But I am an *American!* Your conduct proves
that you are not one! [*Going, crosses*]

COUNT: [*Preventing her*] Don't run away, my immaculate
petite Americaine! Demme, you've quite overlooked
my condescension—the difference of our stations—you
a species of upper servant—an orphan—no friends.
[*Enter* TRUEMAN *unperceived.*]

GERTRUDE: And therefore more entitled to the respect
and protection of every *true gentleman!* Had you been
one, you would not have insulted me!

COUNT: My charming little orator, patriotism and decla-
mation become you particularly! [*Approaches her*] I
feel quite tempted to taste—

TRUEMAN: [*Thrusting him aside*] An American hickory-
switch! [*Strikes him*] Well, how do you like it?

COUNT: [*Aside*] Old matter-of-fact! Sir, how dare you?

TRUEMAN: My stick has answered that question!

GERTRUDE: Oh! now I am quite safe!

TRUEMAN: Safe! not a bit safer than before! All women

would be safe, if they knew how virtue became them! As for you, Mr. Count, what have you to say for yourself? Come, speak out!

COUNT: Sir,—aw—aw—you don't understand these matters!

TRUEMAN: That's a fact! Not having had *your* experience, I don't believe I *do* understand them!

COUNT: A piece of pleasantry—a mere joke—

TRUEMAN: A joke was it? I'll show you a joke worth two of that! I'll teach you the way we natives joke with a puppy who don't respect an honest woman! [*Seizing him*]

COUNT: Oh! oh! demme—you old ruffian! let me go. What do you mean?

TRUEMAN: Oh! a piece of pleasantry—a mere joke—very pleasant, isn't it?

[*Attempts to strike him again;* COUNT *struggles with him. Enter* MRS. TIFFANY *hastily, in her bonnet and shawl.*]

MRS. TIFFANY: What is the matter? I am perfectly *abimé* with terror. Mr. Trueman, what has happened?

TRUEMAN: Oh! we have been *joking!*

MRS. TIFFANY: [*To* COUNT, *who is re-arranging his dress*] My *dear* Count, I did not expect to find you here—how kind of you!

TRUEMAN: Your *dear* Count has been showing his *kindness* in a very *foreign* manner. Too *foreign*, I think, he found it to be relished by an *unfashionable native!* What do you think of a puppy who insults an innocent girl all in the way of *kindness?* This Count of yours—this importation of—

COUNT: My dear Madam, demme, permit me to explain. It would be unbecoming—demme—particularly unbecoming of you—aw—aw—to pay any attention to this ignorant person. [*Crosses to* TRUEMAN] Anything that he says concerning a man of my standing—aw—the truth is, Madam—

TRUEMAN: Let us have the truth by all means—if it is only for the novelty's sake!

COUNT: [*Turning his back to* TRUEMAN] You see, Madam, hoping to obtain a few moments' private conversation

with Miss Seraphina—with *Miss Seraphina*, I say—
and—aw—and knowing her passion for flowers, I found
my way to your very tasteful and *recherché* conservatory. [*Looks about him approvingly*] Very beautifully
arranged—does you great credit, Madam! Here I en-
countered this young person. She was inclined to be
talkative; and I indulged her with—with a—aw—
demme—a few *common places!* What passed between
us was mere *harmless badinage*—on *my* part. You,
Madam, you—so conversant with our European manners—you are aware that when a man of fashion—that
is, when a woman—a man is bound—amongst noble-
men, you know—

MRS. TIFFANY: I comprehend you perfectly—*parfitte-
ment,* my dear Count.

COUNT: [*Aside*] 'Pon my honor, that's very obliging of
her.

MRS. TIFFANY: I am shocked at the plebeian forwardness
of this conceited girl!

TRUEMAN: [*Walking up to* COUNT] Did you ever keep a
reckoning of the lies you tell in an hour?

MRS. TIFFANY: Mr. Trueman, I blush for you! [*Crosses to*
TRUEMAN]

TRUEMAN: Don't do that—you have no blushes to spare!

MRS. TIFFANY: It is a man of rank whom you are addressing, Sir!

TRUEMAN: A rank villain, Mrs. Antony Tiffany! A *rich
one* he would be, had he as much *gold* as *brass!*

MRS. TIFFANY: Pray pardon him, Count; he knows nothing of *how ton!*

COUNT: Demme, he's beneath my notice. I tell you what,
old fellow—[TRUEMAN *raises his stick as* COUNT *approaches; the latter starts back.*] the sight of him dis-
composes me—aw—I feel quite uncomfortable—aw—
let us join your charming daughter? [*To* TRUEMAN] I
can't do you the honor to shoot you, Sir—you are beneath me—a nobleman can't fight a commoner! Good
bye, old Truepenny! I—aw—I'm insensible to your insolence!

[*Exeunt* COUNT *and* MRS. TIFFANY.]

TRUEMAN: You won't be insensible to a cowhide in spite
of your nobility! The next time he practices any of his

foreign fashions on you, Gertrude, you'll see how I'll wake up his sensibilities!

GERTRUDE: I do not know what I should have done without you, Sir.

TRUEMAN: Yes, you do—you know that you would have done well enough! Never tell a lie, girl! not even for the sake of pleasing an old man! When you open your lips, let your heart speak. Never tell a lie! Let your face be the looking-glass of your soul—your heart its clock—while your tongue rings the hours! But the glass must be clear, the clock true, and then there's no fear but the tongue will do its duty in a woman's head!

GERTRUDE: You are very good, Sir.

TRUEMAN: That's as it may be!—[*Aside*] How my heart warms towards her! Gertrude, I hear that you have no mother?

GERTRUDE: Ah! no, Sir; I wish I had.

TRUEMAN: [*Aside, and with emotion*] So do I! Heaven knows, so do I! And you have no father, Gertrude?

GERTRUDE: No, Sir—I often wish I had!

TRUEMAN: [*Hurriedly*] Don't do that, girl! don't do that! Wish you had a mother—but never wish that you had a father again! Perhaps the one you had did not deserve such a child!

[*Enter* PRUDENCE.]

PRUDENCE: Seraphina is looking for you, Gertrude.

GERTRUDE: I will go to her. [*Crosses*] Mr. Trueman, you will not permit me to thank you, but you cannot prevent my gratitude! [*Exit*]

TRUEMAN: [*Looking after her*] If falsehood harbors there, I'll give up searching after truth! [*Crosses, retires up the stage musingly, and commences examining the flowers*]

PRUDENCE: [*Aside*] What a nice old man he is, to be sure! I wish he would say something! [*Crosses, walks after him, turning when he turns; after a pause*] Don't mind me, Mr. Trueman!

TRUEMAN: Mind you? Oh! no, don't be afraid [*Crosses*]— I wasn't minding you. Nobody seems to mind you much!

[*Continues walking and examining the flowers—* PRUDENCE *follows.*]

PRUDENCE: Very pretty flowers, ain't they? Gertrude takes care of them.

TRUEMAN: Gertrude? So I hear—[*Advancing*] I suppose you can tell me now who this Gertrude—

PRUDENCE: Who she's in love with? I *knew* you were going to say that! I'll tell you all about it! Gertrude, she's in love with—Mr. Twinkle! and he's in love with her. And Seraphina, she's in love with Count Jolly—what-d'ye-call-it; but Count Jolly don't take to her at all—but Colonel Howard—he's the man—he's desperate about her!

TRUEMAN: Why you feminine newspaper! Howard in love with that quintessence of affectation! Howard—the only frank, straightforward fellow that I've met since—I'll tell him my mind on the subject! And Gertrude hunting for happiness in a rhyming dictionary! The girl's a greater fool than I took her for! [*Crosses*]

PRUDENCE: So she is—you see I know all about them!

TRUEMAN: I see you do! You've a wonderful knowledge—wonderful—of *other people's concerns!* It may do here, but take my word for it, in the county of Catteraugus you'd get the name of a great *busybody*. But perhaps you know that too?

PRUDENCE: Oh! I always know what's coming. I feel it beforehand all over me. I knew something was going to happen the day you came here—and what's more I can always tell a married man from a single—I felt right off that you were a bachelor!

TRUEMAN: Felt right off I was a bachelor did you? You were sure of it—sure?—quite sure? [PRUDENCE *assents delightedly*.] Then you felt wrong!—A bachelor and a widower are not the same thing!

PRUDENCE: Oh! but it all comes to the same thing—a widower's as good as a bachelor any day! And besides I knew that you were a farmer *right off*.

TRUEMAN: On the spot, eh? I suppose you saw cabbages and green peas growing out of my hat?

PRUDENCE: No, I didn't—but I knew all about you. And I knew—[*Looking down and fidgeting with her apron*] I knew you were for getting married soon! For last night I dreamt I saw your funeral going along the streets, and the mourners all dressed in white. And a funeral is a sure sign of a wedding, you know! [*Nudging him with her elbow*]

TRUEMAN: [*Imitating her voice*] Well, I can't say that I *know* any such thing! you know! [*Nudging her back*]

PRUDENCE: Oh! it does, and there's no getting over it! For my part, I like farmers—and I know all about setting hens and turkeys, and feeding chickens, and laying eggs, and all that sort of thing!

TRUEMAN: [*Aside*] May I be shot if mistress newspaper is not putting in an advertisement for herself! This is your city mode of courting, I suppose, ha, ha, ha!

PRUDENCE: I've been west, a little; but I never was in the county of Catteraugus, myself.

TRUEMAN: Oh! you were not? And you have taken a particular fancy to go there, eh?

PRUDENCE: Perhaps I shouldn't object—

TRUEMAN: Oh!—ah!—so I suppose. Now pay attention to what I am going to say, for it is a matter of great importance to yourself.

PRUDENCE: [*Aside*] Now it's coming—I know what he's going to say!

TRUEMAN: The next time you want to tie a man for life to your apron-strings, pick out one that don't come from the county of Catteraugus—for greenhorns are scarce in those parts, and modest women plenty! [*Exit*]

PRUDENCE: Now who'd have thought he was going to say that! But I won't give him up yet—I won't give him up. [*Exit*]

ACT III

Scene 1

MRS. TIFFANY's *Parlor. Enter* MRS. TIFFANY, *followed by* MR. TIFFANY.

TIFFANY: Your extravagance will ruin me, Mrs. Tiffany!

MRS. TIFFANY: And your stinginess will ruin me, Mr. Tiffany! It is totally and *toot a fate* impossible to convince you of the necessity of *keeping up appearances*. There is a certain display which every woman of fashion is forced to make!

TIFFANY: And pray who made *you* a woman of fashion?

MRS. TIFFANY: What a vulgar question! All women of fashion, Mr. Tiffany—

TIFFANY: In this land are *self-constituted,* like you, Madam—and *fashion* is the cloak for more sins than charity ever covered! It was for *fashion's* sake that you insisted upon my purchasing this expensive house—it was for *fashion's* sake that you ran me in debt at every exorbitant upholsterer's and extravagant furniture warehouse in the city—it was for *fashion's* sake that you built that ruinous conservatory—hired more servants than they have persons to wait upon—and dressed your footman like a harlequin!

MRS. TIFFANY: Mr. Tiffany, you are thoroughly plebeian, and insufferably *American,* in your grovelling ideas! And, pray, what was the occasion of these very *mal-ap-pro-pos* remarks? Merely because I requested a paltry fifty dollars to purchase a new style of headdress—a *bijou* of an article just introduced in France.

TIFFANY: Time was, Mrs. Tiffany, when you manufactured your own French headdresses—took off their first

34

gloss at the public balls, and then sold them to your shortest-sighted customers. And all you knew about France, or French either, was what you spelt out at the bottom of your fashion plates—but now you have grown so fashionable, forsooth, that you have forgotten how to speak your mother tongue!

MRS. TIFFANY: Mr. Tiffany, Mr. Tiffany! Nothing is more positively vulgarian—more *unaristocratic*—than any allusion to the past!

TIFFANY: Why I thought, my dear, that *aristocrats* lived principally upon the past—and traded in the market of fashion with the bones of their ancestors for capital?

MRS. TIFFANY: Mr. Tiffany, such vulgar remarks are only suitable to the counting house; in my drawing room you should—

TIFFANY: Vary my sentiments with my locality, as you change your *manners* with your *dress!*

MRS. TIFFANY: Mr. Tiffany, I desire that you will purchase Count d'Orsay's *Science of Etiquette*, and learn how to conduct yourself—especially before you appear at the grand ball, which I shall give on Friday!

TIFFANY: Confound your balls, Madam; they make *footballs* of my money, while you dance away all that I am worth! A pretty time to give a ball when you know that I am on the very brink of bankruptcy!

MRS. TIFFANY: So much the greater reason that nobody should suspect your circumstances, or you would lose your credit at once. Just at this crisis a ball is absolutely *necessary* to save your reputation! There is Mrs. Adolphus Dashaway—she gave the most splendid fête of the season—and I hear on very good authority that her husband has not paid his baker's bill in three months. Then there was Mrs. Honeywood—

TIFFANY: Gave a ball the night before her husband shot himself—perhaps you wish to drive me to follow his example? [*Crosses*]

MRS. TIFFANY: Good gracious! Mr. Tiffany, how you talk! I beg you won't mention anything of the kind. I consider black the most unbecoming color. I'm sure I've done all that I could to gratify you. There is that vulgar old torment, Trueman, who gives one the lie fifty times a day—haven't I been very civil to him?

TIFFANY: Civil to his *wealth*, Mrs. Tiffany! I told you that
he was a rich, old farmer—the early friend of my
father—my own benefactor—and that I had reason to
think he might assist me in my present embarrass-
ments. Your civility was *bought*—and like most of your
own purchases has yet to be *paid* for. [*Crosses*]

MRS. TIFFANY: And will be, no doubt! The condescension
of a woman of fashion should command any price. Mr.
Trueman is insupportably indecorous—he has insulted
Count Jolimaitre in the most outrageous manner. If the
Count was not so deeply interested—so *abimé* with
Seraphina, I am sure he would never honor us by his
visits again!

TIFFANY: So much the better—he shall never marry my
daughter!—I am resolved on that. Why, Madam, I am
told there is in Paris a regular matrimonial stock company, who fit out indigent dandies for this market. How
do I know but this fellow is one of its creatures, and
that he has come here to increase its dividends by marrying a fortune?

MRS. TIFFANY: Nonsense, Mr. Tiffany. The Count, the
most fashionable young man in all New York—the intimate friend of all the dukes and lords in Europe—not
marry my daughter? Not permit Seraphina to become
a Countess? Mr. Tiffany, you are out of your senses!

TIFFANY: That would not be very wonderful, considering
how many years I have been united to you, my dear.
Modern physicians pronounce lunacy infectious!

MRS. TIFFANY: Mr. Tiffany, he is a man of fashion—

TIFFANY: Fashion makes fools, but cannot *feed* them. By
the bye, I have a request—since you are bent upon
ruining me by this ball, and there is no help for it—I
desire that you will send an invitation to my confidential clerk, Mr. Snobson.

MRS. TIFFANY: Mr. Snobson! Was there ever such an *you-
nick* demand! Mr. Snobson would cut a pretty figure
amongst my fashionable friends! I shall do no such
thing, Mr. Tiffany.

TIFFANY: Then, Madam, the ball shall not take place.
Have I not told you that I am in the power of this man?
That there are circumstances which it is happy for you
that you do not know—which you cannot compre-

hend—but which render it essential that you should be civil to Mr. Snobson? Not you merely, but Seraphina also? He is a more appropriate match for her than your foreign favorite.

MRS. TIFFANY: A match for Seraphina, indeed! [*Crosses*] Mr. Tiffany, you are determined to make a *fow pas*.

TIFFANY: Mr. Snobson intends calling this morning. [*Crosses*]

MRS. TIFFANY: But, Mr. Tiffany, this is not reception day—my drawing-rooms are in the most terrible disorder—

TIFFANY: Mr. Snobson is not particular—he must be admitted.
[*Enter* ZEKE.]

ZEKE: Mr. Snobson.
[*Enter* SNOBSON. *Exit* ZEKE.]

SNOBSON: How dye do, Marm? [*Crosses*] How are you? Mr. Tiffany, your most!—

MRS. TIFFANY: [*Formally*] Bung jure. Comment vow portè vow, Monsur Snobson?

SNOBSON: Oh, to be sure—very good of you—fine day.

MRS. TIFFANY: [*Pointing to a chair with great dignity*] Sassoyez vow, Monsur Snobson.

SNOBSON: [*Aside*] I wonder what she's driving at? I ain't up to the fashionable lingo yet! Eh? What? Speak a little louder, Marm?

MRS. TIFFANY: [*Aside*] What ignorance!

TIFFANY: I presume Mrs. Tiffany means that you are to take a seat.

SNOBSON: Ex-actly—very obliging of her—so I will. [*Sits*] No ceremony amongst friends, you know—and likely to be nearer—you understand? *O.K.*, all correct. How *is* Seraphina?

MRS. TIFFANY: Miss Tiffany is not visible this morning. [*Retires up*]

SNOBSON: Not visible? [*Jumping up; Crosses*] I suppose that's the English for can't see her? Mr. Tiffany, Sir— [*Walking up to him*] what am I to understand by this *de-fal-ca-tion*, Sir? I expected your word to be as good as your bond—beg pardon, Sir—I mean *better*—considerably better—no humbug about it, Sir.

TIFFANY: Have patience, Mr. Snobson. [*Rings bell*]

[*Enter* ZEKE.]

Zeke, desire my daughter to come here.

MRS. TIFFANY: [*Coming down*] A-dolph—I say, A-dolph—
[ZEKE *straightens himself and assumes foppish airs, as he turns to* MRS. TIFFANY.]

TIFFANY: Zeke.

ZEKE: Don't know any such nigga, Boss.

TIFFANY: Do as I bid you instantly, or off with your livery and quit the house!

ZEKE: Wheugh! I'se all dismission!

[*Exit*]

MRS. TIFFANY: A-dolph, A-dolph! [*Calling after him*]

SNOBSON: [*Aside*] I brought the old boy to his bearings, didn't I though! Pull that string, and he is sure to work right. Don't make any stranger of me, Marm—I'm quite at home. If you've got any odd jobs about the house to do up, I sha'n't miss you. I'll amuse myself with Seraphina when she comes—we'll get along very cosily by ourselves.

MRS. TIFFANY: Permit me to inform you, Mr. Snobson, that a French mother never leaves her daughter alone with a young man—she knows your sex too well for that!

SNOBSON: Very *dis*-obliging of her—but as we're none French—

MRS. TIFFANY: You have yet to learn, Mr. Snobson, that the American *ee-light*—the aristocracy—the *how-ton*—as a matter of conscience, scrupulously follow the foreign fashions.

SNOBSON: Not when they are foreign to their interests, Marm—for instance—
[*Enter* SERAPHINA.]
There you are at last, eh, Miss? How d'ye do? Ma said you weren't visible. Managed to get a peep at her, eh, Mr. Tiffany?

SERAPHINA: I heard you were here, Mr. Snobson, and came without even arranging my toilette; you will excuse my negligence?

SNOBSON: Of everything but *me*, Miss.

SERAPHINA: I shall never have to ask your pardon for *that*, Mr. Snobson.

MRS. TIFFANY: Seraphina—child—really—

[*As she is approaching* SERAPHINA, MR. TIFFANY *plants himself in front of his wife.*]

TIFFANY: Walk this way, Madam, if you please. [*Aside*] To see that she fancies the surly fellow takes a weight from my heart.

MRS. TIFFANY: Mr. Tiffany, it is highly improper and not at all *distingué* to leave a young girl—

[*Enter* ZEKE.]

ZEKE: Mr. Count Jolly-made-her!

MRS. TIFFANY: Good gracious! The Count—Oh, dear!— Seraphina, run and change your dress—no, there's not time! A-dolph, admit him. [*Exit* ZEKE.] Mr. Snobson, get out of the way, will you? Mr. Tiffany, what are you doing at home at this hour?

[*Enter* COUNT JOLIMAITRE, *ushered by* ZEKE.]

ZEKE: [*Aside*] Dat's de genuine article ob a gemman. [*Exit.*]

MRS. TIFFANY: My dear Count, I am overjoyed at the very sight of you.

COUNT: Flattered myself you'd be glad to see me, Madam—knew it was not your *jour de reception*.

MRS. TIFFANY: But for you, Count, all days—

COUNT: I thought so. Ah, Miss Tiffany, on my honor, you're looking beautiful. [*Crosses*]

SERAPHINA: Count, flattery from you—

SNOBSON: What? Eh? What's that you say?

SERAPHINA: [*Aside to him*] Nothing but what etiquette requires.

COUNT: [*Regarding* MR. TIFFANY *through his eyeglass*] Your worthy Papa, I believe? Sir, your most obedient. [MR. TIFFANY *bows coldly;* COUNT *regards* SNOBSON *through his glass, shrugs his shoulders and turns away.*]

SNOBSON: [*To* MRS. TIFFANY] Introduce me, will you? I never knew a Count in all my life—what a strange-looking animal!

MRS. TIFFANY: Mr. Snobson, it is not the fashion to introduce in France!

SNOBSON: But, Marm, we're in America. [MRS. TIFFANY *crosses to* COUNT. *Aside*] The woman thinks she's somewhere else than where she is—she wants to make an *alibi?*

MRS. TIFFANY: I hope that we shall have the pleasure of seeing you on Friday evening, Count?

COUNT: Really, Madam, my invitations—my engagements—so numerous—I can hardly answer for myself; and you Americans take offence so easily—

MRS. TIFFANY: But Count, everybody expects you at our ball—you are the principal attraction—

SERAPHINA: Count, you *must* come!

COUNT: Since you insist—aw—aw—there's no resisting you, Miss Tiffany.

MRS. TIFFANY: I am so thankful. How can I repay your condescension! [COUNT *and* SERAPHINA *converse.*] Mr. Snobson, will you walk this way?—I have *such* a cactus in full bloom—remarkable flower! Mr. Tiffany, pray come here—I have something particular to say.

TIFFANY: Then speak out, my dear. [*Aside to her*] I thought it was highly improper just now to leave a girl with a young man?

MRS. TIFFANY: Oh, but the Count—that is different!

TIFFANY: I suppose you mean to say there's nothing of *the man* about him?

[*Enter* MILLINETTE *with a scarf in her hand.*]

MILLINETTE: [*Aside*] Adolph tell me he vas here. Pardon, Madame, I bring dis scarf for Mademoiselle.

MRS. TIFFANY: Very well, Millinette; you know best what is proper for her to wear.

[MR. *and* MRS. TIFFANY *and* SNOBSON *retire up; she engages the attention of both gentlemen.* MILLINETTE *crosses towards* SERAPHINA, *gives the* COUNT *a threatening look, and commences arranging the scarf over* SERAPHINA's *shoulders.*]

MILLINETTE: Mademoiselle, *permettez-moi.* [*Aside to* COUNT] *Perfide!* [*To* SERAPHINA] If Mademoiselle vil stand *tranquille* one *petit* moment. [*Turns* SERAPHINA's *back to the* COUNT, *and pretends to arrange the scarf. Aside to* COUNT] I must speak vid you today, or I tell all—you find me at de foot of de stair ven you go. *Prends garde!*

SERAPHINA: What is that you say, Millinette?

MILLINETTE: Dis scarf make you so very beautiful, Mademoiselle—*Je vous salue, mes dames.* [*Curtsies. Exit*]

COUNT: [*Aside*] Not a moment to lose! Miss Tiffany, I have an unpleasant—a particularly unpleasant piece of intelligence—you see, I have just received a letter from my friend—the—aw—the Earl of Airshire; the truth is, the Earl's daughter—beg you won't mention it—has distinguished me by a tender *penchant*.

SERAPHINA: I understand—and they wish you to return and marry the young lady; but surely you will not leave us, Count?

COUNT: If *you* bid me stay—I shouldn't have the conscience—I couldn't *afford* to tear myself away. [*Aside*] I'm sure that's honest.

SERAPHINA: Oh, Count!

COUNT: Say but one word—say that you shouldn't mind being made a Countess—and I'll break with the Earl tomorrow.

SERAPHINA: Count, this surprise—but don't think of leaving the country, Count—we could not pass the time without you! I—yes—yes, Count—I do consent!

COUNT: [*Aside, while he embraces her*] I thought she would! Enchanted, rapture, bliss, ecstasy, and all that sort of thing—words can't express it, but you understand. But it must be kept a secret—positively it *must!* If the rumor of our engagement were whispered abroad—the Earl's daughter—the delicacy of my situation, aw—you comprehend? It is even possible that our nuptials, my charming Miss Tiffany, *our nuptials* must take place in private!

SERAPHINA: Oh, that is quite impossible!

COUNT: It's the latest fashion abroad—the very latest. Ah, I knew that would determine you. Can I depend on your secrecy?

SERAPHINA: Oh, yes! Believe me.

SNOBSON: [*Coming forward in spite of* MRS. TIFFANY's *efforts to detain him*] Why, Seraphina, haven't you a word to throw to a dog?

TIFFANY: [*Aside*] I shouldn't think she had after wasting so many upon a puppy.

[*Enter* ZEKE, *wearing a three-cornered hat.*]

ZEKE: Missus, de bran new carriage am below.

MRS. TIFFANY: Show it up—I mean—very well, A-dolph.

[*Exit* ZEKE.] Count, my daughter and I are about to take an airing in our new *voyture*—will you honor us with your company?

COUNT: Madam, I—I have a most *pressing* engagement. A letter to write to the *Earl of Airshire*—who is at present residing in the *Isle of Skye*. I must bid you good morning.

MRS. TIFFANY: Good morning, Count.

[*Exit* COUNT.]

SNOBSON: *I'm* quite at leisure, [*Crosses to* MRS. TIFFANY] Marm. Books balanced—ledger closed—nothing to do all the afternoon—I'm for you.

MRS. TIFFANY: [*Without noticing him*] Come, Seraphina, come!

[*As they are going* SNOBSON *follows them.*]

SNOBSON: But Marm—I was saying, Marm, I am quite at leisure—not a thing to do; have I, Mr. Tiffany?

MRS. TIFFANY: Seraphina, child—your red shawl—remember—Mr. Snobson, *bon swear!*

[*Exit, leading* SERAPHINA]

SNOBSON: Swear! Mr. Tiffany, Sir, am I to be fobbed off with a *bon swear?* D—n it, I will swear!

TIFFANY: Have patience, Mr. Snobson; if you will accompany me to the counting house—

SNOBSON: Don't count too much on me, Sir. I'll make up no more accounts until these are settled! I'll run down and jump into the carriage in spite of her *bon swear*. [*Exit*]

TIFFANY: You'll jump into a hornet's nest, if you do! Mr. Snobson, Mr. Snobson! [*Exit after him*]

Scene 2

Housekeeper's room.

Enter MILLINETTE.

MILLINETTE: I have set dat bête, Adolph, to vatch for

him. He say he would come back so soon as Madame's
voiture drive from de door. If he not come—but he
vill—he vill—he *bien étourdi*, but he have *bon coeur*.
[*Enter* COUNT.]

COUNT: Ah! Millinette, my dear, you see what a goodnatured dog I am to fly at your bidding—.

MILLINETTE: Fly? Ah! *trompeur!* Vat for you fly from
Paris? Vat for you leave me—and I love you so much?
Ven you sick—you almost die—did I not stay by you—
take care of you—and you have no else friend? Vat for
you leave Paris?

COUNT: Never allude to disagreeable subjects, *mon enfant!* I was forced by uncontrollable circumstances to
fly to the land of liberty—

MILLINETTE: Vat you do vid all de money I give you?
The last sou I had—did I not give you?

COUNT: I dare say you did, ma petite— [*Aside*] Wish
you'd been better supplied! Don't ask any questions
here—can't explain now—the next time we meet—

MILLINETTE: But, ah! ven shall ve meet—ven? You not
deceive me, not any more.

COUNT: Deceive you! I'd rather deceive myself. [*Aside*]
I wish I could! I'd persuade myself you were once more
washing linen in the Seine!

MILLINETTE: I vill tell you ven ve shall meet—On Friday
night Madame give one grand ball—you come *sans
doute*—den ven de supper is served—de Americans
tink of noting else ven de supper come—den you steal
out of de room, and you find me here—and you give
me one grand *explanation!*

[*Enter* GERTRUDE, *unperceived.*]

COUNT: Friday night—while supper is serving—*parole
d'honneur* I will be here—I will explain everything—
my sudden departure from Paris—my—demme, my
countship—everything! Now let me go—if any of the
family should discover us—

GERTRUDE: [*Who during the last speech has gradually
advanced*] They might discover more than you think it
advisable for them to know!

COUNT: The devil!

MILLINETTE: *Mon Dieu!* Mademoiselle Gertrude!

COUNT: [*Recovering himself*] My dear Miss Gertrude, let me explain—aw—aw—nothing is more natural than the situation in which you find me—

GERTRUDE: I am inclined to believe that, Sir.

COUNT: Now—'pon my honor, that's not fair. Here is Millinette will bear witness to what I am about to say—

GERTRUDE: Oh, I have not the slightest doubt of that, Sir.

COUNT: You see, Millinette happened to be lady's-maid in the family of—of—the Duchess Chateau D'Espagne—and I chanced to be a particular friend of the Duchess—*very particular* I assure you! Of course I saw Millinette, and she, demme, she saw me! Didn't you, Millinette?

MILLINETTE: Oh! *oui*—Mademoiselle, I knew him ver vell.

COUNT: Well, it is a remarkable fact that—being in correspondence with this very Duchess—at this very time—

GERTRUDE: That is sufficient, Sir—I am already so well acquainted with your extraordinary talents for improvisation that I will not further tax your invention—

MILLINETTE: Ah! Mademoiselle Gertrude do not betray us—have pity!

COUNT: [*Assuming an air of dignity*] Silence, Millinette! My word has been doubted—the word of a nobleman! I will inform my friend, Mrs. Tiffany, of this young person's audacity. [*Going*]

GERTRUDE: [*Aside*] His own weapons alone can foil this villain! Sir—Sir—Count! [*At the last word the* COUNT *turns.*] Perhaps, Sir, the least said about this matter the better!

COUNT: [*Delightedly*] The least said? We won't say anything at all. [*Aside*] She's coming round—couldn't resist me! Charming Gertrude—

MILLINETTE: *Quoi?* Vat that you say?

COUNT: [*Aside to her*] My sweet, adorable Millinette, hold your tongue, will you?

MILLINETTE: [*Aloud*] No, I vill not! If you do look so from out your eyes at her again, I vill tell all!

COUNT: [*Aside*] Oh, I never could manage two women at once—jealousy makes the dear creatures so spiteful. The only valor is in flight! Miss Gertrude, I wish you good morning. Millinette, *mon enfant, adieu.* [*Exit*]

MILLINETTE: But I have one word more to say. Stop, Stop! [*Exit after him*]

GERTRUDE: [*Musingly*] Friday night, while supper is serving, he is to meet Millinette here and explain— what? This man is an impostor! His insulting me—his familiarity with Millinette—his whole conduct—prove it. If I tell Mrs. Tiffany this she will disbelieve me, and one word may place this so-called Count on his guard. To convince Seraphina would be equally difficult, and her rashness and infatuation may render her miserable for life. No—she shall be saved! I must devise some plan for opening their eyes. Truly, if I *cannot* invent one, I shall be the first woman who was ever at a loss for a stratagem—especially to punish a villain or to shield a friend. [*Exit*]

ACT IV

Scene 1

Ballroom splendidly illuminated. A curtain hung at the further end. MR. *and* MRS. TIFFANY, SERAPHINA, GERTRUDE, FOGG, TWINKLE, COUNT, SNOBSON, COLONEL HOWARD, *a number of guests—some seated, some standing. As the curtain rises, a cotillion is danced;* GERTRUDE *dancing with* HOWARD, SERAPHINA *with* COUNT.

COUNT: [*Advancing with* SERAPHINA *to the front of the stage*] Tomorrow then—tomorrow—I may salute you as my bride—demme, my Countess!
[*Enter* ZEKE, *with refreshments.*]

SERAPHINA: Yes, tomorrow. [*As the* COUNT *is about to reply,* SNOBSON *thrusts himself in front of* SERAPHINA.]

SNOBSON: You said you'd dance with me, Miss—now take my fin, and we'll walk about and see what's going on. [COUNT *raises his eyeglass, regards* SNOBSON, *and leads* SERAPHINA *away;* SNOBSON *follows, endeavoring to attract her attention, but encounters* ZEKE, *bearing a waiter of refreshments; stops, helps himself, and puts some in his pockets.*] Here's the treat! get my tomorrow's luncheon out of Tiff.
[*Enter* TRUEMAN, *yawning and rubbing his eyes.*]

TRUEMAN: What a nap I've had, to be sure! [*Looks at his watch*] Eleven o'clock, as I'm alive! [*To* TIFFANY, *who approaches*] Just the time when country folks are comfortably *turned in*, and here your grand *turn-out* has hardly begun yet!

GERTRUDE: [*Advancing*] I was just coming to look for you, Mr. Trueman. I began to fancy that you were paying a visit to dreamland.

TRUEMAN: So I was, child—so I was—and I saw a face—like yours—but brighter!—even brighter. [*To* TIFFANY] There's a smile for you, man! It makes one feel that the world has something worth living for in it yet! Do you remember a smile like that, Antony? Ah! I see you don't—but I do—I do! [*Much moved*]

HOWARD: [*Advancing*] Good evening, Mr. Trueman. [*Offers his hand*]

TRUEMAN: That's right, man; give me your whole hand! When a man offers me the tips of his fingers, I know at once there's nothing in him worth seeking beyond his fingers' ends.

[TRUEMAN *and* HOWARD, GERTRUDE *and* TIFFANY *converse.*]

MRS. TIFFANY: [*Advancing*] I'm in such a fidget lest that vulgar old fellow should disgrace us by some of his plebeian remarks! What it is to give a ball, when one is forced to invite vulgar people!

[MRS. TIFFANY *advances towards* TRUEMAN; SERAPHINA *stands conversing flippantly with the gentlemen who surround her; amongst them is* TWINKLE, *who, having taken a magazine from his pocket, is reading to her, much to the undisguised annoyance of* SNOBSON.]

Dear me, Mr. Trueman, you are very late—quite in the fashion, I declare!

TRUEMAN: Fashion! And pray what is *fashion*, madam? An agreement between certain persons to live without using their souls! to substitute etiquette for virtue—decorum for purity—manners for morals! to affect a shame for the works of their Creator! and expend all their rapture upon the works of their tailors and dressmakers!

MRS. TIFFANY: You have the most *ow-tray* ideas, Mr. Trueman—quite rustic, and deplorably *American!* But pray walk this way.

[MRS. TIFFANY *and* TRUEMAN *go up.*]

COUNT: [*Advancing to* GERTRUDE, HOWARD *a short distance behind her*] Miss Gertrude—no opportunity of speaking to you before—in demand, you know!

GERTRUDE: [*Aside*] I have no choice, I must be civil to him. What were you remarking, Sir?

COUNT: Miss Gertrude—charming Ger—aw—aw—[*Aside*]

I never found it so difficult to speak to a woman before.

GERTRUDE: Yes, a very charming ball—many beautiful faces here.

COUNT: Only one!—Aw—aw—one—the fact is— [*Talks to her in dumb show*]

HOWARD: What could old Trueman have meant by saying she fancied that puppy of a Count—that paste jewel thrust upon the little finger of society.

COUNT: Miss Gertrude—aw—'pon my honor—you don't understand—really—aw—aw—will you dance the polka with me?

[GERTRUDE *bows and gives him her hand; he leads her to the set forming;* HOWARD *remains looking after them.*]

HOWARD: Going to dance with him, too! A few days ago she would hardly bow to him civilly—could old Trueman have had reasons for what he said? [*Retires up*] [*Dance, the polka;* SERAPHINA, *after having distributed her bouquet, vinaigrette and fan amongst the gentlemen, dances with* SNOBSON.]

PRUDENCE: [*Peeping in as dance concludes*] I don't like dancing on Friday; something strange is always sure to happen! I'll be on the look out. [*Remains peeping and concealing herself when any of the company approach*]

GERTRUDE: [*Advancing hastily*] They are preparing the supper—now if I can only dispose of Millinette while I unmask this insolent pretender! [*Exit*]

PRUDENCE: [*Peeping*] What's that she said? It's coming! [*Re-enter* GERTRUDE, *bearing a small basket filled with bouquets; approaches* MRS. TIFFANY; *they walk to the front of the stage.*]

GERTRUDE: Excuse me, Madam—I believe this is just the hour at which you ordered supper?

MRS. TIFFANY: Well, what's that to you! So you've been dancing with the Count—how dare you dance with a nobleman—*you?*

GERTRUDE: I will answer that question half an hour hence. At present I have something to propose, which I think will gratify you and please your guests. I have heard that at the most elegant balls in Paris, it is customary—

MRS. TIFFANY: What? What?

GERTRUDE: To station a servant at the door with a basket of flowers. A bouquet is then presented to every lady as she passes in—I prepared this basket a short time ago. As the company walk in to supper, might not the flowers be distributed to advantage?

MRS. TIFFANY: How *distingué!* You are a good creature, Gertrude—there, run and hand the *bokettes* to them yourself! You shall have the whole credit of the thing.

GERTRUDE: [*Aside*] Caught in my own net! But, Madam, I know so little of fashions—Millinette, being French herself, will do it with so much more grace. I am sure Millinette—

MRS. TIFFANY: So am I. She will do it a thousand times better than you—there, go call her.

GERTRUDE: [*Giving basket*] But, Madam, pray order Millinette not to leave her station till supper is ended—as the company pass out of the supper room she may find that some of the ladies have been overlooked.

MRS. TIFFANY: That is true—very thoughtful of you, Gertrude. [*Exit* GERTRUDE.] What a *recherché* idea!
[*Enter* MILLINETTE.]
Here Millinette, take this basket. Place yourself there, and distribute these *bokettes* as the company pass in to supper; but remember not to stir from the spot until supper is over. It is a French fashion, you know, Millinette. I am so delighted to be the first to introduce it—it will be all the rage in the *bow-monde!*

MILLINETTE: [*Aside*] Mon Dieu! dis vill ruin all! Madame, Madame, let me tell you, Madame, dat in France, in Paris, it is de custom to present *les* bouquets ven every body first come—long before de supper. Dis vould be *outré! barbare!* not at all la mode! Ven dey do come in—dat is de fashion in Paris!

MRS. TIFFANY: Dear me! Millinette, what is the difference? besides, I'd have you to know that Americans always improve upon French fashions! here, take the basket, and let me see that you do it in the most *younick* and genteel manner.

[MILLINETTE *poutingly takes the basket and retires up stage. A march. Curtain hung at the further end of the room is drawn back, and discloses a room, in the center of which stands a supper table, beautifully decorated*

*and illuminated; the company promenade two by two
into the supper room;* MILLINETTE *presents bouquets
as they pass;* COUNT *leads* MRS. TIFFANY.]

TRUEMAN: [*Encountering* FOGG, *who is hurrying alone
to the supper room*] Mr. Fogg, never mind the supper,
man! Ha, ha, ha! Of course you are indifferent to suppers!

FOGG: Indifferent! suppers—oh, ah—no, Sir—suppers?
no—no—I'm not indifferent to suppers! [*Hurries away
towards table*]

TRUEMAN: Ha, ha, ha! Here's a new discovery I've made
in the fashionable world! Fashion don't permit the crit-
ters to have *heads* or *hearts,* but it allows them stomachs! [*To* TIFFANY, *who advances*] So it's not fashionable to *feel,* but it's fashionable to *feed,* eh, Antony?
Ha, ha, ha!

[TRUEMAN *and* TIFFANY *retire towards supper room.
Enter* GERTRUDE, *followed by* ZEKE.]

GERTRUDE: Zeke, go to the supper room instantly—whisper to Count Jolimaitre that all is ready, and that he
must keep his appointment without delay—then watch
him, and as he passes out of the room, place yourself
in front of Millinette in such a manner that the Count
cannot see her nor she him. Be sure that they do not
see each other—everything depends upon that.
[*Crosses*]

ZEKE: Missey, consider dat business brought to a scien-
tific conclusion.

[*Exit into supper room. Exit* GERTRUDE.]

PRUDENCE: [*Who has been listening*] What can she want
of the Count? I always suspected that Gertrude, because she is so merry and busy! Mr. Trueman thinks so
much of her too—I'll tell him this! There's something
wrong—but it all comes of giving a ball on a Friday!
How astonished the dear old man will be when he finds
out how much I know! [*Advances timidly towards the
supper room*]

Scene 2

Housekeeper's room; dark stage; table, two chairs.

[*Enter* GERTRUDE, *with a lighted candle in her hand.*]

GERTRUDE: So far the scheme prospers! and yet this imprudence—if I fail? Fail! to lack courage in a difficulty, or ingenuity in a dilemma, are not woman's failings! [*Enter* ZEKE, *with a napkin over his arm, and a bottle of champagne in his hand.*] Well Zeke—Adolph!

ZEKE: Dat's right, Missey; I feels just now as if dat was my legitimate title; dis here's de stuff to make a nigger feel like a gemman!

GERTRUDE: But he is coming?

ZEKE: He's coming! [*Sound of a champagne cork heard*] Do you hear dat, Missey? Don't it put you all in a froth, and make you feel as light as a cork? Dere's nothing like the *union brand,* to wake up de harmonies ob de heart.

[*Drinks from bottle*]

GERTRUDE: Remember to keep watch upon the outside— do not stir from the spot; when I call you, come in quickly with a light—now, will you be gone!

ZEKE: I'm off, Missey, like a champagne cork wid de strings cut. [*Exit*]

GERTRUDE: I think I hear the Count's step. [*Crosses, stage dark; she blows out candle.*] Now if I can but disguise my voice, and make the best of my French. [*Enter* COUNT.]

COUNT: Millinette, where are you? How am I to see you in the dark?

GERTRUDE: [*Imitating* MILLINETTE's *voice in a whisper*] Hush! *parle bas.*

COUNT: Come here and give me a kiss.

GERTRUDE: Non—non— [*Retreating alarmed.* COUNT *follows.*] make haste, I must know all.

COUNT: You did not use to be so deuced particular.

ZEKE: [*Without*] No admission, gemman! Box office closed, tickets stopped!

TRUEMAN: [*Without*] Out of my way; do you want me to try if your head is as hard as my stick?

GERTRUDE: What shall I do? Ruined, ruined! [*She stands with her hands clasped in speechless despair.*]

COUNT: Halloa! they are coming here, Millinette! Millinette, why don't you speak? Where can I hide myself? [*Running about stage, feeling for a door*] Where are all your closets? If I could only get out—or get in somewhere; may I be smothered in a clothes' basket if you ever catch me in such a scrape again! [*His hand accidentally touches the knob of a door opening into a closet.*] Fortune's favorite yet! I'm safe!

[*Gets into closet and closes door. Enter* PRUDENCE, TRUEMAN, MRS. TIFFANY, *and* COLONEL HOWARD, *followed by* ZEKE, *bearing a light; lights up.*]

PRUDENCE: Here they are, the Count and Gertrude! I told you so! [*Stops in surprise on seeing only* GERTRUDE]

TRUEMAN: And you see what a lie you told!

MRS. TIFFANY: Prudence, how dare you create this disturbance in my house? To suspect the Count, too—a nobleman!

HOWARD: My sweet Gertrude, this foolish old woman would—

PRUDENCE: Oh! you needn't talk—I heard her make the appointment—I know he's here—or he's been here. I wonder if she hasn't hid him away! [*Runs peeping about the room*]

TRUEMAN: [*Following her angrily*] You're what I call a confounded—troublesome—meddling—old—prying— [*As he says the last word,* PRUDENCE *opens closet where the* COUNT *is concealed.*] Thunder and lightning!

PRUDENCE: I told you so!

[*They all stand aghast;* MRS. TIFFANY, *with her hands lifted in surprise and anger;* TRUEMAN, *clutching his stick;* HOWARD, *looking with an expression of bewildered horror from the* COUNT *to* GERTRUDE.]

MRS. TIFFANY: [*Shaking her fist at* GERTRUDE] You depraved little minx! this is the meaning of your dancing with the Count!

COUNT: [*Stepping from the closet and advancing*] [*Aside*]

I don't know what to make of it! Millinette not here!
Miss Gertrude—Oh! I see—a disguise—the girl's desperate about me—the way with them all.

TRUEMAN: I'm choking—I can't speak—Gertrude—no—
no—it is some horrid mistake! [*Partly aside, changes
his tone suddenly*] The villain! I'll hunt the truth out
of him, if there's any in— [*Crosses, approaches* COUNT
threateningly] Do you see this stick? You made its first
acquaintance a few days ago; it is time you were better
known to each other.

[*As* TRUEMAN *attempts to seize him,* COUNT *escapes,
crosses and shields himself behind* MRS. TIFFANY,
TRUEMAN *following.*]

COUNT: You ruffian! would you strike a woman?—
Madam—my dear Madam—keep off that barbarous old
man, and I will explain! Madam, with—aw—your natural *bon gout*—aw—your fashionable refinement—aw—
your—aw—your knowledge of *foreign customs*—

MRS. TIFFANY: Oh! Count, I hope it ain't a *foreign custom*
for the nobility to shut themselves up in the dark with
young women? We think such things *dreadful* in
America.

COUNT: Demme—aw—hear what I have to say, Madam—
I'll satisfy all sides—I am perfectly innocent in this
affair—'pon my honor I am! That young lady shall inform you that I am so herself!—can't help it, sorry for
her. Old matter-of-fact won't be convinced any other
way. [*Aside*] That club of his is so particularly unpleasant! Madam, I was summoned here *malgré moi*, and
not knowing whom I was to meet—Miss Gertrude, favor the company by saying whether or not you
directed—that—aw—aw—that colored individual to
conduct me here?

GERTRUDE: Sir, you well know—

COUNT: A simple yes or no will suffice.

MRS. TIFFANY: Answer the Count's question instantly,
Miss.

GERTRUDE: I did—but—

COUNT: You hear, Madam—

TRUEMAN: I won't believe it—I can't! Here, you nigger,
stop rolling up your eyes, and let us know whether she
told you to bring that critter here?

ZEKE: I'se refuse to gib ebidence; dat's de device ob de skilfullest counsels ob de day! Can't answer, Boss—neber git a word out ob dis child—Yah! yah! [*Exit*]

GERTRUDE: Mrs. Tiffany—Mr. Trueman, if you will but have patience—

TRUEMAN: Patience! Oh, Gertrude, you've taken from an old man something better and dearer than his patience—the one bright hope of nineteen years of self-denial—of nineteen years of— [*Throws himself upon a chair, his head leaning on table*]

MRS. TIFFANY: Get out of my house, you *ow*dacious—you ruined—you *abimé* young woman! You will corrupt all my family. Good gracious! don't touch me—don't come near me. Never let me see your face after tomorrow. Pack. [*Goes up*]

HOWARD: Gertrude, I have striven to find some excuse for you—to doubt—to disbelieve—but this is beyond all endurance! [*Exit*]

[*Enter* MILLINETTE *in haste.*]

MILLINETTE: I could not come before— [*Stops in surprise at seeing the persons assembled*] Mon Dieu! vat does dis mean?

COUNT: [*Aside to her*] Hold your tongue, fool! You will ruin everything. I will explain tomorrow. Mrs. Tiffany—Madam—my dear Madam, let me conduct you back to the ballroom. [*She takes his arm.*] You see I am quite innocent in this matter; a man of my standing, you know—aw—aw—you comprehend the whole affair.

[*Exit* COUNT *leading* MRS. TIFFANY.]

MILLINETTE: I will say to him von vord, I will! [*Exit*]

GERTRUDE: Mr. Trueman, I beseech you—I insist upon being heard—I claim it as a right!

TRUEMAN: Right? How dare you have the face, girl, to talk of rights? [*Comes down*] You had more rights than you thought, but you have forfeited them all! All rights to love, respect, protection, and to not a little else that you don't dream of. Go, go! I'll start for Catteraugus tomorrow—I've seen enough of what fashion can do! [*Exit*]

PRUDENCE: [*Wiping her eyes*] Dear old man, how he takes on! I'll go and console him! [*Exit*]

GERTRUDE: This is too much! How heavy a penalty has my imprudence cost me!—his esteem, and that of one dearer—my home—my— [*Burst of lively music from ballroom*] They are dancing, and I—I should be weeping, if pride had not sealed up my tears.

[*She sinks into a chair. Band plays the polka behind till Curtain falls.*]

ACT V

MRS. TIFFANY's *Drawing Room—same Scene as Act I.*
GERTRUDE *seated at a table, with her head leaning on
her hand; in the other hand she holds a pen. A sheet of
paper and an ink-stand before her.*

GERTRUDE: How shall I write to them? What shall I say?
Prevaricate I cannot— [*Rises and comes forward*] and
yet if I write the truth—simple souls! how can they
comprehend the motives for my conduct? Nay—the
truly pure see no imaginary evil in others! It is only
vice that, reflecting its own image, suspects even the
innocent. I have no time to lose—I must prepare them
for my return. [*Resumes her seat and writes*] What a
true pleasure there is in daring to be frank! [*After writing a few lines more pauses*] Not so frank either—there
is one name that I cannot mention. Ah! that he should
suspect—should despise me. [*Writes*]
[*Enter* TRUEMAN.]
TRUEMAN: There she is! If this girl's soul had only been
as fair as her face—yet she dared to speak the truth, I'll
not forget that! A woman who refuses to tell a lie has
one spark of heaven in her still. [*Approaches her*] Gertrude, [GERTRUDE *starts and looks up.*] what are you
writing there? Plotting more mischief, eh, girl?
GERTRUDE: I was writing a few lines to some friends in
Geneva.
TRUEMAN: The Wilsons, eh?
GERTRUDE: [*Surprised, rising*] Are you acquainted with
them, Sir?
TRUEMAN: I shouldn't wonder if I was. I suppose you

56

have taken good care not to mention the dark room—
that foreign puppy in the closet—the pleasant surprise—and all that sort of thing, eh?

GERTRUDE: I have no reason for concealment, Sir, for I
have done nothing of which I am ashamed!

TRUEMAN: Then I can't say much for your modesty.

GERTRUDE: I should not wish you to say more than I
deserve.

TRUEMAN: [*Aside*] There's a bold minx!

GERTRUDE: Since my affairs seem to have excited your
interest—I will not say *curiosity*—perhaps you even
feel a desire to inspect my correspondence? There,
[*Handing the letter*] I pride myself upon my good nature—you may like to take advantage of it?

TRUEMAN: [*Aside*] With what an air she carries it off! Take
advantage of it? So I will. [*Reads*] What's this? "French
chambermaid—Count—impostor—infatuation—Seraphina—Millinette—disguised myself—expose him."
Thunder and lightning! I see it all! Come and kiss me,
girl! [GERTRUDE *evinces surprise.*] No, no—I forgot—
it won't do to come to that yet! She's a rare girl! I'm out
of my senses with joy! I don't know what to do with
myself! Tol, de rol, de rol, de ra! [*Capers and sings*]

GERTRUDE: [*Aside*] What a remarkable old man! Then
you do me justice, Mr. Trueman?

TRUEMAN: I say I don't! Justice? You're above all dependence upon justice! Hurrah! I've found one true woman
at last! *True?* [*Pauses thoughtfully*] Humph! I didn't
think of that flaw! Plotting and maneuvering—not
much truth in that! An honest girl should be above
stratagems!

GERTRUDE: But my *motive*, Sir, was good.

TRUEMAN: That's not enough—your *actions* must be *good*
as well as your *motives*! Why could you not tell the
silly girl that man was an impostor?

GERTRUDE: I did inform her of my suspicions—she ridi-
culed them; the plan I chose was an imprudent one,
but I could not devise—

TRUEMAN: I hate devising! Give me a woman with the
firmness to be *frank!* But no matter—I had no right to
look for an angel out of Paradise; and I am as happy—
as happy as a Lord! that is, ten times happier than any

Lord ever was! Tol, de rol, de rol! Oh! you—you—I'll thrash every fellow that says a word against you!

GERTRUDE: You will have plenty of employment then, Sir, for I do not know of one just now who would speak in my favor!

TRUEMAN: Not *one*, eh? Why, where's your dear Mr. Twinkle? I know all about it—can't say that I admire your choice of a husband! But there's no accounting for a girl's taste.

GERTRUDE: Mr. Twinkle! Indeed you are quite mistaken!

TRUEMAN: No—really? Then you're not taken with him, eh?

GERTRUDE: Not even with his rhymes.

TRUEMAN: Hang that old mother meddle-much! What a fool she has made of me. And so you're quite free, and I may choose a husband for you myself? Heart-whole, eh?

GERTRUDE: I—I—I trust there is nothing *unsound* about my heart.

TRUEMAN: There it is again. Don't prevaricate, girl! I tell you an *evasion* is a *lie in contemplation,* and I hate lying! Out with the truth! Is your heart *free* or not?

GERTRUDE: Nay, Sir, since you *demand* an answer, permit *me* to demand by what right you ask the question? [*Enter* HOWARD.] Colonel Howard here!

TRUEMAN: I'm out again! What's the Colonel to her? [*Retires up*]

HOWARD: [*Crosses to her*] I have come, Gertrude, to bid you farewell. Tomorrow I resign my commission and leave this city, perhaps forever. You, Gertrude, it is you who have exiled me! After last evening—

TRUEMAN: [*Coming forward to* HOWARD] What the plague have you got to say about last evening?

HOWARD: Mr. Trueman!

TRUEMAN: What have you got to say about last evening? and what have you to say to that little girl at all? It's Tiffany's precious daughter you're in love with.

HOWARD: Miss Tiffany? Never! I never had the slightest pretension—

TRUEMAN: That lying old woman! But I'm glad of it! Oh! Ah! Um! [*Looking significantly at* GERTRUDE *and then at* HOWARD] I see how it is. So you don't choose to marry Seraphina, eh? Well now, whom do you choose to marry? [*Glancing at* GERTRUDE]

HOWARD: I shall not marry at all!

TRUEMAN: You won't? [*Looking at them both again*] Why you don't mean to say that you don't like— [*Points with his thumb to* GERTRUDE]

GERTRUDE: Mr. Trueman, I may have been wrong to boast of my good nature, but do not presume too far upon it.

HOWARD: You like frankness, Mr. Trueman, therefore I will speak plainly. I have long cherished a dream from which I was last night rudely awakened.

TRUEMAN: And that's what you call speaking plainly? Well, I differ with you! But I can guess what you mean. Last night you suspected Gertrude there of— [*Angrily*] of what no man shall ever suspect her again while I'm above ground! You did her injustice—it was a mistake! There, now that matter's settled. Go, and ask her to forgive you—she's woman enough to do it! Go, go!

HOWARD: Mr. Trueman, you have forgotten to whom you dictate.

TRUEMAN: Then you won't do it? You won't ask her pardon?

HOWARD: Most undoubtedly I will not—not at any man's bidding. I must first know—

TRUEMAN: You won't do it? Then if I don't give you a lesson in politeness—

HOWARD: It will be because you find me your *tutor* in the same science. I am not a man to brook an insult, Mr. Trueman! but we'll not quarrel in presence of the lady.

TRUEMAN: Won't we? I don't know that—

GERTRUDE: Pray, Mr. Trueman—Colonel Howard, pray desist, Mr. Trueman, for my sake! [*Taking hold of his arm to hold him back*] Colonel Howard, if you will read this letter it will explain everything.

[*Hands letter to* HOWARD, *who reads*]

TRUEMAN: He don't deserve an explanation! Didn't I tell him that it was a mistake? Refuse to beg your pardon! I'll teach him, I'll teach him!

HOWARD: [*After reading*] Gertrude, how have I wronged you!

TRUEMAN: Oh, you'll beg her pardon now?
[*Between them*]

HOWARD: Hers, Sir, and yours! Gertrude, I fear—

TRUEMAN: You needn't—she'll forgive you. You don't know these women as well as I do—they're always ready to pardon; it's their nature, and they can't help it. Come along, I left Antony and his wife in the dining room; we'll go and find them. I've a story of my own to tell! As for you, Colonel, you may follow. Come along. Come along! [*Leads out* GERTRUDE, *followed by* HOWARD]

[*Enter* MR. *and* MRS. TIFFANY, MR. TIFFANY *with a bundle of bills in his hand.*]

MRS. TIFFANY: I beg you won't mention the subject again, Mr. Tiffany. Nothing is more plebeian than a discussion upon economy—nothing more *ungenteel* than looking over and fretting over one's bills!

TIFFANY: Then I suppose, my dear, it is quite as ungenteel to *pay* one's bills?

MRS. TIFFANY: Certainly! I hear the *ee-light* never condescend to do anything of the kind. The honor of their invaluable patronage is sufficient for the persons they employ!

TIFFANY: *Patronage* then is a newly invented food upon which the working classes fatten? What convenient appetites poor people must have! Now listen to what I am going to say. As soon as my daughter marries Mr. Snobson—

[*Enter* PRUDENCE, *a three-cornered note in her hand.*]

PRUDENCE: Oh, dear! oh, dear! what shall we do! Such a misfortune! Such a disaster! Oh, dear! oh, dear!

MRS. TIFFANY: Prudence, you are the most tiresome creature! What *is* the matter?

PRUDENCE: [*Pacing up and down the stage*] Such a disgrace to the whole family! But I always expected it. Oh, dear! Oh, dear!

MRS. TIFFANY: [*Following her up and down the stage*] What are you talking about, Prudence? Will you tell me what has happened?

PRUDENCE: [*Still pacing,* MRS. TIFFANY *following*] Oh! I can't, I can't! You'll feel so dreadfully! How could she do such a thing! But I expected nothing else! I never did, I never did!

MRS. TIFFANY: [*Still following*] Good gracious! what do you mean, Prudence? Tell me, will you tell me? I shall get into such a passion! What *is* the matter?

PRUDENCE: [*Still pacing*] Oh, Betsy, Betsy! That your daughter should have come to that! Dear me, dear me!

TIFFANY: Seraphina? Did you say Seraphina? What has happened to her? what has she done?

[*Following* PRUDENCE *up and down the stage on the opposite side from* MRS. TIFFANY]

MRS. TIFFANY: [*Still following*] What *has* she done? What *has* she done?

PRUDENCE: Oh! something dreadful—dreadful—shocking!

TIFFANY: [*Still following*] Speak quickly and plainly—you torture me by this delay—Prudence, be calm, and speak! What is it?

PRUDENCE: [*Stopping*] Zeke just told me—he carried her travelling trunk himself—she gave him a whole dollar! Oh, my!

TIFFANY: Her trunk? where? where?

PRUDENCE: Round the corner!

MRS. TIFFANY: What did she want with her trunk? You are the most vexatious creature, Prudence! There is no bearing your ridiculous conduct!

PRUDENCE: Oh, you will have worse to bear—worse! Seraphina's gone!

TIFFANY: Gone! Where?

PRUDENCE: Off!—eloped—eloped with the Count! Dear me, dear me! I always told you she would!

TIFFANY: Then I am ruined! [*Stands with his face buried in his hands*]

MRS. TIFFANY: Oh, what a ridiculous girl! And she might have had such a splendid wedding! What could have possessed her?

TIFFANY: The devil himself possessed her, for she has ruined me past all redemption! Gone, Prudence, did you say gone? Are you *sure* they are gone?

PRUDENCE: Didn't I tell you so! Just look at this note— one might know by the very fold of it—

TIFFANY: [*Snatching the note*] Let me see it! [*Opens the note and reads*] "My dear Ma—When you receive this I shall be a *countess!* Isn't it a sweet title? The Count and I were forced to be married privately, for reasons which I will explain in my next. You must pacify Pa, and put him in a good humor before I come back, though now I'm to be a countess I suppose I shouldn't care!" Undutiful huzzy! "We are going to make a little excursion and will be back in a week. Your dutiful daughter—Seraphina." A man's curse is sure to spring up at his own hearth—here is mine! The sole curb upon that villain gone, I am wholly in his power! Oh! the first downward step from honor—he who takes it cannot pause in his mad descent and is sure to be hurried on to ruin!

MRS. TIFFANY: Why, Mr. Tiffany, how you do take on! And I dare say to elope was the most fashionable way after all!

[*Enter* TRUEMAN, *leading* GERTRUDE, *and followed by* HOWARD.]

TRUEMAN: Where are all the folks? Here, Antony, you are the man I want. We've been hunting for you all over the house. Why—what's the matter? There's a face for a thriving city merchant! Ah! Antony, you never wore such a hang-dog look as that when you trotted about the country with your pack upon your back! Your shoulders are no broader now—but they've a heavier load to carry—that's plain!

MRS. TIFFANY: Mr. Trueman, such allusions are highly improper! What would my daughter, *the Countess*, say!

GERTRUDE: The Countess? Oh! Madam!

MRS. TIFFANY: Yes, the Countess! My daughter Seraphina, the Countess *dee* Jolimaitre! What have you to say to that? No wonder you are surprised after your *recherché, abimé* conduct! I have told you already, Miss Gertrude, that you were not a proper person to enjoy the inestimable advantages of my patronage. You are dismissed—do you understand? Discharged!

TRUEMAN: Have you done? Very well, it's my turn now. Antony, perhaps what I have to say don't concern you as much as some others—but I want you to listen to

me. You remember, Antony, [*His tone becomes serious*]
a blue-eyed, smiling girl—

TIFFANY: Your daughter, Sir? I remember her well.

TRUEMAN: None ever saw her to forget her! Give me your
hand, man. There—that will do! Now let me go on. I
never coveted wealth—yet twenty years ago I found
myself the richest farmer in Catteraugus. This cursed
money made my girl an object of speculation. Every
idle fellow that wanted to feather his nest was sure to
come courting Ruth. There was one—my heart misgave
me the instant I laid eyes upon him—for he was a city
chap, and not over fond of the truth. But Ruth—ah! she
was too pure herself to look for guile! His fine words
and his fair looks—the old story—she was taken with
him—I said, "no"—but the girl liked her own way better than her old father's—girls always do! and one
morning—the rascal robbed me—not of my money—he
would have been welcome to that—but of the only treasure I cherished—my daughter!

TIFFANY: But you forgave her!

TRUEMAN: I did! I knew she would never forgive herself—that was punishment enough! The scoundrel
thought he was marrying my gold with my daughter—
he was mistaken! I took care that they should never
want; but that was all. She loved him—what will not
woman love? The villain broke her heart—mine was
tougher, or it wouldn't have stood what it did. A year
after they were married, he forsook her! She came back
to her old home—her old father! It couldn't last long—
she pined—and pined—and—then—she died! Don't
think me an old fool—though I am one—for grieving
won't bring her back. [*Bursts into tears*]

TIFFANY: It was a heavy loss!

TRUEMAN: So heavy that I should not have cared how
soon I followed her, but for the child she left! As I
pressed that child in my arms, I swore that my unlucky
wealth should never curse it, as it had cursed its
mother! It was all I had to love—but I sent it away—
and the neighbors thought it was dead. The girl was
brought up tenderly but humbly by my wife's relatives
in Geneva. I had her taught true independence—she

had hands—capacities—and should use them! Money
should never buy her a husband! For I resolved not to
claim her until she had made her choice, and found the
man who was willing to take her for herself alone. She
turned out a rare girl! and it's time her old grandfather
claimed her. Here he is to do it! And there stands
Ruth's child! Old Adam's heiress! Gertrude, Gertrude!—my child!

[GERTRUDE *rushes into his arms.*]

PRUDENCE: [*After a pause*] Do tell; I want to know! But
I knew it! I always said Gertrude would turn out somebody, after all!

MRS. TIFFANY: Dear me! Gertrude an heiress! My dear
Gertrude, I always thought you a very charming girl—
quite YOU-NICK—an heiress! [*Aside*] I must give her a
ball! I'll introduce her into society myself—of course
an heiress must make a sensation!

HOWARD: [*Aside*] I am too bewildered even to wish her
joy. Ah! there will be plenty to do that now—but the
gulf between us is wider than ever.

TRUEMAN: Step forward, young man, and let us know
what you are muttering about. I said I would never
claim her until she had found the man who loved her
for herself. I *have* claimed her—yet I never break my
word—I think I *have* found that man! and here he is.
[*Strikes* HOWARD *on the shoulder*] Gertrude's yours!
There—never say a word, man—don't bore me with
your thanks—you can cancel all obligations by making
that child happy! There—take her!—Well, girl, and
what do you say?

GERTRUDE: That I rejoice too much at having found a
parent for my first act to be one of disobedience! [*Gives
her hand to* HOWARD]

TRUEMAN: How very dutiful! and how disinterested!
[TIFFANY *retires up—and paces the stage, exhibiting
great agitation.*]

PRUDENCE: [*To* TRUEMAN] All the *single folks* are getting
married!

TRUEMAN: No they are not. You and I are single folks,
and we're not likely to get married.

MRS. TIFFANY: My dear Mr. Trueman—my sweet Gertrude, when my daughter, the Countess, returns, she

will be delighted to hear of this *deenooment!* I assure
you that the *Countess* will be quite charmed!

GERTRUDE: The Countess? Pray, Madam, where *is* Seraphina?

MRS. TIFFANY: The Countess *dee* Jolimaitre, my dear, is
at this moment on her way to—to Washington! Where
after visiting all the fashionable curiosities of the day—
including the *President*—she will return to grace her
native city!

GERTRUDE: I hope you are only jesting, Madam? Seraphina is not married?

MRS. TIFFANY: Excuse me, my dear, my daughter had this
morning the honor of being united to the Count *dee*
Jolimaitre!

GERTRUDE: Madam! He is an impostor!

MRS. TIFFANY: Good gracious! Gertrude, how can you
talk in that disrespectful way of a man of rank? An heiress, my dear, should have better manners! The Count—
[*Enter* MILLINETTE, *crying.*]

MILLINETTE: Oh! Madame! I will tell everyting—oh! dat
monstre! He break my heart!

MRS. TIFFANY: Millinette, what is the matter?

MILLINETTE: Oh! he promise to marry me—I love him
much—and now Zeke say he run away vid Mademoiselle Seraphina!

MRS. TIFFANY: What insolence! The girl is mad! Count
Jolimaitre marry my *femmy de chamber!*

MILLINETTE: Oh! Madame, he is not one Count, not at
all! Dat is only de title he go by in dis country. De
foreigners always take de large title ven dey do come
here. His name *à Paris* vas Gustave Treadmill. But he
not one Frenchman at all, but he do live one long time
à Paris. First he live vid Monsieur Vermicelle—dere
he vas de head cook! Den he live vid Monsieur Tire-
nez, de barber! After dat he live vid Monsieur le
Comte Frippon-fin—and dere he vas le Comte's valet!
Dere, now I tell everyting I feel one great deal better!

MRS. TIFFANY: Oh! good gracious! I shall faint! Not a
Count! What will everybody say? It's no such thing! I
say he *is* a Count! One can see the foreign *jenny says
quoi* in his face! Don't you think I can tell a Count
when I see one? I say he *is* a Count!

[*Enter* SNOBSON, *his hat on, his hands thrust in his pockets, evidently a little intoxicated.*]

SNOBSON: I won't stand it! I say I won't!

TIFFANY: [*Rushing up to him. Aside*] Mr. Snobson, for heaven's sake—

SNOBSON: Keep off! I'm a hard customer to get the better of! You'll see if I don't come out strong!

TRUEMAN: [*Quietly knocking off* SNOBSON's *hat with his stick*] Where are your manners, man?

SNOBSON: My business ain't with you, Catteraugus; you've waked up the wrong passenger! [*Aside*] Now the way I'll put it into Tiff will be a caution. I'll make him wince! That extra mint julep has put the true pluck in me. Now for it! Mr. Tiffany, Sir—you needn't think to come over me, Sir—you'll have to get up a little earlier in the morning before you do *that,* Sir! I'd like to know, Sir, how you came to assist your daughter in running away with that foreign loafer? It was a downright swindle, Sir. After the conversation I and you had on that subject she wasn't your property, Sir.

TRUEMAN: What, Antony, is that the way your city clerk bullies his boss?

SNOBSON: You're drunk, Catteraugus—don't expose yourself—you're drunk! Taken a little too much toddy, my old boy! Be quiet! I'll look after you, and they won't find it out. If you want to be busy, you may take care of my *hat*—I feel so deuced weak in the chest, I don't think I *could* pick it up myself. [*Aside*] Now to put the screws to Tiff. Mr. Tiffany, Sir—you have broken your word, as no virtuous individual—no honorable member—of—the—com—mu—ni—ty—

TIFFANY: [*Aside to him*] Have some pity, Mr. Snobson, I beseech you! I had nothing to do with my daughter's elopement! I will agree to anything you desire—your salary shall be doubled—trebled—

SNOBSON: [*Aloud*] No you don't. No bribery and corruption.

TIFFANY: [*Aside to him*] I implore you to be silent. You shall become partner of the concern, if you please—only do not speak. You are not yourself at this moment.

SNOBSON: Ain't I, though? I feel *twice* myself. I feel like two Snobsons rolled into one, and I'm chock full of the spunk of a dozen! Now Mr. Tiffany, Sir—

TIFFANY: [*Aside to him*] I shall go distracted! Mr. Snobson, if you have one spark of manly feeling—

TRUEMAN: Antony, why do you stand disputing with that drunken jackass? Where's your nigger? Let him kick the critter out, and be of use for once in his life.

SNOBSON: Better be quiet, Catteraugus. This ain't your hash, so keep your spoon out of the dish. Don't expose yourself, old boy.

TRUEMAN: Turn him out, Antony!

SNOBSON: He daren't do it! Ain't I up to him? Ain't he in my power? Can't I knock him into a cocked hat with a word? And now he's got my steam up—I *will* do it!

TIFFANY: [*Beseechingly*] Mr. Snobson—my friend—

SNOBSON: It's no go—steam's up—and I don't stand at anything!

TRUEMAN: You won't *stand* here long unless you mend your manners—you're not the first man I've *upset* because he didn't know his place.

SNOBSON: I know where Tiff's place is, and that's in the *States' Prison!* It's bespoke already. He would have it! He wouldn't take pattern of me, and behave like a gentleman! He's a *forger*, Sir! [TIFFANY *throws himself into a chair in an attitude of despair; the others stand transfixed with astonishment.*] He's been forging Dick Anderson's endorsements of his notes these ten months. He's got a couple in the bank that will send him to the wall anyhow—if he can't make a raise. I took them there myself! Now you know what he's worth. I said I'd expose him, and I have done it!

MRS. TIFFANY: Get out of the house! You ugly, little, drunken brute, get out! It's not true. Mr. Trueman, put him out; you have got a stick—put him out!

[*Enter* SERAPHINA, *in her bonnet and shawl—a parasol in her hand.*]

SERAPHINA: I hope Zeke hasn't delivered my note. [*Stops in surprise at seeing the persons assembled*]

MRS. TIFFANY: Oh, here is the Countess! [*Advances to embrace her*]

TIFFANY: [*Starting from his seat, and seizing* SERAPHINA *violently by the arm*] Are—you—married?

SERAPHINA: Goodness, Pa, how you frighten me! No, I'm not married, *quite*.

TIFFANY: Thank heaven.

MRS. TIFFANY: [*Drawing* SERAPHINA *aside*] What's the matter? Why did you come back?

SERAPHINA: The clergyman wasn't at home—I came back for my jewels—the Count said nobility couldn't get on without them.

TIFFANY: I may be saved yet! Seraphina, my child, you will not see me disgraced—ruined! I have been a kind father to you—at least I have tried to be one—although your mother's extravagance made a *madman* of me! The Count is an impostor—you seemed to like him— [*pointing to* SNOBSON] [*Aside*] Heaven forgive me! Marry *him* and save *me*. You, Mr. Trueman, you will be my friend in this hour of extreme need—you will advance the sum which I require—I pledge myself to return it. My wife—my child—who will support them were I—the thought makes me frantic! You will aid me? You had a child yourself.

TRUEMAN: But I did not *sell* her—it was her own doings. Shame on you, Antony! Put a price on your own flesh and blood! Shame on such foul traffic!

TIFFANY: Save me—I conjure you—for my father's sake.

TRUEMAN: For your *father's* SON's sake I will *not* aid you in becoming a greater villain than you are!

GERTRUDE: Mr. Trueman—Father, I should say—save him—do not embitter our happiness by permitting this calamity to fall upon another—

TRUEMAN: Enough—I did not need your voice, child. I am going to settle this matter my own way. [*Goes up to* SNOBSON—*who has seated himself and fallen asleep—tilts him out of the chair*]

SNOBSON: [*Waking up*] Eh? Where's the fire? Oh! it's you, Catteraugus.

TRUEMAN: If I comprehend aright, you have been for some time aware of your principal's forgeries? [*As he says this, he beckons to* HOWARD, *who advances as witness.*]

SNOBSON: You've hit the nail, Catteraugus! Old chap saw that I was up to him six months ago; left off throwing dust into my eyes—

TRUEMAN: Oh, he did!

SNOBSON: Made no bones of forging Anderson's name at my elbow.

TRUEMAN: Forged at your elbow? You saw him do it?

SNOBSON: I did.

TRUEMAN: Repeatedly.

SNOBSON: Re—pea—ted—ly.

TRUEMAN: Then you, Rattlesnake, if he goes to the States' Prison, you'll take up your quarters there too. You are an accomplice, an *accessory!*

[TRUEMAN *walks away and seats himself.* HOWARD *rejoins* GERTRUDE. SNOBSON *stands for some time bewildered.*]

SNOBSON: The deuce, so I am! I never thought of that! I must make myself scarce. I'll be off! Tif, I say, Tif! [*Going up to him and speaking confidentially*] That drunken old rip has got us in his power. Let's give him the slip and be off. They want men of genius at the West—we're sure to get on! You—you can set up for a writing master, and teach copying *signatures*; and I— I'll give lectures on *temperance!* You won't come, eh? Then I'm off without you. Good bye, Catteraugus! Which is the way to California? [*Steals off*]

TRUEMAN: There's one debt your city owes me. And now let us see what other nuisances we can abate. Antony, I'm not given to preaching; therefore I shall not say much about what you have done. Your face speaks for itself—the crime has brought its punishment along with it.

TIFFANY: Indeed it has, Sir! In *one year* I have lived a *century* of misery.

TRUEMAN: I believe you, and upon one condition I will assist you—

TIFFANY: My friend—my first, ever kind friend—only name it!

TRUEMAN: You must sell your house and all these gewgaws, and bundle your wife and daughter off to the country. There let them learn economy, true independence, and home virtues, instead of foreign follies. As for yourself, continue your business—but let moderation, in future, be your counsellor, and let *honesty* be your confidential clerk.

TIFFANY: Mr. Trueman, you have made existence once more precious to me! My wife and daughter shall quit the city tomorrow, and—

PRUDENCE: It's all coming right! It's all coming right! We'll go to the county of Catteraugus. [*Walking up to* TRUEMAN]

TRUEMAN: No, you won't—I make that a stipulation, Antony; keep clear of Catteraugus. None of your fashionable examples there!

[JOLIMAITRE *appears in the Conservatory and peeps into the room unperceived.*]

COUNT: What can detain Seraphina? We ought to be off!

MILLINETTE: [*Turns round, perceives him, runs and forces him into the room*] Here he is! Ah, Gustave, mon cher Gustave! I have you now and we never part no more. Don't frown, Gustave, don't frown—

TRUEMAN: Come forward, Mr. Count! and for the edification of fashionable society confess that you're an impostor.

COUNT: An impostor? Why, you abominable old—

TRUEMAN: Oh, your feminine friend has told us all about it, the cook—the valet—barber and all that sort of thing. Come, confess, and something may be done for you.

COUNT: Well then, I do confess I am no count; but really, ladies and gentlemen, I may recommend myself as the most capital cook.

MRS. TIFFANY: Oh, Seraphina!

SERAPHINA: Oh, Ma!

[*They embrace and retire up.*]

TRUEMAN: Promise me to call upon the whole circle of your fashionable acquaintances with your own advertisements and in your cook's attire, and I will set you up in business tomorrow. Better turn stomachs than turn heads!

MILLINETTE: But you will marry me?

COUNT: Give us your hand, Millinette! Sir, command me for the most delicate *paté*—the daintiest *croquette à la royale*—the most transcendent *omelette soufflée* that ever issued from a French pastry-cook's oven. I hope you will pardon my conduct, but I heard that in America, where you pay homage to titles while you profess to scorn them—where *Fashion* makes the basest coin current—where you have no kings, no princes, no *no-bility*—

TRUEMAN: Stop there! I object to your use of that word. When justice is found only among lawyers—health among physicians—and patriotism among politicians, *then* may you say that there is no *nobility* where there are no titles! But we *have* kings, princes, and nobles in abundance—of *Nature's stamp*, if not of *Fashion's*— we have honest men, warm hearted and brave, and we have women—gentle, fair, and true, to whom no *title* could add *nobility*.

EPILOGUE

PRUDENCE: I told you so! And now you hear and see.
  I told you *Fashion* would the fashion be!
TRUEMAN: Then both its point and moral I distrust.
COUNT: Sir, is that liberal?
HOWARD: Or is it just?
TRUEMAN: The guilty have escaped!
TIFFANY: Is, therefore, sin
  Made charming? Ah! there's punishment within!
  Guilt ever carries his own scourge along.
GERTRUDE: Virtue her own reward!
TRUEMAN: You're right, I'm wrong.
MRS. TIFFANY: How we have been deceived!
PRUDENCE: I told you so.
SERAPHINA: To lose at once a title and a beau!
COUNT: A count no more, I'm no more of *account*.
TRUEMAN: But to a nobler title you may mount,
  And be in time—who knows?—an honest man!
COUNT: Eh, Millinette?
MILLINETTE: Oh, *oui*—I know you can!
GERTRUDE: [*To audience*] But, ere we close the scene, a
    word with you—
  We charge you answer—Is this picture true?
  Some little mercy to our efforts show,
  Then let the world your honest verdict know.
  Here let it see portrayed its ruling passion,
  And learn to prize at its just value—*Fashion*.

CURTAIN

A MAN'S WORLD

A Play in Four Acts

RACHEL CROTHERS

———————◆•◆◆———————

First performed 1909

CHARACTERS

FRANK WARE
LIONE BRUNE
CLARA OAKES
KIDDIE
MALCOLM GASKELL
FRITZ BAHN
WELLS TREVOR
EMILE GRIMBEUX

ACT ONE

FRANK WARE's living room in an old house in lower New York. Eight o'clock a winter evening.

ACT TWO

A room in the same house, occupied by CLARA and LIONE. Four weeks later. Two o'clock in the afternoon.

ACT THREE

Six hours later. Same scene as Act One.

ACT FOUR

Immediately following Act Three. Same scene.

ACT I

Time—the present—eight o'clock a winter evening.

*Scene—*FRANK WARE'S *living room in an old house in lower New York. There is a door at center back leading into hall. One at left leading into sleeping room. A wide window cuts off the upper right corner diagonally. Another window is down right. At left a large old-fashioned fireplace of white marble. Low open book shelves fill the wall spaces. In the upper corner left is a large round table on which are magazines, a lamp—a box of cigarettes and a bowl of red apples. At left center a very large upholstered davenport facing the fire at a slanting angle. Below the fire a large armchair.*

At back a baby grand piano stands right of the door center—the keyboard facing the window—a single chair before it. Below piano a small round table holding books and a work basket—a chair at left of this table. Well out from the window right is a large table desk with a chair on either side. The desk holds a student's lamp—magazines, newspapers, brass desk furnishings—and a great quantity of mss., letters, etc.

On the book shelves are vases, several busts in bronze and white—old bowls, a large Victory in white, and a great quantity of pictures on the walls—water colors, oils, sketches—all good.

The walls and ceilings are done in faded, old frescoes—

and there is a center gas chandelier of an old-fashioned design.

The furniture is all old, but solid and the general air is that of past elegance grown shabby and invaded by up-to-date comfort and cheerfulness.

At curtain—KIDDIE WARE, *a sturdy boy of seven, is lying full length on sofa looking into fire. After a slight pause he rises—punches pillow and sulkily crosses to piano. With one finger he plays* Can you come out to-night boys *three times, with one note always wrong. He then crosses to window and looks eagerly out into the street. There is a soft rap at the door center. Pause—and the rap is repeated.*

KIDDIE: [*Lifelessly*] Come.

FRITZ: [*Opening the hall door*] Wie gehts. Hello.

KIDDIE: [*Without turning*] Hello!

   [FRITZ BAHN *is a young German. He is in evening clothes and carries a shabby topcoat, a cap and a violin case.*]

FRITZ: Where is de Frankie mutter?

KIDDIE: [*Still not turning*] She hasn't come yet.

FRITZ: Ach! She is late. Don't you worry. She come soon. It is not eight o'clock all ready. [*Goes to child at window*]

KIDDIE: I want Frankie.

FRITZ: Ach Gott, so do I—but we don't get everything we want.

KIDDIE: [*Still not turning from window*] Why don't she come?

FRITZ: I tink she has had a very busy day with dot old publisher down town today. She will be so tired. Un? Yah, I tink it. Don't look all de time on de outside. She not come so. Look a liddle on de inside an she come. So.

KIDDIE: Light all the gas. She likes it.

FRITZ: [*Lighting the gas*] So. Dere iss one—dere iss two—dere iss dree. So. Better? Un? Who lighted the first one for you all ready?

KIDDIE: Old Grumper, when she brought my supper. She
   was awful cross tonight.

FRITZ: No, iss dot so?

KIDDIE: Light the lamp.

FRITZ: [*Lighting student lamp on desk*] Oh, yah. De light
   at de shrine. So. We are ready for her. Un? Wat did you
   do today?

KIDDIE: Nothing.

FRITZ: Nothing? Didn't you go to school?

KIDDIE: Yes.

FRITZ: And didn't that nice girl wat takes care of you,
   take you to de park dis afternoon?

KIDDIE: Yes.

FRITZ: And did she go home already?

KIDDIE: Yes.

FRITZ: And you was alone dis evening waiting for de
   Frankie mutter. Ain't you going to smile yet? Wat will
   make you smile now? Shall I tell you—oh—such a
   funny story aboud Chris Kringle, wat's coming down
   your chimney next month already? [KIDDIE *shakes his
   head.*] No? shall I—

KIDDIE: [*Solemnly*] Be a monkey.

FRITZ: [*Hopping on a chair and imitating a monkey*] Ach
   Gott! Dot iss too easy.

KIDDIE: I like that.

FRITZ: Well I am glad you like something.

KIDDIE: [*Going to kick the end of a couch*] I want Frankie
   to come.

FRITZ: Du Leiber! Can't you forget a liddle? She come
   soon, now. I tink she iss eating her dinner all ready
   down in de restaurant.

KIDDIE: She's going to take me to dinner to eat with her
   down in that restaurant, she said so.

FRITZ: No! How fine! I will haf to get invited on that
   time. You tink I can?

KIDDIE: Sing a song.

FRITZ: All my tricks, un? [*Going to piano he begins a
   German song—extravagantly—after first few bars—
   loud voices are heard in hall singing same tune.* WELLS
   and EMILE *bang on the door and enter arm in arm
   singing.*]

WELLS: For heaven's sake, can't you hear anything but your own voice.

EMILE: Que faites—vous? Oh, la, la, Tenez! Ou est la divinite?—Ou est Divinite?

[WELLS TREVOR *is a happy go lucky young American, good looking and goodnatured. He wears a shabby lounging coat.* EMILE GRIMEAUX *is a small Frenchman of the unmistakable artist type. He wears a blue working blouse.*]

WELLS: Where's Frankie? Kiddie?

KIDDIE: She hasn't come home yet.

FRITZ: [*Rising from piano and going to* WELLS *thumping him in the ribs*] It's too early all ready. Don't you know anything?

EMILE: Um—he knows nossing.

WELLS: I know a good sport when I see one. [*Going to* KIDDIE] Kiddie, old man, doesn't care when Frank gets home, do you? He can take care of himself, can't you? [WELLS *doubles his fist and makes a pass at* KIDDIE, *to which* KIDDIE *quickly responds. They move to center going on with mock fight.*]

FRITZ: Gif it to him, Kiddie. Goot! See! Ach du lieber Himmel! Keep at him! You have him going! [WELLS *doubles back to left towards the couch.* KIDDIE *is excited with his victory.*]

EMILE: Voila! See ze liddle champion! En garde! Bien! Voila!

FRITZ: Reach for de chin.

EMILE: Non, no,—Kick him wiz se feet! [WELLS *falls full length backwards on couch among pillows.* KIDDIE *wildly excited.*]

FRITZ: [*Snatching a newspaper from the desk and giving it to* KIDDIE] Here—here—fan him! You must be goot to a man when he iss down.

WELLS: [*Gasping*] Where am I?

FRITZ: You are wid friends. [KIDDIE *takes paper and holding it at arm's length, in both hands, fans* WELLS *laboriously.*] Haf you got your wind all ready?

EMILE: [*Laughing*] I wonder where iss a cigarette. Oh— le voila!

WELLS: Let me have that paper, Kiddie. Did you see a criticism of Frank's book this morning?

EMILE: Non—I had not ze time. I haf painted all day like mad. I have had ze most wonderful—

WELLS: Here you are. [*Finding the article*] *The Beaten Path* is the strongest thing that Frank Ware has ever done. Her first work attracted wide attention when we thought Frank Ware was a man, but now that we know she is a woman we are more than ever impressed by the strength and scope of her work. She has laid her scenes this time on the East side in the wretched poverty of the tenement houses, and the marvel is that any woman could see and know so much and depict crime and degradation so boldly. Her great cry is for women— to make them better by making them freer. It is decidedly the most striking book of the year. [KIDDIE *with a heavy sigh goes back to the window.*] Bully good criticism.

FRITZ: It's a bully good book.

WELLS: You bet it is. Where does she get her stuff, anyway? After all, that's the point! How does she get it?

EMILE: Sere iss only one way. [*Rising and stretching himself complacently, standing with back to fire*] A woman only gets what a man gives her. [FRITZ *draws* KIDDIE *away from the window and sitting right of desk, takes him on his knee.*]

WELLS: [*Still lying on couch*] Lione says the man is Gaskell.

EMILE: Zut! Gaskell has not ze romanse—ze mystery—ze charm for a secret love.

FRITZ: [*Attracting* KIDDIE's *attention from the others by showing him a trick with his fingers*] Can you do dot? It iss not so easy. Un?

WELLS: I'm hanged if I can tell whether it *is Gaskell* or not—but if it is—why the devil won't she marry him? I tell you Malcolm Gaskell's going to be a big man some day. He's got the grip on this newspaper all right, all right, and he's not going to let go till he's got a darned good thing.

EMILE: Zat would be nossing to her. She wants ze love of ze poet—ze artist. It is not—

FRITZ: Wat are you talking about? It is not dis—it is not dat. It is not nobody.

EMILE: Oh, la, la! She is a very brilliant woman, but she

cannot do what is impossible. She cannot write like a
man unless a man help her—and no man could make
her write like zat unless she love him.

FRITZ: [*Frowning fiercely and shaking his head at*
EMILE, *takes up picture to show* KIDDIE] Mine gracious! Look at dis beautiful ladies.

KIDDIE: I don't like 'em.

FRITZ: Ach Gott! Der is Fraulein Keppel who used to
sing wid dot beautiful voice when I played in the or-
chestra in Berlin.

KIDDIE: There ain't anything funny in that old paper. Why
don't they have Buster Brown every day?

FRITZ: Ach no. They have to keep Buster so we can tell
ven it iss Sunday.

WELLS: [*In a lower voice to* EMILE] You can't see beyond
the love idea. Frank isn't a Frenchwoman. What if there
is a man helping her—it might be only a business deal.

EMILE: Oh—mon enfant!

FRITZ: [*Rising quickly as he puts* KIDDIE *to the floor*]
You are two big fools. [*To* KIDDIE] Kiddie, why don't
you go down to the lower hall and wait dere for Frankie
mutter?

KIDDIE: [*Going up to hall door*] I'll stay by the door and
when she comes in, I'll jump out at her. [*He goes out.*]

FRITZ: [*Going out into hall after him*] Oh my! Dot will
be so funny! She will jump so high.

EMILE: [*At fireplace*] Au revoir, mon mignon.

WELLS: So long, old man.

KIDDIE: [*Calling from the hall*] I'm going to slide down
the banisters.

FRITZ: [*In the door way*] Don't break your neck, all
ready. I vill watch! Ach Got! Be careful! Der you go.
[*He closes door and goes down center.*] So you—her
friends—are talking too.

EMILE: Oh—la—la!

FRITZ: You have listened to de gossip, de—

WELLS: [*Throwing down paper and sitting up*] Oh, come
off, Fritz. Don't get excited. I say I don't know whether
it's a love affair or not. *If* it is Gaskell—

FRITZ: If—if—if! Why do you always use dot mean little
"if"? Are you cowards? Are you afraid to say it is a
lie?

EMILE: She does not deny it.

FRITZ: She would not stoop to deny it.

WELLS: I think Frank has had some grand smash up of a love affair sometime. I don't know whether Kiddie's her child or not—don't care—none of my business—but after she's had the courage to adopt the boy, and refuses to explain who he is—after she's made people respect her and accept the situation—I can't see for the life of me, why she lets *another* thing come up for people to talk about.

FRITZ: There *is* no other thing! That iss a lie.

EMILE: How do you know?

FRITZ: *You* know—*you* know it iss a lie! Why don't you kill it?

EMILE: How can you kill a lie about a woman?

FRITZ: Wid de truth.

EMILE: Mais! What *is* ze truth?

FRITZ: De truth iss—that she is a good woman and you are too small too liddle—too—too—too bad in your mind to know wat dot means.

EMILE: [*Following him to center*] Prenez-garde! I am a Frenchman!

FRITZ: Yah, dot iss yust it. You don't know a good woman when you see one.

EMILE: "Good!" I said nossing about good or bad. It iss you—you who make her bad. You say she must live like zis or like zat—or like one little way *you* think—or she iss bad! Bah! What is bad? She iss good because she has a great heart—a great nature. She is brave enough to keep ziz child wiz her—and snap ze fingers at ze world. She is kind as an angel—she is free—she is not afraid—but she must love because she is too great to live without love. Does zat make her bad? Allons donc! Because she does not tell who ze lover is does zat make her bad? Bah! It is you who are too small— too little too bete—too German to understand.

FRITZ: Oh, yah! yah, yah. You can talk wid your French talk. You mix up de good and de bad like you mix your black and white paint till you get a dirty something and say it iss beautiful. You say—"Oh, yah, she iss a good woman," and you damn her wid dat nasty liddle shrug of dat nasty liddle shoulder.

EMILE: Wat do you—

FRITZ: You cannot do dat wid me. You are her friend or you are not her friend. You know dat she is what I know she is, and if you don't stop winking and wiggling and smiling—I vill—

EMILE: You will? What will you? It is not to you to tell me what I sink of her. You are only jealous. You say zer is no ozzer man because you are crazy wiz ze jealous. Hein! If you was ze man you would not care what I zink—[FRITZ *rushes at* EMILE.]

WELLS: [*Springing up from couch and going between them*] Drop it, you fools!

KIDDIE: [*Bursting into the room and getting behind the hall door*] Don't tell 'er where I am.

FRANK: [*Coming in with a rush*] Oh, I'm so frightened! Something jumped out at me and ran up the stairs. Where's my Kiddie man to save me? Where is he I say.

EMILE: Il n'est pas ici. I do not see him.

WELLS: Didn't you see him? He went down to meet you. [KIDDIE *and* FRANK *both cautiously peer near edge of the door which is between them until they see each other and* KIDDIE *springs into* FRANK's *arms.*]

FRANK: [*Catching* KIDDIE *to her and covering his face with kisses*] My Kiddie man! Was I long? I tried so hard not to be late tonight. I must have a bigger hug than that.

KIDDIE: [*With a bear like hug*] You was awful scared—wasn't you?

FRANK: 'Deed I was—all to pieces!

KIDDIE: She jumped awful high, Fritz!

FRITZ: Yah, I told you.

FRANK: Well, how are you? You're lucky dogs to be so poor that you don't have to work. [*She smiles at them all with the frank abandon of being one of them— strong, free, unafraid, with the glowing charm of a woman at the height of her development. Her clothes are simple and not new—but have a certain artistic individuality and style.*]

EMILE: Zen why do you kill yourself to get rich?

FRANK: I have to get rich for my Kiddie, don't I? See what you think of that, boy. [*Giving him a small package*]

FRITZ: [*Helping* FRANK *off with her coat*] Have you had some dinner?

FRANK: Yes, I had a bite down town, but I'm hungry.

FRITZ: [*Putting her cloak on piano*] I will get you someding.

WELLS: No, I'll chase out and get it.

EMILE: I will make you a salad, toute de suite.

FRANK: [*Sitting on the couch*] No—no—no. Stay where you are—all of you. I know what I want. It's an apple. Give it to me, Wells. Oh—This is good! Be it ever so high up, there's no place like home. Take off my gloves, will you, Emile? Somebody might poke up the fire a bit. [*To* KIDDIE *who is struggling with the toy*] Can't you make it go, old man? Wind it up for him, Fritz. [EMILE *having taken the gloves off goes back of couch and takes off her hat.* FRITZ *takes the toy and sits on the floor tailor fashion.* KIDDIE *sits in front of him with his back to audience. There is a long pause.* WELLS, *peeling and slicing the apple sits on the left arm of couch, holding the slices out to* FRANK *on the end of the knife.*] What's the matter with you all? Anybody had bad luck? You're a cheerful set. Why don't you talk? Amuse me. What are you good for? You look as cross as sticks, Fritz. Have you had a fight?

EMILE: Oui. We have had a grand fight.

FRANK: What about?

EMILE: About you.

FRANK: That's good. Who was on my side?

EMILE: We were all on your side, only in ze different way.

FRANK: What's your way? [KIDDIE *runs to* FRANK, *sitting on her lap.*]

EMILE: I say I have ze advantage of zem all—because I can put you in my pictures as I see you—as I understand you. You are in zem all—many women—in many moods. Mon Dieu! I have had a wonderful day! I have painted every minute till ze light is gone.

FRANK: You look it.

EMILE: I haf got it today—what I want—and it iss you zat I see in ziz picture.

FRITZ: [*Working with the toy on the floor*] Nobody else vill see it.

EMILE: Ah, not ze nose—ze ears—ze chin, maybe—I am not, painting the photograph. I am painting the soul— ze soul of a woman.

FRITZ: How can you paint what you know nudding about?

FRANK: [*Laughing*] How's the play, Wells?

WELLS: I rewrote the great third act today. May I read it to you in the morning?

FRANK: Yes. [*As* KIDDIE *hugs her*] Aw—Kiddie—between you and the apple I am choking to death. What have you been doing today, Fritz?

FRITZ: [*Reaching for the toy which has run away from him*] I have been gifing a five dollar violin lesson for a dollar fifty.

WELLS: Cash?

FRITZ: Yah.

WELLS: Then you haven't got any kick coming.

FRANK: Go and see that thing, Kiddie. Don't you like it? [KIDDIE *goes to sit on the floor again.*]

FRITZ: [*Winding the toy*] One of his legs is a liddle longer than he really ought to be.

KIDDIE: Make him go.

FRANK: What are you doing in your glad rags, Fritz? You ought not to be sitting on the floor so dressed up.

FRITZ: I am going to play Lione's accompaniments. She says it is a very fashionable function.

FRANK: Oh, yes, I remember. Get up and brush yourself off. What is she going to sing?

FRITZ: [*Rising and going to piano*] She is going to sing dis for an encore.

WELLS: [*Putting apple and tray back on table up left*] Lione's encores are her long suite.

FRANK: That's because she always sings Fritzie's songs for them. [FRITZ *plays a tender little German song, singing a strain here and there.* WELLS *whistles.* FRANK *closes her eyes listening.*] Um—sweet. I could tell that was Fritzie's in the moon. Come and listen, Kiddie. [KIDDIE *runs to kneel on couch by* FRANK *with his head on her shoulder.* LIONE'S *voice is heard singing the song from the hall. She throws open the hall door on a high note.* WELLS *and* EMILE *applaud her with good natured guying.* LIONE BRUNE *is a tall woman with rather striking beauty of a bold type, emphasized by her black gown which is very low and long.*]

WELLS: Bravo! Bravo! Make your entrance again, my dear,—and I'll throw the lights on the door.

LIONE: I'm on now. You're too late for the cue.

FRANK: No one will dispute your Italian blood tonight, Lione.

LIONE: [*Sweeping down to fire*] Why should they dispute it?

WELLS: [*Imitating her*]—Why should they—but they do.

EMILE: A man say to me ze ozzer day—"Wat iss Miss Brune?" and I say—"Can you not see by ze look—ze voice—ze temperament?" And he says to me—"You mean Irish?"

LIONE: Beast! [*Sitting in arm chair down left*]

WELLS: Italian extraction. Lione from Lena—Bruné—from Brown.

LIONE: That's brilliant dialogue, Wells. Put it in a play. Give me a cigarette, Emile. [EMILE *lights a cigarette for her.* FRITZ *plays again—they all whistle or sing for a moment with comfortable abandon.* CLARA OAKES *opens the door. She is a medium-sized woman of about thirty-seven—with a generally drab and nondescript appearance, looking thrown into her clothes which are somewhat passé. One refractory lock of hair falls over her face and her hat is on one side of her head—both of these she constantly tries to adjust. She speaks in a nervous gasping way and is just now very much out of breath.*]

CLARA: Hello, everybody.

ALL: "Hello Clara."

LIONE: [*Condescendingly*] Ah, cara mia, where have you been all day?

CLARA: Did you miss me, dearest?

LIONE: Of course I did. I wanted you to hook my gown.

CLARA: I am so sorry.

FRANK: Sit down, child.

CLARA: [*Sitting on the edge of the couch by* FRANK] I went into Cousin Mabel's and she asked me to stay to dinner. So I did of course.

WELLS: Of course. Don't miss any of Cousin Mabel's dinners, Clara.

CLARA: [*Still out of breath*] She sent me home in the motor.

FRANK: Too bad she didn't send you all the way up stairs in it.

CLARA: Yes. I ran up three flights I was in such a hurry to see you. I have an idea.

LIONE: Well, sit back and either take your hat off or pin it on straight.

CLARA: Oh, is it crooked?

EMILE: It make ze whole room crooked—out of drawing. I cannot see anything else.

CLARA: [*Struggling with her hat and hair*] Well—I'm going to give an exhibition.

FRITZ: [*From the piano where he is still playing very softly*] Ach gott!

WELLS: What?

LIONE: Now, Clara, don't be a fool.

EMILE: And what are you going to exhibit?

FRANK: Be quiet. [*To* CLARA] Go on. Why shouldn't you give an exhibition? I wish to goodness you'd finish that miniature of Kiddie you began about six months ago.

CLARA: I will. I'll get to work at it right away. I'll make it *the* important picture of the exhibition.

FRANK: Kiddie can be there and walk up and down in front of it to show how good it is.

WELLS: I wouldn't run any unnecessary risks, Clara.

CLARA: You mean thing!

FRANK: Shut up, Wells. [*Throwing a pillow at him*]

CLARA: You just wait—you just wait, you people. You don't believe in me. You don't think I am in earnest. I'll show you. I am going to get to work right away.

EMILE: Oh, you have some orders, zen?

CLARA: No—I didn't mean that. But Cousin Mabel says she'll let me do her miniature.

LIONE: *Let* you? For nothing?

CLARA: Well, yes. I don't mind that.

WELLS: Good Lord! [*An uproar from the others*]

CLARA: Now, listen!

FRANK: Listen! Listen! Go on, Clara.

CLARA: Then if she likes it, she'll interest other people. That's what I've always wanted her to do, you know.

Because if Cousin Mabel really wanted to she could do anything with her social position.

LIONE: Your Cousin Mabel and her social position make me sick. Why doesn't she give you an income?

CLARA: Oh, I couldn't accept that.

WELLS: You couldn't—if you didn't get it.

CLARA: You don't understand how conservative my people are.

LIONE: How stingy—you mean.

EMILE: Why don't you tell them all to go to ze devil?

CLARA: Oh, I couldn't do that. I can't afford to cut loose entirely from my family—though of course they object horribly to my working.

LIONE: They're a pack of snobs. Why don't they boost you along in society then, if they object to this?

CLARA: Well, I really think if I succeeded, they wouldn't mind so much.

LIONE: No—you bet. They'd all be running after you then.

EMILE: Zat is ze trouble. You are still hanging to ze petticoats of your fashionable world—and what do it do for you? Look at me—I am alone in a strange country. I have no influence—no rich friends. I am working for ze art—not for ze money.

FRITZ: [*Rising, getting pipe from overcoat and going to window*] Dat is a good thing den.

EMILE: Bah! What is money?

WELLS: Don't ask me.

EMILE: Why don't you live for your art—and starve for it if it must be.

FRITZ: Yah! And when you are hungry—eat one of your beautiful miniatures.

EMILE: Art has nossing to do wiz money.

WELLS: No, but money has something to do with art.

EMILE: In America, yes. Oui—zat is ze truth—ze sad truth. You have no art in America—and what you have is French. [*A laugh of tolerance from the others*]

LIONE: I suppose you'll be swelling it, Frank, now that you don't have to make any sacrifices for the sake of your work.

FRANK: I never have made any for it.

LIONE: I'd be ashamed to confess it.

FRANK: Neither have you—none of you have. We're all working for money. We'd be fools if we didn't.

LIONE: Well—really—I thought you had a few ideals.

FRANK: Never mind ideals. I've got a little talent and I'm trying to sell it. So are we all—because we haven't got anything else to sell. It's only genius that forgets money. Only the glory of creating that compensates for being hungry. No—no—talent wants three meals a day—genius can live in spite of none.

WELLS: Well, by God—I guess you're right. Frank, I want to sell—and I'm going to hang on. I think I've got a chance—not because my plays are any good—but because other people's are so damned bad. [*All laugh and there is a general movement.*]

FRANK: [*Rising*] Come, Kiddie, say good night.

KIDDIE: Aw—

FRANK: Not another minute. Past time now.

FRITZ: Gute nacht—mine kint.

KIDDIE: Gute nacht.

EMILE: Bonne nuit, mon petit. Dormez bien.

KIDDIE: Good night.

EMILE: Comment? Que dis tu? Ah! Mon Dieu! I will never make you a Frenchman if you do not speak ze language.

FRITZ: Don't speak den, Kiddie.

WELLS: Good night, old man—I'll have to practice an uppercut for you.

KIDDIE: I'll do you up again.

CLARA: [*Catching* KIDDIE *as he passes her*] Good night, angel sweetheart. [*Kissing him on both cheeks*]

KIDDIE: [*Rubbing his cheek*] Night.

FRANK: Excuse me two minutes, good people.
   [*She follows* KIDDIE *out closing the door.*]

CLARA: [*After pause*] Dear Frank is so devoted to Kiddie.

LIONE: Yes, isn't she—as devoted—as a mother.

CLARA: Oh, I didn't mean *that*. That is—I—I—you—know what I mean. [*She looks from one to the other much embarrassed. A conscious pause*] Oh, dear, I'm always saying the wrong thing. You know I just love Frank. I wouldn't criticize her for the world. Of course I do think you have to be very broad minded when you

come into this atmosphere. Cousin Mabel says I am
getting entirely too liberal—but then she—

WELLS: You're very liberal with your hair pins—they're
all over the place. [*Giving her two from the floor*]

CLARA: Oh, thank you, Wells. She also said my hair was
too loose and that I was getting just like a bohemian.
[*Laughing foolishly*] She doesn't like it—but then she
doesn't understand—you know.

WELLS: That's it. She doesn't understand. Cousin Mabel
doesn't understand. You tell her it takes more than
loose hair to make a bohemian—and you're getting to
be an out and outer.

CLARA: [*Rising, laughing again—nervous—but immensely flattered*] Oh, no, I'm not.

EMILE: Oui—oui—I can see it. It is there—that something—mysterious and illusive—the true mark of ze
bohemian.

CLARA: Oh, don't say that. I—I think I'm just as I always
was.

WELLS: No, Clara, you're not. The change is so subtle
that you don't know it yourself. But we feel it, you
know.

LIONE: You want to be careful, Clara.

CLARA: Why what do you mean? Oh, dear!

FRITZ: You better make your hair tight again all ready.

CLARA: Well—I'm sure I don't know what you mean. I
don't believe it any way. I'm going. [*Running out the
hall door*]

LIONE: [*Calling to her*] I'm coming. Clara, get my coat
out, will you?

WELLS: Poor Clara, she'd like to tiptoe through bohemia,
but she's afraid of her petticoats.

EMILE: She will never be an artist.

FRITZ: But she makes very nice little pictures all ready.

LIONE: [*Sneeringly*] Nobody said she didn't. You have
charity to burn.

FRITZ: I would like to give some of it away.

LIONE: Oh, you mean I am uncharitable. Just because I'm
not a fool and can see what's what as plain as the nose
on your face.

WELLS: [*Dreading LIONE's temper*] Well, I must skip.

I've got to rewrite a whole play tonight. Come on,
Emile. [*Pulling* EMILE *to the door*]

EMILE: No, I vill not—

WELLS: Come on. Come on. Good night. Hope you make
a hit tonight, Lione. [*He pulls* EMILE *out, closing the
door.*]

LIONE: Pray, what did you mean by that speech?

FRITZ: You seem to tink you know.

LIONE: I wish you wouldn't imply before other people
that you think I'm uncharitable to Frank. I have the
greatest charity. I don't care what she has done, or is
doing, or how many lovers she has. All I ask is that she
doesn't *pose*. It's absurd the attitude she takes of being
strong minded and independent and it makes me sick—
simply *sick* to see her fool you and lead you around by
the nose.

FRITZ: Sh! Be careful!

LIONE: Anybody—*anybody* can see that it's Gaskell.
She's flirting with you and fooling you and using you
as a blind—

FRITZ: What if she do lof Gaskell? What of it?

LIONE: What of it?

FRITZ: Dot—don't mean der is anything wrong or dot
dere iss any reason for everybody in de house to talk
and whisper and hint.

LIONE: I don't know whether you are so simple that you
don't see—or so crazy about her that you lie for her.

FRITZ: Lie for her? Ah, Lione, why do you do dis? Are
you out of your head? You are making it all up.

LIONE: Don't you say that to me. I not only believe what
I say—but something else.

FRITZ: What?

LIONE: Have you ever thought—Does Kiddie make you
think of anyone?

FRITZ: What do you mean?

LIONE: I'll tell you some day—when I'm sure.

FRITZ: I don't understand you. [*He turns sharply and
goes to lower window. She follows him.*]

LIONE: You're a fool! a fool—a fool! I'm only trying to
save you. Now you've made me angry, Fritz, and I
won't sing well.

FRITZ: Oh, yes, you will. You are very beautiful tonight.

LIONE: You only say that to— [*Lifting her face to him*] Do you really think I am, Fritzie?

FRITZ: I tink it, yah. Und I tink it iss time to go already.

LIONE: Come on then—I'll get my coat.

FRITZ: You get your coat und I come.

LIONE: You want to see *her*. Stay with her then. I don't want you to go with me.

FRITZ: I will come as soon as I—

LIONE: Stay with her. I won't be made a fool of.

FRITZ: I vill come in ten minutes.

LIONE: I don't want you. [*Rushing out and closing the door with a bang*]

FRITZ: [*Calling*] I will come. [FRITZ *sighs and going to piano, plays again as* FRANK *enters. She goes quietly to her desk—drawing pen and paper towards her.* FRITZ *goes to stand at left of desk. She smiles up at him with comfortable affection.*]

FRITZ: You are tired tonight, yah? Un?

FRANK: A little Fritz.

FRITZ: Und you must work yet?

FRANK: I'm going out later.

FRITZ: Oh, no. Don't do dot!

FRANK: Oh, I must. If I get what I'm after tonight I'll have a fine study. I'm going to have supper with a girl from the East side.

FRITZ: I vill be back. I vill go with you.

FRANK: Indeed you won't.

FRITZ: But, I don't want you to go—alone—at night.

FRANK: Now—now—Fritzie—if you get fidgety—

FRITZ: Oh—but de talk—de talk—I can't stand it for you. When you go out like dis people don't believe it is for your work. They say you have a lover—they say he writes your books.

FRANK: That's very flattering. It means that they think they are too good for a woman to do.

FRITZ: But you see you make dem talk when you do foolish things.

FRANK: Foolish? You mean going out alone? Good Heavens! You don't suppose I'm going to give up all my chances of seeing and knowing and understanding just because a few silly people are talking about me?

FRITZ: But you are a woman. You must not expect people to trust you—too much.

FRANK: I'm not going to spend my life explaining.

FRITZ: [Sitting at left of desk] No—but you—

FRANK: Oh, Fritz, don't. You've been so nice and so comfortable. And now you're beginning to worry. You see how much better it would have been for both of us if I'd never told you anything about myself and about Kiddie.

FRITZ: Don't say that. You have to talk to somebody—sometimes. Don't say you are sorry you told me, dot was de most natural ting I haf ever seen you do.

FRANK: Natural? Surely, I am nothing but natural. I'm a natural woman—because I've been a free one. Living alone with my father all those years made me so. He took me with him every possible place.

FRITZ: Ah—but he was with you to protect you.

FRANK: I didn't need much protection. Dad wanted me to see—to know—to touch all kinds of life—and I surely did. He developed all his stories by telling them aloud to me. He used to walk up and down the little library and talk out his characters. So I began to balance men and women very early—and the more I knew—the more I thought the women had the worst of it.

FRITZ: Something has made you bitter to men.

FRANK: Kiddie has made me bitter. Poor little nameless fellow! I shall never forget the night his mother came to us. I didn't know her very well—she was only one of the hundreds of American girls studying in Paris—but she came to me because she wanted to get away from her own set. We kept her and she died when Kiddie was born—and then we kept him—because we didn't know what else in God's world to do with him—and then we loved him—and after father died—some how that poor, little, helpless baby was the greatest comfort in the world to me. I couldn't bear Paris without dad, so I came back to America. Kiddie was two then, and we set up house in this old place three years ago—and here we are—and it's nobody's business who he is. I don't *know* who his father was; I don't *care* who

he was—but my name is better for the boy than his—
for mine is honest.

FRITZ: I tink it iss a too bad ting to be a woman wid a big
mind, a big soul. Yah, I tink it. But I am glad you are
one already.

FRANK: Dear old Fritz!

FRITZ: I only wonder wat vill be de end.

FRANK: Kiddie will be the end of everything for me.

FRITZ: No—he vill not. Someday you vill lof a strong
man—and he vill change it all.

FRANK: You don't believe me of course. But, it's Kiddie—
Kiddie I am living for. Everything I believe about men
and women has been so intensified by him that he has
become a sort of symbol to me of what women suffer
through men—and he's given me a purpose—something to do.

FRITZ: I tink Malcolm Gaskell has cut me out wid—Kiddie.

FRANK: Nonsense! Nobody could do that.

FRITZ: I am not so sure. I think Gaskell can get most
anything he want—if he try.

FRANK: Why don't you like him, Fritz?

FRITZ: He isn't de kind of a man dot every body knows
all about and can trust de first time you see him.

FRANK: Yes, he is. That's just what Gaskell is. Whatever
his faults may be at least they're honest, right out from
the shoulder!

FRITZ: I am not—so sure. [*A pause*] Don't be sorry tomorrow that you haf talked a liddle tonight. It's gute
for you—und don't tink I don't understand. Gute nacht.
[*Giving her his hand*]

FRANK: Good night, Fritz. [FRITZ *goes up to table by
piano and picks up his violin case and overcoat. There
is a knock at hall door.*]

FRANK: Open the door. [FRITZ *opens door and* MALCOLM
GASKELL *stands in the doorway. He is a tall, powerful
looking man, about forty. The face is strong and reck-
less.*]

FRITZ: Speaking of the devil—here iss the old boy himself.

GASKELL: Hello, Bahn, you here? Good evening, Miss
Ware.

FRANK: Good evening, Mr. Gaskell.

FRITZ: Yah—I am here—but I am going. She is very tired and very busy.

GASKELL: You must have stayed too long. [*To* FRANK] Why didn't you send him away?

FRITZ: She did.

GASKELL: That's good. I came to borrow a book.

FRANK: Help yourself.

GASKELL: [*Going to table up left and selecting book he sits carelessly on couch.*] Thanks. [FRITZ *still stands by door watching* GASKELL.] You don't seem to be going?

FRITZ: No, I'm holding the door open for you.

GASKELL: I'd rather you'd shut it for me.

FRITZ: Vell—I haf done my best—you see he is going to stay. [FRANK *watches both men, much amused.* FRITZ *starts to go as* LIONE *appears in doorway. She wears a long coat and is drawing on her gloves petulantly.*]

LIONE: Well—really, I thought you were coming for me.

FRITZ: Yah—I am just coming.

LIONE: I am not in the habit of going after my escorts.

FRITZ: Ach—Lione.

LIONE: It's frightfully late. Of course some people are such *sirens.* [*With a withering glance at* FRANK] Oh—Mr. Gaskell—too. You're so popular, Frank.

FRANK: I am with some people. You don't appreciate me, Lione.

LIONE: At least I understand you. I'm ready, Fritz. [*She sweeps out*—FRITZ *following meekly, nodding to* FRANK *as he closes door.*]

GASKELL: You ought to look out for the stiletto under that Italian cloak. I am sure she's got it ready for you.

FRANK: Don't laugh.

GASKELL: [*Rising and going center*] Why not?

FRANK: It isn't a joke—poor girl.

GASKELL: It is decidedly a joke to see that big tempestuous Lione bow down to the little pink and white Fritz.

FRANK: You're decidedly off when you call Fritz pink and white.

GASKELL: He couldn't be that and love you, I suppose?

FRANK: [*Sitting sidewise in the chair at left of desk*] What did you come for?

GASKELL: Your book. I want to read it again. You haven't given me a copy.

FRANK: Why don't you buy one and help the sale?

GASKELL: I did buy one—but I threw it away—it irritated me.

FRANK: Then you don't need another one.

GASKELL: No—I don't need it—I admit, but I want it. I want to read it again. I want to see why people are talking about it.

FRANK: You don't see then?

GASKELL: I don't see why they say it's so strong. It's clever as the deuce and it's got a lot of you in it— but it isn't big. Our paper gave you a darned good criticism. Did you see it? [*Handing her a paper from his pocket*]

FRANK: [*Taking paper and getting scissors from desk she goes to couch.*] Yes, I saw it. Much obliged to your paper.

GASKELL: [*Following her*] Your story's all right—a man couldn't have done it any better—your people are clean cut as a man's.

FRANK: Oh, thank you.

GASKELL: [*Standing with his back to fire looking down at her*] But—it's only a story. You haven't got at the social evil in the real sense. You couldn't tackle that. It's too big for you. You've taken the poverty and the wrongs of the woman on the East side as an effective background for your story, and you've let your daredevil profligate girl rail against men and the world. She says some darn good things—more or less true—but— you don't get *at* the thing. You keep banging away about woman—woman and what she could do for herself if she would. Why—this is a man's world. Women'll never change anything.

FRANK: Oh! [*Smiling*]

GASKELL: Man sets the standard for woman. He knows she's better than he is and he demands that she be— and if she isn't she's got to suffer for it. That's the whole business in a nut shell—and you know it.

FRANK: Oh, don't begin that again. I know your arguments backwards.

GASKELL: How did you happen to come here anyway? This isn't a good place for you to live.

FRANK: Why did you?

GASKELL: Oh, this is all right for a man.

FRANK: Rather good for me too. The house is filled with independent women who are making their own living.

GASKELL: And you also have a little court of admirers here—all more or less in love with you—all curious—most of them doubting and all of them gossiping about you to beat the band. Don't you know that?

FRANK: Let's talk about something else for a change.

GASKELL: Hang it! Somebody's got to tell you. You can't live the way you do and do the things you do—without running your head into a noose—just as any other woman would.

FRANK: I don't know why you take the trouble to say all this.

GASKELL: I don't know why I do myself, for Lord knows, I wouldn't stop you in anything you're trying to do. I like your pluck. I say go on. I understand you—but you needn't think for a moment anybody else does. I don't question you. I take you just as you are. I suppose you think this Dutchman understands you?

FRANK: He isn't impertinent to say the least.

GASKELL: No, I suppose not. He wouldn't dare to disagree with you.

FRANK: Oh, yes he would. Fritz has a mind of his own and a very strong character. He is a genius besides. If he only had a chance to be heard. I wish you'd do something for him, you know so many people. You've got a lot of influence in that direction. Don't you want to?

GASKELL: Do you really want me to?

FRANK: Oh, awfully. He has the real thing—you know he has. Don't you know it?

GASKELL: Oh, I suppose so,—the real thing is fiddling— but that's not much for a man.

FRANK: He's here without friends—without money. He ought to be heard.

GASKELL: What do you want me to do?

FRANK: Talk him up to somebody. He can't do that sort of thing for himself. He's too sensitive and too fine.

GASKELL: Sensitive and fine—be hanged. That won't get him any where.

FRANK: [*Rising to go back to desk with the clipping*] I hate you when you say things like that.

GASKELL: [*Catching her hand as she passes him*] Do you hate me! Do you?

FRANK: Then don't be so—

GASKELL: So what—? Don't you think I'm—What do you think of me? Tell me.

FRANK: I think you don't mean half you say.

GASKELL: Oh, yes, I do. And a good deal more. You don't mean half *you* say—they're only ideals.

FRANK: Oh!

GASKELL: You'll acknowledge it some day—when you care for a man. You won't give a hang for anything you ever believed then.

FRANK: Oh, yes, I will—and I'll care what he believes.

GASKELL: [*Bending close to her*] You'll believe that you've got to live while you are young and you'll believe that love is the only thing that counts much for a woman.

FRANK: No—no—no!

GASKELL: It is. Women are only meant to be loved—and men have got to take care of them. That's the whole business. You'll acknowledge it some day—when you do—love somebody.

FRANK: It would only make me feel more—more than ever the responsibility of love of life. [*She moves back from him—looking at him while she speaks.*]

GASKELL: [*After a pause*] Come out after awhile and have a bite of supper with me. Will you?

FRANK: Oh, couldn't—possibly. [*Sitting at her desk and drawing a MS. towards her*]

GASKELL: Please.

FRANK: No—really I can't. I have to work.

GASKELL: Well—get to work and I'll come back for you—any time you say.

FRANK: Can't. I'm going out at twelve anyway.

GASKELL: Oh, that's different—if you're going out to supper anyway.

FRANK: I'm going to have supper with a girl from the East side.

GASKELL: Why in the name of heaven are you going at twelve o'clock?

FRANK: She is going to bring her sweetheart for me to see and he can't get off any other time.

GASKELL: I'll go with you.

FRANK: No, you—

GASKELL: Yes, I will.

FRANK: Indeed you won't. I want them to be natural and talk. She's had a tragic story and this fellow knows all about it and is going to marry her. She is helping me a lot in my club for girls over there—she can get at them because she's been through it all and has come out a fine, decent woman.

GASKELL: I can't see for the life of me why you go banging around over there—wasting your time—getting into all sorts of disagreeable things. What's the use?

FRANK: What's the use? I call it some use to get hold of about a dozen girls a year and make them want to lead decent lives.

GASKELL: [*After a pause*] Are you going to let your Fritz go with you?

FRANK: Of course not.

GASKELL: Thought perhaps you would. He makes a pretty good watch dog trotting around after you. Doesn't he?

FRANK: He makes a pretty good friend. [*Rising*] You must skip now. I've got to get to work!

GASKELL: I don't want to go.

FRANK: Come on. [*They walk together to door.*]

GASKELL: [*Standing in the open door*] You're awfully hard on me.

FRANK: Poor you!

GASKELL: That's right. You don't know how nice I could be if you didn't fight with me.

FRANK: You always begin it.

GASKELL: Will you come to dinner tomorrow night and see a show? Will you—will you? [*After a pause she nods smilingly.*] Good. [*Taking her hand*] And we won't fight? [*She shakes her head.*] Not a bit?

FRANK: [*Drawing her hand away*] Not a bit.

GASKELL: If you were only as kind to me as you are to—
everybody else—I'd be—

FRANK: You wouldn't like me at all.

GASKELL: Try it.

FRANK: I couldn't. Nobody could get on with you without
fighting.

GASKELL: Oh, don't say that.

FRANK: It's the truth. You're a headstrong, domineering—

GASKELL: Just because I don't crawl at your feet the way
the other fellows do. Do you hate me?

FRANK: You said that before. Skip now. Goodnight.

GASKELL: [*Taking book out of pocket*] Are you going to
give me this?

FRANK: I said no.

GASKELL: But I've got it.

FRANK: [*Putting her hand on the book*] But I haven't
given it to you.

GASKELL: You'll never give me anything. I'll have to fight
for it. [*He snatches her hand and kisses her wrist and
arm and goes out—closing the door. Hesitating she
puts her hand over the arm where he kissed it and puts
her arm on the door hiding her face in it.*]

CURTAIN

ACT II

Scene—a room in the same house, occupied by CLARA *and* LIONE. *Long double windows at back. A single door at left leading into hall. A single door at right opening into a closet. An old-fashioned fireplace below closet at right.*

Down right below the fireplace a large hassock. Before upper end of fireplace a large armchair. To the right of windows at back a couch bed—covered with a dark cover, and holding two pillows. Before the windows are two screens for holding pictures. They have only a single panel and stand on spreading feet, and are made of a plainwood and brown canvas. To the left of windows is a washstand, with bowl, pitcher, etc., of flowered china. Above the door at left is a bureau crowded with toilet articles, a small china bowl, a few books, cigarettes, matches, etc.

Half hiding the bureau and washstand is a large screen of four leaves. Below the screen an upright piano, and at left center a good sized round table with a chair between it and the piano. A chair to right of table, and one below it to the left.

At left below the door is another couch bed, covered with a dark cover, and holding several pillows. On the table center are a brass tea service and a dozen teacups and saucers of various kinds—and a white lace cover.

On the piano are piles of music and a small clock. The

mantel holds a brass candle stick, a few ornaments and a great many photographs.

The furniture is old-fashioned, heavy black walnut. The walls are covered with a dull faded paper—which is badly torn above the couch at right. There are a few effective pictures—watercolors, prints, etc., on the walls.

Time—four weeks later, two o'clock in the afternoon.

*At curtain—*LIONE, *with the front of her skirt turned up and a towel pinned over it as an apron, is sitting on the couch down left, polishing a brass candle stick with a flannel rag.* CLARA *wears a skirt and shirtwaist, which do not meet in the back, and a much besmeared painting apron. The same lock of hair of act one is constantly falling over her face and she mechanically pushes it back.*

CLARA: [*Going to take a workbasket from the table to put it on bureau at left*] Oh, dear! I hope it pays for all the trouble. Cousin Mabel may have one of her headaches at the last minute and not come at all. She's really awfully pleased with her miniature. It flatters her horribly. I do want to be honest and true in my work, but what are you going to do? No woman will accept a miniature unless it does flatter her.

LIONE: I hope to goodness somebody gives you an order after this affair. I'm ruining my hands cleaning these things.

CLARA: Don't do them well. We'll never be ready by four o'clock. It's two now. [*Taking hat from armchair and dropping on her knees before the couch up right. She draws a hatbox from under the bed and puts the hat in it.*]

LIONE: If your cousin doesn't come, I'd never speak to her again in all my life, if I were you.

CLARA: [*Getting flat on the floor to reach a dress box under the bed*] Oh, pooh! She wouldn't care whether I did or not.

LIONE: Your cousin Mabel's a damned snob—that's what she is.

CLARA: [*Taking a shabby afternoon gown from the box*]

Oh, she doesn't mean to be. She's just like everybody else in her world. [*Examining the gown*]

LIONE: I hate 'em. Ignorant, idle, society women. That's all they are.

CLARA: You'd give your ears to be one though.

LIONE: [*Rising and leaving candles on couch, as she goes to look at herself at bureau*] I wouldn't. I wouldn't give up my career for anything on earth.

CLARA: Yes, that's what I used to think—but somehow, I'm not so keen about my—Goodness, this is mussed and shabby! Absolutely the only rag I've got to wear. [*Hanging the gown on the chandelier below the fireplace she pushes the box back—and arranges the cover on couch.*] Oh, I must get the rest of the miniatures up. Here's Kiddie's picture. Where's the best place to put this?

LIONE: I think Frank's got an awful nerve to let you display it at all.

CLARA: Why?

LIONE: Why? Because people will ask who he is.

CLARA: Oh, well, I'll just say he's a little boy that Frank Ware adopted.

LIONE: [*Going to put a candle stick on mantel*] Yes, that sounds well.

CLARA: Well, it's plausible. [*Putting the miniature on the screen and standing back to see how it looks*]

LIONE: Not to me. The men say she isn't in love with Gaskell. Why, she is, head over heels—and sometimes I think—

CLARA: What?

LIONE: Sometimes—I think— [*Going to* CLARA] —*he* is Kiddie's father.

CLARA: What? Oh, horrible, Lione. She never saw Gaskell till she came here.

LIONE: Yes, so *they* say. Let me see Kiddie's picture. Frank used to live in Paris, and so did Gaskell.

CLARA: Oh, Goodness! I never dreamed of such a thing.

LIONE: [*Going to sit at right of table and looking closely at miniature*] Several times I've thought—

CLARA: You'd better keep on working. The tea table isn't ready at all. I hope to goodness nobody looks behind this screen.

LIONE: [*Starting as she looks at picture*] It isn't imagination. I do see it—as true as I live.

CLARA: What's the matter?

LIONE: Look! Come here.

FRITZ: [*Calling as he knocks*] Can I come in?

CLARA: Yes, come. [FRITZ *enters carrying a screen like the others. He is in his shirtsleeves.*] Oh, you angel! Put it over there. The screens are perfectly splendid. I'm so grateful. Really I am. You're so clever to have made them. I never could have afforded to have them if you hadn't—

FRITZ: [*Putting screen near the others*] I like to do it.

CLARA: You're a genius, Fritz.

FRITZ: Yah—but I am too many kinds of a one. Dat iss my trouble.

CLARA: [*As they adjust the screens*] You ought to stick to your violin. That's where your genius is.

FRITZ: Yah. But de great American public doesn't seem to know it.

CLARA: Yes—I know—I know. Isn't it awful? I hope to goodness somebody gives me at least one order from this exhibition.

FRITZ: Oh, yah, you get some.

CLARA: I wish I were as cheerful as you are. Did you ask Emile if I could have his tapestry for this afternoon?

FRITZ: Ach du lieber! You ask him. He vill not gif it to me. Dot tapestry is de apple core of his eye.

CLARA: I'm going to ask him now. It won't hurt it a bit and I want it awfully to put above that couch over there—to hide the hole in the paper. [*She goes out.*]

FRITZ: [*Going to look over* LIONE's *shoulder*] What are you looking at?

LIONE: [*Hiding the miniature*] Nothing.

FRITZ: Let me see.

LIONE: I've just decided something. Something I've halfway believed for a long time.

FRITZ: What is dot?

LIONE: I don't know that I'll tell you.

FRITZ: Please.

LIONE: I've found out something and you'll pretend not to see it.

FRITZ: How do you know that unless you tell me what it iss?

LIONE: Because I know *you*.

FRITZ: Tell me, please—please. You have very pretty eyes.

LIONE: Had you forgotten that?

FRITZ: No.

LIONE: It's the last woman who comes along with you, Fritz.

FRITZ: Every woman keeps her own place in a man's heart.

LIONE: What I don't understand about you is—how can you let a woman flirt with you when you know she is crazy about another man.

FRITZ: You mean Frank? She does not flirt with me. She iss a friend.

LIONE: Will you admit that she's in love with Gaskell?

FRITZ: She don't want to love any man.

LIONE: Oh, is that what she tells you?

FRITZ: No—no—she tells me nodding. Dat iss what I tink.

LIONE: You do? Well, you're about as wise as a kitten. I know she's in love with Gaskell and I think she always has been—that is—long before she came here.

FRITZ: Ach! Why? Why you tink dot? She never know him.

LIONE: [*Lifting the miniature*] Whom does Kiddie look like?

FRITZ: What do you mean?

LIONE: Look.

FRITZ: No, no—I will not look.

LIONE: [*Catching his arm*] Why won't you look? Are you afraid to?

FRITZ: No—no—I am not afraid. Why should I be?

LIONE: Why you are so excited?

FRITZ: I am not excited.

LIONE: You are. Oh! You see the resemblance too, do you?

FRITZ: What resemblance? I don't know what you are talking about.

LIONE: Don't you? Who is he like through the eyes?

FRITZ: Who? He iss like himself.

LIONE: [*Holding the picture before him*] It's Malcolm Gaskell!

FRITZ: [*Closing his eyes*] Ach Gott! What do you mean?

LIONE: You know what it means. Frank came here alone with this child. There is a mystery about her—then Gaskell comes—they're in love with each other and pretend not to be. I'll bet anything you like, Gaskell is this boy's father.

FRITZ: You have made it all up.

LIONE: You either know it's the truth or you're *afraid* it is. I'll tell her that I know.

FRITZ: No.

LIONE: I will—I will—I will. There's no reason why I shouldn't and there's every reason why I should.

FRITZ: Listen to me. If you will promise to keep still—if you will promise to say nodding to anybody about it, I will tell you what I tink.

LIONE: [*Looking at him keenly*] What's that?

FRITZ: Frank has told us he is de child of a woman who died.

LIONE: Yes—but who is the father?

FRITZ: *She* don't know who de fadder was. But when Gaskell first came here *I* see dis resemblance and *I* believe he is de boy's fadder. Maybe he don't know it—maybe he do—but Frank don't know it. I am as sure of dat as I am standing here.

LIONE: Fritz, you must think I'm an awful fool. Of all the cock and bull stories I ever heard—that's the worst.

FRITZ: It might—it might be. Dis iss a strange und funny old world.

LIONE: But it isn't as funny as that. Oh, Fritz, I want to save you from this woman, from her influence.

FRITZ: She iss de best influence dot efer came into my life.

LIONE: What's going to come of it?

FRITZ: Nodding.

LIONE: You love her?

FRITZ: You are two women, Lione. You and I used to haf such good times togedder. I lof your voice, Lione, you haf someding great in it. I like to play for you when you sing. You are so jolly and so sweet when you—

when you are nice. Why can't it always be so? Why can't we always be friends?

LIONE: She's changed everything. She's spoiled everything. She's ruining your life—and I'm trying to save you.

FRITZ: No—Lione—you don't—

LIONE: I've wasted my friendship on you—wasted it—wasted it—!

CLARA: [*Opening the door*] Yes—yes—if I get an order from this exhibition I'll blow you all to a supper. [EMILE *follows. He is in his blouse and carries a large tapestry over his shoulder.* WELLS *comes next carrying a quantity of curious daggers, foils, Indian weapons, etc.*]

EMILE: Where will you have it?

CLARA: There—over there. [*Pointing above couch up right*] Put that stuff on the arm chair, Wells—till we put it up. I'm so much obliged.

WELLS: [*Striding across the room with the tapestry dragging he stops center and recites elaborately.*] Clara, I've composed an ode to the occasion. Ahem!

Clara, Clara's giving a show,
She makes miniatures, you know;
She gives you cake, she gives you tea,
She's polite as she can be.
But don't just eat her cake and tea,
She would like some cash you see.
Don't say just—"How charming, dear.
Oh, how quaint and sweet and queer!"
But let her paint your pretty faces
With a rose bud and the laces.
Then the checks that you have sent
Will pay our Clara's board and rent.
[*The others laugh and applaud.*]

WELLS: [*Suddenly seeing* CLARA's *gown hanging below fireplace, and springing back*] Great Heavens! Is that your astral body?

CLARA: No, it's my last year's body.

EMILE: Where did you say to put zis?

CLARA: [*Going to couch right*] Right over this. It will cover the hole.

EMILE: Mais! Mon Dieu! Ze tapestry will not show. It belong to Napoleon.

WELLS: [*Holding out Indian hatchet*] This belonged to George Washington.

CLARA: Get up there, Emile. You take the other end, Wells, and I'll get you some tacks.

WELLS: [*As he and* EMILE *get on couch*] Where are you going to put the weapons of warfare?

CLARA: [*Going to bureau and taking tacks out of china bowl*] Right over the tapestry.

EMILE: Sacre! You are not going to put ze relics of your savages with ze tapestry of Napoleon!

CLARA: [*With tacks in her mouth*] Why not? It will be effective and nobody will notice whether they really go together or not.

EMILE: Zat is ze American. You mix your Art until nobody knows what you mean.

CLARA: I don't want it to *mean* anything. I want it to cover the hole. Here— [*Holding up shabby slipper and tacks*]

EMILE: [*Taking slipper*] What is zis for?

CLARA: To pound with, of course.

WELLS: You wouldn't expect that artistic temperament to have a hammer, would you? Go on. Hold up your end and fire away, Napoleon. Don't stop for details. [EMILE *and* WELLS *begin to hang the tapestry.* LIONE *has sat on the floor by the couch down left and taking a box from under it gets out teaspoons which she rubs with a towel.*]

CLARA: That isn't straight. Lift your end—

FRANK: [*Coming in carrying a large bunch of roses in a paper. She is wearing a very charming afternoon gown and hat.*] Hello, everybody.

ALL: [*Except* LIONE] Hello! Hello, Frank!

FRANK: How're you getting on? Oh, how nice you're going to look.

CLARA: And how nice *you* look.

FRANK: I bought these for your tea table.

CLARA: You darling! Just what I wanted. But, how awfully extravagant!

FRANK: Not extravagant at all. Marked down on the corner. Not warranted to last over night—but I think they'll get through the afternoon. Have you got anything to put them in?

CLARA: Nothing high enough.

FRANK: Get the tall vase out of my room—will you, Fritz? And isn't there anything else you want?

LIONE: We have everything we want thank you.

FRANK: You're lucky. Here's the key, Fritz, will you get the vase?

FRITZ: Yah, I get it. [*Going out with the key*]

CLARA: [*Moving the large screen so the bureau and wash stand are hidden*] You'll sit here, Frank, when you serve the tea.

FRANK: [*Squeezing into the chair between the table and piano*] Give me room enough to get in.

CLARA: Oh, well, you can get in before the people come. Now, Emile, listen. You said you'd help Frank with the tea. When you take the cups away don't move the screen what ever you do. Just hand them around like this. See—

EMILE: Bien.

CLARA: And Mrs. Grumper will be behind the screen *washing*.

WELLS: What?

CLARA: Washing cups, you goose!

WELLS: Oh!

CLARA: And all you have to do, Emile—

WELLS: All you have to do is to whisper—"One wash."

FRANK: [*Laughing*] What are you going to have—just tea?

CLARA: Heavens yes. Don't you think it's enough?

FRANK: Oh, of course. I only wanted to know.

WELLS: Nothing else—on the side?

CLARA: Oh, I wouldn't dare. Cousin Mabel would say there was drinking and carousing going on.

WELLS: Give Cousin Mabel a drink or two and she might pay for her picture.

FRANK: Kiddie's quite excited about his picture being displayed. [LIONE *looks up at* FRANK *quickly and watches her a moment.*] He said this morning—"Don't you think I ought to be there and see if they could guess who it is?"

CLARA: Bless his heart!

WELLS: Yes, you might make it a guessing party, Clara.

LIONE: To guess who Kiddie is, you mean? [*There is a slight pause as they all look from* LIONE *to* FRANK.]

WELLS: I meant to guess which is Kiddie's picture.

FRANK: We might all guess now—what Lione means. [*A pause*—LIONE *rises, puts spoons on table—looks at* FRANK *and goes up to window.*]

FRITZ: [*Enters with medium sized glass vase*] Here you are.

FRANK: No, you aren't. That isn't it at all. I meant the tall one.

FRITZ: Ach du lieber! Dis iss all I see.

FRANK: [*Rising*] I'll get it.

FRITZ: No—I'll go back. I am sorry.

FRANK: I'd rather go—thank you. I want to get something else. Oh, Clara,—don't you want some more pillows and rugs and things?

CLARA: I'd just love them.

FRANK: And are you going to wear that? [*Pointing to the gown hanging on the chandelier*]

CLARA: Yes—It's all I've got.

FRANK: Don't you think it would be rather pretty with that little lace jacket of mine over it?

CLARA: Oh, heavenly! May I?

FRANK: Of course. [CLARA *pushes her lock of hair back.*] And I wish you'd let me do your hair. I'd love to try it a different way.

CLARA: You're an angel. I wish you would. I don't seem to be able to make it stay up. It drives Cousin Mabel crazy. Wells says it's temperament, you know. [*Giggling*]

FRANK: Well, lets see if we can't hold your temperament in a little.

CLARA: You're awfully good, Frank. Really you are.

FRANK: Nonsense! Fritz, will you come and help me bring some things? Fritz!

FRITZ: Yah?

FRANK: Will you come and help me bring some things?

FRITZ: Oh, yah, I come. [*He goes out with* FRANK *closing the door.*]

CLARA: Frank's a dear. She's got the biggest heart.

EMILE: I do not sink Fritz tinks her heart is quite big enough. He would like to get in.

WELLS: [*Kicking* EMILE *and looking at* LIONE] You don't know anything about her heart.

CLARA: I wish I did. I think it would be awfully inter-

esting to know whether she really cares for Gaskell or
not.

WELLS: Give us more bric-a-brac, Clara, if you want it all
up.

CLARA: Oh, yes, use it all. [*Giving* WELLS *another
weapon from chair*]

EMILE: I tell you she love somebody. Zat iss her charm—
her mystery. She could not be what she iss wiz out
love.

WELLS: She's a mystery to me all right, all right.

CLARA: She certainly is to me.

LIONE: She certainly is not to me. Look here—all of you.
[*Holding out the picture*] Whom does Kiddie look like?

CLARA: Oh, gracious! What do you mean?

LIONE: Simply what I say. Whom does he look like?

EMILE: You mean like Frank?

LIONE: No, no. Not like Frank. Look now—through the
eyes.

CLARA: I don't see it—and I ought to if anybody does—
I painted it. What do you mean, Lione, anybody we
know?

WELLS: You couldn't very well see a resemblance to anybody you didn't know.

CLARA: Well, dear me. I don't see—through the eyes—
Oh, Heaven's—yes—I do.

LIONE: You see it! Wait!—Don't say anything.

WELLS: Oh, you can imagine anything.

LIONE: You can't imagine anything as strong as that.

CLARA: Yes—I actually—

EMILE: Ah! Mon Dieu! I see what you mean. It is Gaskell.

WELLS: What—

EMILE: Ah! C'est extraordinaire!

LIONE: [*Looking triumphantly at* WELLS] We *all* see it.

WELLS: Rot—rot! Nothing of the sort. I don't see the
slightest—

LIONE: We see it. All of us.

CLARA: I think I do—I did. It sort of comes and goes.

WELLS: Especially goes. I don't see it.

LIONE: You're blind. Look—it's Gaskell. That child looks
like Malcolm Gaskell—and *any*body can see it. Unless
they don't want to.

EMILE: Mais oui! I see it. It is here, the eyes. For *you*—

Clara, it iz wonderful—you haf caught ze trick wiz ze eyes.

LIONE: Of course it's there.

CLARA: Oh my! I think it's awful. What do you mean, Lione? I don't know what you mean.

WELLS: Nothing. It doesn't mean anything.

LIONE: Oh, no. Nobody means anything—nobody knows anything—nobody says anything—but you all *think* what I do—and you haven't got the courage to say so. I have you know. I believe in saying what you think—and not pretending to be fooled.

WELLS: Well, now, what of it? What if what you imply is true. What of it? What's the good of digging it up?

CLARA: Oh, dear! I don't believe it at all.

EMILE: I tell you all—all ze time—you are foolish as babies not to understand.

WELLS: Oh, yes, you understand a lot, you do. I say, what's the use of talking about it? Let it alone.

LIONE: Oh, very well, if that's the sort of thing you accept and believe in—that's your affair—but I don't propose to help a woman of that sort keep up appearances by pretending that I don't see what's right under my nose.

CLARA: Oh, dear! I never was in anything like this before. I think you have to have strict ideas even if you are broadminded. I do think—Oh, dear! I don't know what to think.

EMILE: You amuse me—all. You pretend to live in ze world of art and freedom and yet you make ze grand fight about—about what? What are you talking about? What do you expect—you funny Americans. She is a great woman—she must live and love and—

LIONE: You needn't say that to me. I don't—[FRANK *knocks and opens the door.* LIONE *puts the miniature back in her blouse.* FRANK *has taken off her hat and coat. She carries a sofa pillow under each arm, and the lace coat. She has also the vase and the two framed pictures in silver frames in her hands.* FRITZ *follows with four pillows and a rug.*]

FRANK: [*Laughing*] We met old Grumper in the hall and she thought the house was on fire. [*An uncomfortable pause*] You don't seem to think that is funny. [*Putting vase on table and throwing the two pillows onto the couch left she hangs the coat over screen.*] This is the vase I meant. [FRITZ *goes behind piano and filling vase from pitcher puts it on table and remains up center.*]

WELLS: Come on, girls, your lunch is ready. Sorry we didn't know you'd be home, Frank. We've only got enough for four.

FRANK: That's all right. I've had my luncheon.

LIONE: Come on, Clara.

CLARA: You don't mind my going, do you, Frank?

FRANK: Of course not. I'll do the flowers for you.

WELLS: We've only got salad and cheese. Thought the girls wouldn't have time to go out today—so we're setting them up.

FRANK: How nice of you!

EMILE: [*To* FRANK] You are an angel. Je vous adore.

CLARA: I hate to go and leave you—but—

LIONE: Come on, Clara, don't keep everybody waiting— [LIONE *goes out.*]

WELLS: [*Catching* CLARA *by left hand and pulling her to door*] On, Clara, on, to the feast. On, Clara, let us be mad and gay while life is fleeting. [*Exit* WELLS, EMILE, *and* CLARA *laughing.*]

FRANK: Weren't you invited to the party?

FRITZ: Nein. No, I was not invited.

FRANK: Put the pillows on the other couch. I do hope this affair does Clara some good. The screens are splendid. Where's Kiddie's picture? Do you know?

FRITZ: A—no, I don't know.

FRANK: [*Going to look on the screens*] I don't see it.

FRITZ: Oh, I think she has not yet hung them all.

FRANK: It looks as if she had. I don't see it. Funny! Is it on that one?

FRITZ: No.

FRANK: Here's a vacant space. Maybe she's taken it down. I wonder where it is. Oh!

FRITZ: What it is?

FRANK: I just thought of something.

FRITZ: What is dot you tink of?

FRANK: I thought maybe Lione took it down. I have a sort of feeling about the miniature from something she said just now. Fritz, tell me honestly. Do they talk about it much? Do they? Oh, they do.

FRITZ: Frankie, I want you to do something. You must tell them—more about Kiddie.

FRANK: No! Fritz, do you doubt what I've told you about him?

FRITZ: If I do not believe you, I believe nodding in de world. But—

FRANK: But what?

FRITZ: But you see you haf gifen me your confidence. You haf only tell a little to dem—just enough to make dem doubt—and it hurts you.

FRANK: All I want to do is to keep still and help Kiddie make his life clean and honest, and then let the world judge him by himself. I don't see anything foolish in that.

FRITZ: That's all very well for him—but you must think of yourself too—your reputation.

FRANK: Now, see here, Fritz, I care just as much about my reputation as any woman in the world, but this talk is only idle gossip and curiosity and I'm not going to let that force me to do a thing that I know isn't right.

FRITZ: Den I ask you something else—Tell Lione—

FRANK: No!

FRITZ: You tink I'm crazy—but I tell you if you make Lione your friend—if you make her understand you— she will kill all de talk—she will be a help. You need a woman on your side, and if once you get Lione, she fight for you—and she wipe up de floor mit everybody else.

FRANK: I don't want to buy her friendship.

FRITZ: No—no, it would not be dot. She—I tell you she need you, too. She need a good woman friend. Lione has a big heart, if it is—if it just get hold de right ting. She fight you now—but it is only like a big child dat don't know how to control its badness. If you just get her once—you could make her lof you, if you try—but first she has got to belief you.

FRANK: You're a funny, dear old boy, Fritz. I'm just as much to blame as Lione when we scrap.

FRITZ: Will you do it? Will you tell her? Will you?

FRANK: Yes, I will.

FRITZ: Ah—I am so glad. [*There is a knock at the hall door.*]

FRANK: Yes, come in.

GASKELL: [*Opening door wearing his hat and coat*] Hello! [*Looking jealously from one to the other*]

FRANK: [*Moving toward* GASKELL] Oh, hello, what are you doing here this time of day? Did you come to the exhibition? You're rather early. It doesn't begin till four o'clock.

GASKELL: Oh, is this the day for the show? No—I came to—I went to your room, Bahn, and I went to yours— [*To* FRANK] There's a concert on for this afternoon— and the young violinist who was booked to play is laid up—fell and broke his arm this morning. The manager—Holbrooke, is a friend of mine, and called me up because I had spoken to him about you. [*Nodding to* FRITZ]

FRANK: Oh—

GASKELL: Will you go on? Will you play? Chance of your life. Crackerjack audience.

FRANK: Oh, your chance has come at last, Fritz! It's too splendid—I could cry—it's too splendid. You'll play the concerto and then you must play your own slumber song. It's too splendid—I can't believe it. [*Turning to* GASKELL] Think what it means to him—Oh, Fritz! I'm so glad. I'm so—What will you play, Fritz?

FRITZ: I cannot play.

FRANK: What?

FRITZ: I cannot play.

FRANK: What do you mean?

FRITZ: Dot is what I mean. I cannot play.

FRANK: Have you gone mad? It's the chance of your life, as Mr. Gaskell says. Are you fooling? Here's the opportunity—in your hand—are you going to take it?

FRITZ: We cannot always take what comes. [*Looks at* GASKELL] I cannot take dis. [*He goes out closing the door.* FRANK *and* GASKELL *stare at the door for an instant.*]

FRANK: I don't understand.

GASKELL: Impudent, pigheaded—irresponsible set— every one of them. How do they expect to get along if they don't take a chance when you hand it out to them? Bohemians! Geniuses! Damn fools, I say.

FRANK: Oh, Fritz isn't like that. There's something else—

some reason. What was the matter with him? Something came over him—I don't—

GASKELL: Why, it's me—that's what's the matter with him. He won't take it from me, because he's so jealous of you he's crazy. If I'd known he was such a fool, I'd have had them send to him direct, so he wouldn't have known I had anything to do with it. That would have pleased you? But I thought the safest and quickest way to get him was to come and find him myself. Sorry I've balled it up. You're friend's so fine and sensitive I don't know how to handle him.

FRANK: Don't be unjust to Fritz just because you've lost your temper. I must say I don't blame you for that—he did seem awfully rude and ungrateful, but I know he didn't mean it. He—

GASKELL: Mean it? Good Lord, what did he mean then?

FRANK: That's just what I don't know.

GASKELL: You're trying to find another reason for what's just plain ordinary jealousy. Do you want me to keep out of his way?

FRANK: Don't be ridiculous.

GASKELL: [*Taking both her hands*] Do you want me to clear out and let you alone?

FRANK: [*Trying to draw her hands away*] This has nothing to do with the case.

GASKELL: Yes, it has. Everything to do with it. He doesn't make any more difference to me than a mosquito—but if you—good God, I love you—and you know it. [*He catches her to him and kisses her, then slowly lets her go. She puts her hands over her face and turns away.*]

GASKELL: I—you've kept me outside. I know he knows— the whole business—what ever it is. You've shut me out. But I know you're making a mistake by making a mystery of your life.

FRANK: You mean I ought to tell about Kiddie—explain and prove every bit of my life?

GASKELL: I don't put it that way. I mean everything ought to be—open—understood.

FRANK: I thought you said you accepted me just as you see me here—just as you accept a man.

GASKELL: In the beginning I thought I did. But, when a man loves a woman—the whole world changes to him.

He wants to protect her—he wants to understand her. He wants to look into her eyes and see the truth.

FRANK: You're afraid of what you might see in mine?

GASKELL: Tell me—whatever it is.

FRANK: Why should I?

GASKELL: Frank, don't fool with me. I love you. That's why I ask. That's why I care. I want to understand you. Why won't you tell me? Have you told this other man?

FRANK: He never asked me.

GASKELL: Do you love him? Are you going to marry him? Are you? You've got to tell me that. Are you going to marry him?

FRANK: No.

GASKELL: Then I'm going to make you love me. I love you. I love you—I tell you. This child is the most important thing in your life. I ask you to tell me what he is to you.

FRANK: How dare you say that to me?

GASKELL: Because I love you. That gives me the right.

FRANK: What if I said to you: "I love you, but I don't believe you. You must prove to me that everything in your life has been just what *I* think it ought to be."

GASKELL: I'm a man. You're a woman. I love you. I have the right to know your life.

FRANK: You mean if Kiddie were my own child, you couldn't ask me to marry you?

GASKELL: Is he?

FRANK: And if he were? Can't a woman live through that and be the better for it? How dare a man question her! How dare he!

GASKELL: Do you mean—[LIONE *throws open the door and stops in supercilious surprise.*]

LIONE: Oh—I beg your pardon! I didn't know Mr. Gaskell was here. I should have knocked.

GASKELL: It's always a pretty good idea to knock, don't you think?

LIONE: Oh, I don't know. I'm such an open, frank sort of a person that somehow it never occurs to me that I ought to knock at the door of my own room. [EMILE, WELLS *and* CLARA *follow her in.*]

FRANK: There are some people who think all doors ought

to be open—always—even to the innermost rooms of one's soul—so that all the curious world may walk in and look about and see if he approves of what he finds there.

LIONE: Do you mean I am one of those?

FRANK: You know whether you are or not.

LIONE: If you mean I am curious about you, you're mistaken. I'm not curious—and I am not deceived.

FRANK: Deceived?

LIONE: No. The real situation is too apparent for me to pretend not to see it.

FRANK: You'll have to speak plainer than that.

LIONE: Do you really want to discuss it here?

FRANK: I do.

LIONE: Well, really, if you insist. A certain resemblance in Kiddie's miniature attracted my attention. We all see it.

WELLS: I object, Lione—

EMILE: If you please—

CLARA: How can you, Lione?

FRANK: Where is Kiddie's miniature? I couldn't find it.

CLARA: It must be there.

FRANK: No, it isn't.

CLARA: Why, I—

LIONE: [*Holding it out to* FRANK] Here it is.

FRANK: A certain resemblance—you say? [FRITZ *comes into the open door.*]

LIONE: [*Looking at* FRITZ] We all see it.

FRITZ: [*Stepping forward*] You have broken your promise.

LIONE: No! I promised if you told the truth—but you told me an absurd thing. Fritz saw it too, but he has a different explanation, of course.

FRITZ: [*Looking at* FRANK *in agony of appeal*] No! Don't—

GASKELL: What do you all mean? What resemblance are you talking about? Confound your impertinence! What do you mean?

LIONE: I'll tell you—

FRITZ: No, you will not.

LIONE: I will. Why shouldn't I? I will.

FRITZ: No, I say you will not.

GASKELL: Tell it—tell it! Say it. What do you mean?

LIONE: I mean—

FRANK: You needn't. They mean that Kiddie looks like me. [*A pause. They stare at* FRANK *as she walks out quietly.*]

CURTAIN

ACT III

Time—six hours later. Eight o'clock the same evening.

Scene—same as Act I. Chandelier and both lamps are lighted—shades are drawn in windows.

*At curtain—*FRANK *wearing a house gown of striking simplicity, is seated by table sewing.* KIDDIE *on the couch, is reading aloud.*

KIDDIE: [*Reading*] And—Fido—runs and—gets—the ball—f-r-o-m—from—the water—and takes—it—to his m-a-s-t-e-r.

FRANK: Master.

KIDDIE: Master—and Willie—takes—it—to his f-a-t-h-e-r?

FRANK: You know that.

KIDDIE: No, I don't.

FRANK: Look at it again.

KIDDIE: F-a-t fatter.

FRANK: No—no.

KIDDIE: F-a-t-h—father.

FRANK: Of course.

KIDDIE: What's my father?

FRANK: Why do you ask that?

KIDDIE: 'Cause today at school two boys were talking about their fathers and one said his was a lawyer and one of 'em said his was a barber.

FRANK: A barber?

KIDDIE: Or a banker—I don't remember.

FRANK: Oh!

KIDDIE: And they asked me what mine was. What is he?

FRANK: [*Going to sit beside* KIDDIE] He went away a long time ago—You don't want him. Aren't I a good father? Don't I give you all you need?

KIDDIE: Maybe I don't need one—but I'd like—

FRANK: Like what?

KIDDIE: Oh, I'd just like to see him sittin' round.

FRANK: I love you as much as if I were your father and mother and sisters and brothers and uncles and aunts. You have to be all those to me, too, you know, because I haven't any. We must tell each other everything and keep close and think all the time of how we can make each other happy. Mustn't we?

KIDDIE: If you want to make me happy, why didn't you take me to see my picture this afternoon? That made me very *un*happy.

FRANK: It made me unhappy too, but I really couldn't take you, dearie. Something happened. I really couldn't take you. I'm so sorry.

KIDDIE: But it's just down stairs. I could have gone by myself. [*Looking at her closely*] Have you been crying?

FRANK: No—no. Are my eyes red?

KIDDIE: Your nose is.

FRANK: Do you love me?

KIDDIE: You bet.

FRANK: How much?

KIDDIE: As much as—[*Stretching his arms out full length. There is a knock at door.*]

FRANK: Oh—. You open the door, Kiddie. [KIDDIE *marches to the door and opens it wide.* GASKELL *stands in the doorway.*]

KIDDIE: Goodie! It's Mr. Gaskell.

GASKELL: May I come in?

FRANK: I—don't—

GASKELL: I'm coming. I want to talk to you.

KIDDIE: Don't you want me to hear it?

GASKELL: Well—to be very honest, I would like to talk to just Miss Ware—if you don't mind.

KIDDIE: I've got to pick up my paints I left all over the floor then I'll be back. [*He goes out left closing the door.*]

GASKELL: I've been thinking—since that—since this afternoon. I was a cad. At least that's what I seemed to

you. I don't know what those other duffers were driving
at—Oh, I do know in a way—but—All I mean is that I
love you and ask for your—confidence.

FRANK: I'm not angry now, but I was then—so horribly
angry and hurt. I could tell you who his mother was
and prove it in a hundred ways but don't ask me to do
that. Oh, Malcolm—You must believe me—just *me*.
Look at me. I give you the one love of my life.

GASKELL: [*Catching her in his arms*] Frank!

FRANK: I love you. I love you.

GASKELL: My darling! It was hell to doubt you, but I
couldn't help it, dear. It was only because I love you
so. Because I want you to be the most perfect woman
in the world. Do you understand?

FRANK: And don't you see why I wanted you—of all people in the world to trust me—in every way? Don't you
understand?

GASKELL: No, not quite. [*Sitting beside her*] When will
you marry me?

FRANK: Oh, I don't know.

GASKELL: I want to take care of you. You need it as much
as any woman does. Do you love me?

FRANK: I've tried—not to.

GASKELL: Don't say that. Why?

FRANK: I haven't wanted to love anybody—and when I
knew I was beginning to care—I didn't want to.

GASKELL: When did you know you—cared?

FRANK: Oh—When I began to fight with you. You made
me so awfully angry—and then I was always wretched
until we made up. I began to know your step in the
hall, and when you opened the door and stood there I
knew something strong and sweet, something stronger
than myself was coming in.

GASKELL: I'm a beast in lots of ways and stubborn as a
mule—but I can take care of you and I'll be good to
you.

FRANK: When did you first know *you* cared?

GASKELL: From the first minute I saw you.

FRANK: Oh, every man says that. You know that isn't true.
I wouldn't want it to be. I'll tell you when I first knew
you cared.

GASKELL: When?

FRANK: Do you remember that day—it was—it was Sunday evening about three months ago. You were here and Fritz came in with some roses for me and you didn't look at me for the rest of the evening. You talked to Clara every minute.

GASKELL: Oh, come, I wasn't quite such an ass as that.

FRANK: You were. You were just as silly as you could be, and perfectly adorable. When you'd gone I—

GASKELL: You what—

FRANK: I won't tell you.

GASKELL: Oh, please tell me.

FRANK: No.

GASKELL: Oh, please. What did you do when I'd gone?

FRANK: I won't tell.

GASKELL: I don't believe you love me at all. Do you?

FRANK: Um—you haven't the faintest idea how much.

GASKELL: Well—tell me—tell me how much.

FRANK: I never can. You don't know what it means for a woman to love only one man in all her life.

GASKELL: Oh, now, Frank—

FRANK: It's true. You're the one man, Malcolm. That's why I've tried to resist it because it means so terribly much to me. My life has been filled with other things you know—with Kiddie—and my work. They absorbed me and satisfied me; and when you—when love began to crowd in—to overpower me—I was afraid. It seemed almost like being a traitor to myself. Oh, it means such a—such an overwhelming thing for a woman to give up to love after—she's—she's been—

GASKELL: After she's been as strong and independent as you have been. I'm the luckiest dog on earth. I don't see how I got you.

FRANK: Just because you are you. Oh, don't ever disappoint me. Be big and fine and honest always—let me lean on you and worship you.

GASKELL: Kiss me. [*She puts her head back and he bends over her kissing her.* KIDDIE *opens the door and comes in, standing amazed.*]

KIDDIE: Is that what you were talking about—kissing her?

GASKELL: No, a man never talks much about that.

KIDDIE: [*Going to* FRANK *and throwing his arms about*

her and kissing her fiercely] She says I am the only man that can kiss her.

GASKELL: Well, let me see if I can do it like that.

FRANK: No—no!

KIDDIE: What made you let him do it, Frankie?

GASKELL: I'll tell you.

FRANK: No—no! Please. I'll tell you after awhile, Kiddie—when I put you to bed.

GASKELL: Will you kiss me too?

KIDDIE: I'll kick you. [GASKELL *laughs.*]

FRANK: Oh, Kiddie, you don't mean that.

KIDDIE: Yes, I do. You said I always had to take care of you.

FRANK: Yes—but— [*There is a loud knocking at door center.*] Oh, heavens! Go over there. [*Motioning GASKELL away*]

KIDDIE: I'll tell on you.

FRANK: Kiddie, you won't do that, will you? You never tell tales, you know. Will you? [*He hesitates a second, then shakes his head.*]

GASKELL: [*In a very loud voice, going to door*] If you'll come down to my room with me, Kiddie, I'll give you— [*He opens the door—*CLARA *is there waiting, with the pillows, coat, etc., which were borrowed.*] Oh, I beg your pardon, did you knock?

CLARA: Yes, I did.

GASKELL: I'm afraid I was talking so loud nobody heard you. I say, Kiddie, if you'll come down I'll give you— well, you can tell me what you want most when we get there. [*After slight hesitation* KIDDIE *goes to* GASKELL.]

KIDDIE: I haven't forgiven him, but I'd like to see what he's got. [KIDDIE *goes out center—followed by* GASKELL.]

CLARA: Here's your coat. I am so much obliged. I wore it—but I must say I was rather ashamed to after what happened.

FRANK: I don't care now what happened.

CLARA: Why?

FRANK: Because something else has happened that makes that affair this afternoon seem very insignificant.

CLARA: Does it? I thought you'd be so furious with everyone of us that you'd never speak to us again. I was really afraid to come up—but I did.

FRANK: I am glad you did.

CLARA: But I want to tell you I wasn't in it. I didn't—

FRANK: Let's not talk about it. Sit down. How was the exhibition?

CLARA: A fizzle. A perfect fizzle.

FRANK: Oh, no. I am so sorry.

CLARA: Cousin Mabel didn't come at all. Some people she'd asked were there, and of all the snippy snobs I ever saw! They only stayed a minute and were so out of breath and asked me how I could possibly climb two flights. Only two mind.

FRANK: Good thing they didn't have to come to see me.

CLARA: One woman asked me why I didn't have one of those lovely studios on 57th St. Oh, dear, what's the use. [*Bursting into tears*] I'm so discouraged I don't know what to do.

FRANK: Oh, no, you're not. You're tired and nervous.

CLARA: Yes, I am too discouraged. I've tried just as hard as I can for ten years—and scrimped and scraped and taken snubs and pretended I was ambitious and didn't care for anything but my work, and look at me—don't even know how I am going to pay my next month's rent. I'm so sick and tired of it all I don't know what to do. I'd marry any man that asked me.

FRANK: Now, you're not going to lose your nerve like this.

CLARA: I would. I'd marry anything that could pay the bills. Oh, I am so tired—so tired of it all.

FRANK: Poor little girl. It is a hard fight, isn't it?

CLARA: It doesn't pay. I've been too terribly respectable and conventional all my life to succeed. If I were like you—you're so strong and independent—you believe in women taking care of themselves.

FRANK: I believe in women doing the thing they're most fitted for. You should have married, Clara, when you were a young girl—and been taken care of all your life. Why didn't you? Don't you believe in that?

CLARA: No man has ever asked me to marry him. I've never had a beau—a real beau—in my life. I—I've always been superfluous and plain. Absolutely superfluous. I'm not necessary to one single human being. I'm just one of those everlasting women that the world is full of. There's nobody to take care of me and I'm simply not capable of taking care of myself. I've tried—God knows I've tried—and what is the use? What under Heaven do I get out of it? If I were a man—the most insignificant little runt of a man—I could persuade some woman to marry me—and could have a home and children and hustle for my living—and life would mean something. Oh, I can't bear it, Frank. I can't bear it! I often wish I were pretty and bad and could have my fling and die. [*Sobbing she falls on the couch—huddled and helpless.*]

FRANK: Life has been dull and commonplace and colorless for you—but there are worse things than that. You've learned that life is easier for men than for women—you know what it is to struggle for existence—come and help me in some of the things I'm trying to do for girls. I'd like to have you teach drawing and modeling in this new club we're opening.

CLARA: Oh—would you?

FRANK: Would you be willing to live there? To be one of the women in charge—and help the girls in a personal way?

CLARA: Oh—do you think I could help anybody?

FRANK: Come over and try it, Clara, and see. You'll never wish again that you were pretty and bad, after you've seen a girl come off the streets and get to be a decent woman.

CLARA: I don't think I could actually do anything, but —Oh, heavens, Frank, I would like to get hold of something.

FRANK: You— [*A ra-ta-tat-tat at the door*] That's Fritz.

CLARA: [*Wiping her eyes and blowing her nose*] Oh dear, I don't want to see anyone. I am going out through your bedroom. I—I am so, awfully grateful, Frank, but—I—can't— [*She chokes with tears and hurries out. Another rap—*FRANK *opens the door.*]

FRITZ: I would like to see you.

FRANK: Come in. [*She goes to sit in armchair below the fire and* FRITZ *closing the door goes to couch.*]

FRITZ: You tink I haf broken my promise? You tink I haf been—dot I haf talked about you to Lione. Dot iss

true—but not in de way that you tink. I was very foolish
and I argue wid her and I say a very foolish ting—but
it was not a bad ting—I mean it was not about you at
all. It was about you—but it wasn't. I don't tink anything but what I always haf and dot iss dot you are de
best and most honest woman in de world. Do you believe dot?

FRANK: I want to believe it—but, oh, Fritz, how could
you discuss me at all? I thought you were so different
from the others. I've told you everything. How could
you talk about it?

FRITZ: I know. I know I was one big fool, but I lose my
head—and I said a ting I wish back.

FRANK: And something else that disappointed me awfully
this afternoon. Why on earth didn't you take the chance
Mr. Gaskell gave you to play?

FRITZ: I couldn't.

FRANK: It can't be because of Malcolm Gaskell himself,
can it?

FRITZ: You must not ask me.

FRANK: For goodness sake speak out. I'm sick of suspi-
cion and curiosity. How dare they take Kiddie's picture
down and try to squeeze something out of it? How dare
they? Of course they decided that he looks like me.
Isn't it a joke? Let's not have any more made up scan-
dals. If you have anything against Gaskell go and tell
him so—like a man.

FRITZ: You would like to believe in him above any man
in the world?

FRANK: I do.

FRITZ: Den I will ask him some ding—some body has got
to do it for you—but—if anything bad should come of
dis—

FRANK: Oh—I'm not afraid—and he wouldn't lie to you!

FRITZ: You are very sure of him.—Don't—don't let it—
don't let it—mean too much to you if—if he is not de
man you tink. It *would* mean everything to you, won't
it? Frankie, don't—don't break your heart about a man.
I—I couldn't bear it—if anybody hurt—you. [*He raises
her hand to his lips and she slowly puts her other hand
on his head.*]

FRANK: You—you've been so good to me, Fritz.

FRITZ: Don't tink I don't want to find him worthy of you—I want you to be happy. You know dot, don't you?

FRANK: I do.

FRITZ: He iss a strong man—he iss a success. He can take care of a woman—he has not failed.

FRANK: Neither have you, Fritz.

FRITZ: I haf nodding to offer a woman.

FRANK: You have to offer her what money can't buy for her.

FRITZ: No—the devotion of a lifetime don't count unless a man can say: "I can protect you from hunger and cold and keep you safe for always."—But—but I would like to know dot some man will do dot and dot he is worthy of you.

FRANK: You dear old Fritz! Your friendship is the most beautiful thing in my life. Oh, Fritz, life is so hard! Love is such a sad, mad, awful thing. It is the greatest danger in the world isn't it—the love of men and women. If we could only get along without it. We—you and I must be friends—always, Fritz. [*Her voice breaks. He tries to speak, but turns and goes quickly out.*]

FRITZ: [*Heard in the hall*] No, no, don't go in.

LIONE: I will. Yes, I will. I guess I can see her if you can. [LIONE *rushes in.*] I don't know what Fritz has been telling you and I don't care. You said you wanted me to speak plainly—so I suppose you'd like to hear what I mean and why I mean it. I've come up as soon as I could get here.

FRANK: Well?

LIONE: Oh, we can't be blind, you know, even to please you.

FRANK: You mean Kiddie looks like me—and you draw the self-evident conclusion.

LIONE: Oh, no, not at all. We mean he looks like Malcolm Gaskell.

FRANK: What?

LIONE: Why you ever let him come here—why you ever undertook such a pose and expected to carry it out is more—[*She stops as* FRANK *goes slowly toward her.*]

FRANK: What do you mean?

LIONE: I mean he's your child and Malcolm Gaskell is his father.

FRANK: Lione, don't say that. Don't lie about a thing like
that—it's too awful. Why do you? Kiddie isn't my child.
I can prove it by people who knew his mother.

LIONE: [*Impressed by the blaze of truth in* FRANK's *eyes.*]
Then—who—*who was his father?*

FRANK: I don't know who his father was.

LIONE: For God's sake, do you mean that? Haven't you
ever had a—Haven't you ever seen the resemblance to
Gaskell?

FRANK: No! No! No! No! Of course not! Not the slightest
bit in the world. [*Hurrying to desk and taking miniature out of drawer*] It isn't there at all. He doesn't look
the least bit like him. See—look! [*They bend over the
picture.*] What do you see? Where? What? I don't see
it. Not a thing. Do you?

LIONE: Well—I—you—I—I thought I did.

FRANK: Did they all say they saw it? All of them?

LIONE: Yes—no, not all of them. You can imagine anything in a picture.

FRANK: What did Fritz say?

LIONE: He believes you—and always has. From the first.

FRANK: But *he* saw the resemblance to Gaskell—*thought*
he saw it? [*Starting*] That's what he meant. That's what
he's going to ask Gaskell. Oh, it can't be. It can't be!
Look again. What did you think was like him? I don't
see a thing. I'm telling the truth, as I live. I'd see it if
it were—there. What is it you think is like him? Tell
me. What? What?

LIONE: Through the eyes.

FRANK: The eyes? No—I can't see it. I can't see it. It's
imagination. You can imagine anything in a picture.
You don't see it now do you? Oh, Lione, any man—any
man in the world but Gaskell. [*Sinking into chair at
right of desk*]

LIONE: I'm sorry I stirred this up. I ought to have kept
my mouth shut. It *was* imagination. Let it alone I say.
It's the wildest—most improbable thing in the world.

FRANK: But I've got to know. I've got to know.

LIONE: Let it alone. Good Lord, you can't stir up any
man's life. You're lucky if it looks right on top. If you
love him—take him—that's the point. Let it alone.

FRANK: Um—you don't understand. Who ever Kiddie's

father is I've hated him all these years. Every time I look at Kiddie and think that somewhere in the world is a man who branded him with the shame of—Every time I see a girl who's made a mess of her life because she's loved a man, I think of Kiddie's poor little mother, with the whole burden and disgrace of it—and the man scott free. I tell you it's horrible—the whole thing—the relation between men and women. Women give too much. It's made me afraid to love any man. I've prided myself that I never would—because of Kiddie. Because I saw and went through that—I feel almost as deeply— as bitterly—as if I really were his mother. Don't you see? Don't you see?

LIONE: I suppose it does make a difference when a thing is brought home to you. I've never thought much about the whole business myself. Men are pigs of course. They take all they can get and don't give any more than they have to. It's a man's world—that's the size of it. What's the use of knocking your head against things you can't change? I never believed before that you really meant all this helping women business. What's the use? You can't change anything to save your neck. Men are men.

FRANK: If women decided that men should be equally disgraced for the same sin, they *would* be.

LIONE: Oh, yes—if—if. That's easy enough to preach. When it comes to morality a woman never holds anything against a man. What good would it do if she did? She'd be alone. Why, see here—what if—just suppose—that Malcolm Gaskell *were* Kiddie's father. You love him, and love is no joke with you. You've let yourself go at last. You've found the one man. What are you going to do about it? Throw him over—because you happen to find a little incident in his life that doesn't jibe with your theory? Where will you be? What becomes of you? Um? Not much fun for you for the rest of your life. He's the man you want—take him and thank your lucky stars you have him. That's all I see in it.

FRANK: It's all you say. He's the one man—but if it—were true—

LIONE: Well?

FRANK: If it were true— [*She shakes her head.*]

LIONE: Oh, bosh! Then you can't marry any man—they're all alike. You know—we've worked ourselves up over nothing after all. I've been at the bottom of all that picture business. It was easy enough to sort of hypnotize the others into it. You can see anything in a picture—in Clara's pictures. I've always been looking for something to get hold of about you because I was jealous. I'm a fool about Fritz. [FRANK *quickly puts a hand over* LIONE'S.] I can't sing any more. I can't sleep. I can't eat. I'm a fool and I know it, but I can't help it.

FRANK: Go away from him for awhile, Lione, get away and he'll go after you.

LIONE: Oh, I don't know. I don't know.

FRANK: There it is! Love! What fools it makes us. Oh, I'm afraid of it!

LIONE: I don't believe this thing's true. Brace up. I don't believe it—not for a minute.

FRANK: I don't either—now. But it frightened me when you—

KIDDIE: [*Opening door and pulling* GASKELL *in by the hand*] Come on. He didn't have anything I wanted— but this. [*Showing a large pocket knife.* FRANK *goes quickly into her room.*] It's got four blades. Look at this one.

LIONE: That's a stunner—isn't it?

KIDDIE: I can cut anything with it.

LIONE: Mind you don't cut the legs off the piano.

KIDDIE: I could. I could cut off your legs too. [KIDDIE *goes to curl up in the left end of couch—busy opening the blades of the knife. There is a pause.*]

LIONE: I think Frank wants you, Kiddie.

KIDDIE: Oh, no, she don't.

LIONE: [*Looking at* GASKELL] I've just been telling Frank—

GASKELL: What?

LIONE: That I'm sorry for the row I kicked up this afternoon. I think everything is cleared up now.

GASKELL: A row's a pretty good thing once in a while for clearing the atmosphere.

LIONE: Well, I tell you, you never know anybody through

and through till you fight with them. Good night, Kiddie. [LIONE *and* GASKELL *nod to each other and she goes out closing the door.*]

GASKELL: [*Going to right end of couch*] Don't you think you had better go to bed now—and ask—Miss Ware, if I can't wait to see her?

KIDDIE: What do you want to see her for?

GASKELL: Well, several things.

KIDDIE: I don't know if I'll let you.

GASKELL: Oh, please.

[FRANK *opens her door and stands watching them.*]

KIDDIE: I like you.

GASKELL: I'm glad.

KIDDIE: I'm much obliged for the knife. [*Giving his hand*]

GASKELL: [*Taking* KIDDIE's *hand*] Don't mention it.

KIDDIE: But that isn't why I like you.

GASKELL: Why, then?

KIDDIE: Cause I do. [FRANK *moves a step toward them.*]

GASKELL: [*Taking* KIDDIE's *other hand*] That's the best reason in the world, isn't it?

FRANK: You must say good night, now, Kiddie.

KIDDIE: [*To* GASKELL] Do you mind if I go?

GASKELL: I'll have to stand it. [FRANK *moves above the fireplace still watching them intently.*]

KIDDIE: [*Standing upon arm of couch*] I'm as tall as you are.

GASKELL: [*Turning his back*] Come on.

KIDDIE: [*Climbing on* GASKELL's *back*] Get up! Look, Frankie! [KIDDIE *laughs as* GASKELL *carries him across to the door left and puts him down.*]

GASKELL: Good night, old man.

KIDDIE: Good night—Frankie, you come in ten minutes. [*He goes in closing the door.*]

GASKELL: He gets hold of you when you're alone with him, doesn't he? When he says he likes you—it sort of makes a fellow throw out his chest. What's the matter? Why do you look at me like that?

FRANK: Nothing. Was I staring?

GASKELL: Tired?

FRANK: Perhaps I am a little.

GASKELL: It's been rather an exciting day. Your hands are as cold as ice. Have you got nerves?

FRANK: No—no—I haven't.

GASKELL: You know—the more I think about what you've done for Kiddie—the more I like you for it.

FRANK: Do you?

GASKELL: [*Holding her by the arms*] Yes, I do. It begins to sink into me what the boy means to you—and that you actually believe all your ideas. I begin to see how through your love for the boy—and his mother's tragedy—you've sort of taken up a fight for all women.

FRANK: Yes, yes—that's it.

GASKELL: I never thought before that you actually believed that things ought to be—the same—for men and women.

FRANK: No—I know you didn't.

GASKELL: But I see that you believe it so deeply that you think it's a thing to go by—live by.

FRANK: Of course.

GASKELL: You couldn't get far by it.

FRANK: Not far. No. You wouldn't have asked me to marry you—if Kiddie had been my own child.

GASKELL: Oh, I don't—I—I love you. I want you. But when I knew he was not—the greatest change came that can come to a man. A radiance went over you. I wanted to kneel at your feet and worship you. That's the way all men feel towards good women and you can't change it. No woman with that in her life could be the same to any man—no matter how he loved her— or what he said or swore. It's different. It's different. A man wants the mother of his children to be the purest in the world.

FRANK: Yes, and a man expects the purest woman in the world to forgive him anything—everything. It's wrong. It's hideously wrong.

GASKELL: It's life. Listen to me—sweetheart. I want to help you do the sensible thing—about Kiddie.

FRANK: What do you mean?

GASKELL: Don't you see that you must let it be known positively who his mother was?

FRANK: That's just what I will not do.

GASKELL: Wait. You've hurt yourself by keeping still

about him. What good can you do him by that? You
can't take away the curse that will follow him. He'll
have to fight that himself. Don't you see it would be
much better to tell the whole business while he's little—too little to know anything about it—and then send
him away—put him in some good school?

FRANK: Give him up, you mean?

GASKELL: No, not at all. I don't ask you to do that. Watch
over him of course and be a sort of guardian—but—
clear this thing about yourself. What's the matter?

FRANK: No, turn your head that way—side ways.

GASKELL: What are you looking at? What do you see?
Gray hairs? The whole point, dear girl, is—that you
can't, to save your life—make things right for the boy.

FRANK: You mean I can't take away the shame that his
father put upon him?

GASKELL: Yes.

FRANK: What would you think—of Kiddie's father—if you
ever saw him?

GASKELL: Oh—let's not go into that again. Nobody
knows the circumstances. You can't judge. Think about
what I've said. We won't say anything more about it
now. [*He goes to her and turns her toward him.*] Do
you love me?

FRANK: I shall never—never give Kiddie up.

GASKELL: I wish you'd tell me what you are looking at.
You look as though you saw—Frank!—what's the matter with you?

FRANK: Nothing. Stand over there.

GASKELL: This is very funny.

FRANK: Oh, don't. [*Quickly putting her hand over her
eyes*]

GASKELL: [*Going to her*] Frank—are you ill? For heaven's
sake tell me what—

FRANK: I've got a blinding headache—I can't see anything.

GASKELL: Do you want me to go? [*She nods her head
slowly—staring at him.*] I'm awfully sorry. Why didn't
you tell me before and I wouldn't have—Frank—
there's something the matter. You've got to tell me.
What do you think you see? [*Taking hold of her*]

FRANK: Please go.

GASKELL: Are you angry? Look at me. Tell me what it is.

FRANK: Please—Just go—I want to think. Go now— please—please. I can't see. [*Hurt and a little angry he moves backwards toward door.*] Oh—it can't be—it isn't—it can't be! It can't be! It isn't! It isn't!

GASKELL: What?

FRANK: Did you ever know a girl named—Alice Ellery?

GASKELL: [*After a pause*] Who told you that?

FRANK: Oh, you *did*.

GASKELL: Who told you? Who told you?

FRANK: No one.

GASKELL: Was it anybody here—in this house?

FRANK: How did you—know her? I mean—oh—tell me!

GASKELL: Do you know the whole business?

FRANK: I don't know anything.

GASKELL: You do—you do.

FRANK: No. I don't. I—I'm not prying into your life. It isn't that. But you must tell me something. I've got to know. I've got to know.

[*She drags herself to the couch.* GASKELL *goes to the fire and after a long pause speaks in a low hard tone.*]

GASKELL: It happened about six years ago. I never said anything about marrying her. She knew what she was doing.

FRANK: But, did you—did you desert her?

GASKELL: I didn't! She went away.

FRANK: And you never heard from her?

GASKELL: Never.

FRANK: Never knew what happened to her?

GASKELL: No. She left a note saying she knew then she'd been a fool—and that she couldn't face the rest. I'm not proud of it, you know. I'd give a good deal to wipe it out—but—it happened. Are you going to hold it up against me? Is that one of your theories? Who told you?

FRANK: No one. I knew her. I was in Paris then. She came to me.

GASKELL: And she told you who—?

FRANK: Oh, not that it was you—no—no.

GASKELL: How did you know then?

FRANK: Her child was born in my house.

GASKELL: What?

FRANK: It was Kiddie!

GASKELL: No!

FRANK: They've seen the likeness—I've just seen it. I had to ask you. I had to know.

GASKELL: Kiddie!

FRANK: Kiddie—Kiddie.

GASKELL: Don't take it like that. I love you better than my life. [*Trying to take hold of her*]

FRANK: Oh, don't.

GASKELL: Look here, Frank, we love each other, and we've got to face it.

FRANK: Yes, we've got to face it.

GASKELL: Nothing—nothing can separate us.

FRANK: We are separated.

GASKELL: Only by your ideas.

FRANK: My ideas! They're horrible realities now because it's you.

GASKELL: Frank—

FRANK: Every time I've looked at Kiddie I've cursed the man who ruined his mother and branded him with disgrace.

GASKELL: Frank, stop!

FRANK: I've loathed and despised that man, I tell you— and it's you. Before it was someone else—any one— some one unknown, but now it's you—you—*you*. [*She stops. They both turn with horror, as Kiddie, in his night clothes, stands watching them, a little wondering figure.*]

CURTAIN

ACT IV

Time—immediately following Act III.

Scene—same as Act III.

*At curtain—*FRANK *and* GASKELL *are standing as at end of Act III.*

KIDDIE: Why don't you come, Frankie?

FRANK: [*Moving slowly*] Come, Kiddie. [KIDDIE *hangs his head, then looks up at* GASKELL *slowly.*] Kiddie. [KIDDIE *pushes past her and goes to* GASKELL—FRANK *goes in to her room.*]

KIDDIE: Don't you like me any more? [GASKELL *doesn't answer.*] Do you want me to give the knife back? [*Moving closer to* GASKELL] It's the best knife I ever had. I found another blade—look. [*Taking knife out of pocket and leaning against* GASKELL *to show it*] You open it. Don't you want to? [KIDDIE *looks steadily at* GASKELL *and then puts his hands on* GASKELL'*s chest.*] Are you mad at me? Don't you like me any more? [KIDDIE *throws his arms about* GASKELL'*s neck.* GASKELL *holds him tensely a moment.*]

FRANK: [*Calling from her room*] Come, Kiddie.

KIDDIE: I've got to go now, but I'll see you tomorrow. [*He goes in. There is a knock at hall door. After a moment* GASKELL *opens it.* FRITZ *stands in door way.*]

FRITZ: I came to find you. I went to your room. Are you going back now?

GASKELL: No, I'm going out.

FRITZ: I have something to say to you.

GASKELL: Well, say it.

FRITZ: Not here.

GASKELL: Go on. Miss Ware is putting Kiddie to bed.

FRITZ: I would rather you—

GASKELL: Say what you've got to say now. I'm in a hurry.

FRITZ: I—der has been—you know—der has been some—some talk about—about Kiddie.

GASKELL: Confounded impertinent set here.

FRITZ: Miss Ware is in a wrong position and some one has got to make it right for her.

GASKELL: Look here. You're meddling with something that doesn't concern you.

FRITZ: No, I'm not meddling. Some one has got to do dis for her.

GASKELL: You needn't trouble yourself. You can tell the rest of your curious friends that I know who this boy is.

FRITZ: You know?

GASKELL: And I've asked Miss Ware to marry me. That clears the whole business.

FRITZ: No, it doesn't.

GASKELL: What are you trying to do? I know all about him, I tell you, and if there's any more of this damnable talk they'll answer to me.

FRITZ: You know who the mother was?

GASKELL: I not only knew who she was—I knew *her*. That's enough.

FRITZ: You knew the fadder also?

GASKELL: That has nothing to do with Miss Ware.

FRITZ: Yes, it has. Der has been a horrible thing said here in dis house. Dey say he is her child—and yours.

GASKELL: It's a lie!

FRITZ: Part of it is a lie—but he is *yours*.

GASKELL: Why damn you—what—

FRITZ: Listen to me. I haf seen dis strange and strong resemblance. I haf watch him—I haf watch you—till I haf come to tink you are his fadder. [*A pause*—GASKELL *looks at* FRITZ *then moves away.*] For de love of God if it is true don't marry dis woman without telling her— it will kill her if she ever find it out.

GASKELL: Now see here, Bahn, Miss Ware does know who Kiddie's father is.

FRITZ: No she does not know.

GASKELL: Yes she does and she is going to marry me. That clears the whole thing.

FRITZ: No, it does not clear her name, it will only make dem sure of what dey tink now—that he is her child and yours.

GASKELL: It's a hellish, infernal lie—and I'll—

LIONE: [*Rapping loudly and opening the hall door quickly*] What are you doing? You're shouting so the whole house can hear you. [WELLS *appears in door behind her.*]

GASKELL: Come in here. Shut the door. [LIONE *enters.* WELLS *follows, closing the door.*] So this is what you've been saying about her? You've been lying about a good woman.

LIONE: What have you told him, Fritz?

GASKELL: The whole business and I'll tell you who the boy is. I knew—the—mother. Maybe you'll believe that when I tell you—the boy is mine. [*There is a pause. They all watch* GASKELL *as he goes to stand before fire—his back to them.*] I only found this out a little while ago—from something Miss Ware told me about—his mother who died in her house. I hope this knocks the truth into you.

LIONE: For my part I'm pretty much ashamed of what I've had to do in this.

GASKELL: It's happened. That's the end of it.

WELLS: I consider what has just been said a sacred confidence. I take my oath it will be so with me.

[LIONE *and* FRITZ *and* WELLS *look at each other and slightly bow their heads in acknowledgment of a pledge.*]

GASKELL: Whether Miss Ware will marry me now, I don't know. That's all I have to say. [WELLS *opens the door for* LIONE *and follows her out.* FRITZ *hesitates, takes a short step toward* GASKELL, *turns and goes out—closing the door.* GASKELL *remains looking into the fire as* FRANK *comes back.*] Frank, this thing isn't going to make any difference in our lives, is it?

FRANK: [*Closing the door after her quietly*] Whatever I do, Malcolm, you'll know I do without bitterness—without any spirit of revenge.

GASKELL: You mean if you throw me over?

FRANK: I mean if the future doesn't seem possible for us together.

GASKELL: Why shouldn't it be possible?

FRANK: You know.

GASKELL: No, I don't. This thing has been a shock to you—of course. It's shaken you terribly, but you haven't given me any real reason—any facts why there shouldn't be a future for us. I love you and I am going to have you.

FRANK: [*Moving away from him*] Oh, don't please. I must—I must—

GASKELL: [*Following her*] There's little enough in the world worth having, heaven knows. Why should we miss each other?

FRANK: Kiddie—Kiddie.

GASKELL: Well—well—we love each other. That's the first thing to reckon with.

FRANK: Oh, you don't know yet what I mean.

GASKELL: Talk won't get us anywhere. We've got to look this thing square in the face, as it is. Either you throw me over, or you let me give you the rest of my life and make you happy.

FRANK: Oh, that isn't—

GASKELL: I love you, Frank. I'd lay down my life for you. You're the whole world to me.

FRANK: Love isn't the only thing in the world.

GASKELL: It's the biggest thing. We've found each other. Look at me. You know it's the one perfect thing on earth—a perfect love and we've found it.

FRANK: It never could be perfect while you believe what you do.

GASKELL: What's that got to do with the facts?

FRANK: Do you believe it wasn't wrong—just because you are a man?

GASKELL: Oh—

FRANK: Do you believe that?

GASKELL: [*After a pause*] Yes.

FRANK: Oh!

GASKELL: Good heavens, Frank, I thought you were so much bigger than the average woman. All women kick against this and what good does it do? Why since the beginning of time one thing has been accepted for a man and another for a woman. Why on earth do you beat your head against a stone wall? Why do you try to put your ideals up against the facts?

FRANK: I'm not talking about my ideals now, nor the accepted thing. I'm talking about *you*, that *girl*, this *child*. You think I must excuse what you did—that it really wasn't wrong at all, just because you are a man.

GASKELL: It's too late to say these things to me now. You know—must have known when you first knew me that I'd—well that I'd lived a man's life. When you first loved me why didn't you think of all this?

FRANK: Ah, that's just it—I loved you. I took you as all women take men—without question. Oh, don't you see I'm not looking for something bad in men. If it hadn't been for him—if he hadn't been put into my arms a little helpless, nameless thing—if I hadn't seen that girl suffer the tortures of hell through her disgrace, I probably wouldn't have thought any more about this than most women do.

GASKELL: Isn't our love more to you than that?

FRANK: No!

GASKELL: Good God, Frank! You're a woman. You talk like a woman—you think like a woman. I'm a man. What do you expect? We don't live under the same laws. It was never meant to be. Nature, nature made men different.

FRANK: Don't make nature the excuse for ruining the life of a good girl. Oh, Malcolm— [*Putting her hand on his arm*] Do you think it wasn't wrong?

GASKELL: [*Drawing her to him*] I only know I love you. You said you loved me. I won't give you up.

FRANK: Oh!

GASKELL: You're angry now. When you've had time to think you'll see. Frank, I love you. I love you.

FRANK: [*Getting away from him*] Oh, no, no.

GASKELL: Frank, you're not as cold and hard as that. You're going to forgive me.

FRANK: Oh, I want to forgive you. If you could only see. If your soul could only see. Oh, dear God! Malcolm, tell me, tell me you know it was wrong—that you'd give your life to make it right. Say that you know this thing was a crime.

GASKELL: No! Don't try to hold me to account by a standard that doesn't exist. Don't measure me by your theories. If you love me you'll stand on that and forget everything else.

FRANK: I can't. I can't.

GASKELL: I'm not a man to beg, Frank. Do you want me to go? Is that it? Is this the end?

FRANK: There's nothing else.

GASKELL: Do you mean that?

FRANK: There's nothing else. It is the end.

[*He goes out closing the door.*]

CURTAIN

TRIFLES
A Play in One Act

SUSAN GLASPELL

First performed 1916

CHARACTERS

GEORGE HENDERSON, County Attorney
HENRY PETERS, Sheriff
LEWIS HALE, A Neighboring Farmer
MRS. PETERS
MRS. HALE

THE SETTING

The kitchen in the now abandoned farmhouse of JOHN WRIGHT.

SCENE: *The kitchen in the now abandoned farmhouse of* JOHN WRIGHT, *a gloomy kitchen, and left without having been put in order—unwashed pans under the sink, a loaf of bread outside the breadbox, a dish towel on the table—other signs of incompleted work. At the rear the outer door opens and the* SHERIFF *comes in followed by the* COUNTY ATTORNEY *and* HALE. *The* SHERIFF *and* HALE *are men in middle life, the* COUNTY ATTORNEY *is a young man; all are much bundled up and go at once to the stove. They are followed by the two women—the* SHERIFF'*s wife first; she is a slight wiry woman, a thin nervous face.* MRS. HALE *is larger and would ordinarily be called more comfortable looking, but she is disturbed now and looks fearfully about as she enters. The women have come in slowly, and stand close together near the door.*

COUNTY ATTORNEY: [*Rubbing his hands*] This feels good. Come up to the fire, ladies.

MRS. PETERS: [*After taking a step forward*] I'm not—cold.

SHERIFF: [*Unbuttoning his overcoat and stepping away from the stove as if to mark the beginning of official business*] Now, Mr. Hale, before we move things about, you explain to Mr. Henderson just what you saw when you came here yesterday morning.

COUNTY ATTORNEY: By the way, has anything been moved? Are things just as you left them yesterday?

SHERIFF: [*Looking about*] It's just the same. When it dropped below zero last night I thought I'd better send Frank out this morning to make a fire for us—no use

149

getting pneumonia with a big case on, but I told him not to touch anything except the stove—and you know Frank.

COUNTY ATTORNEY: Somebody should have been left here yesterday.

SHERIFF: Oh—yesterday. When I had to send Frank to Morris Center for that man who went crazy—I want you to know I had my hands full yesterday, I knew you could get back from Omaha by today and as long as I went over everything here myself—

COUNTY ATTORNEY: Well, Mr. Hale, tell just what happened when you came here yesterday morning.

HALE: Harry and I had started to town with a load of potatoes. We came along the road from my place and as I got here I said, "I'm going to see if I can't get John Wright to go in with me on a party telephone." I spoke to Wright about it once before and he put me off, saying folks talked too much anyway, and all he asked was peace and quiet—I guess you know about how much he talked himself; but I thought maybe if I went to the house and talked about it before his wife, though I said to Harry that I didn't know as what his wife wanted made much difference to John—

COUNTY ATTORNEY: Let's talk about that later, Mr. Hale. I do want to talk about that, but tell now just what happened when you got to the house.

HALE: I didn't hear or see anything; I knocked at the door, and still it was all quiet inside. I knew they must be up, it was past eight o'clock. So I knocked again, and I thought I heard somebody say, "Come in." I wasn't sure, I'm not sure yet, but I opened the door— this door [*Indicating the door by which the two women are still standing*] and there in that rocker— [*Pointing to it*] sat Mrs. Wright.

[*They all look at the rocker.*]

COUNTY ATTORNEY: What—was she doing?

HALE: She was rockin' back and forth. She had her apron in her hand and was kind of—pleating it.

COUNTY ATTORNEY: And how did she—look?

HALE: Well, she looked queer.

COUNTY ATTORNEY: How do you mean—queer?

HALE: Well, as if she didn't know what she was going to do next. And kind of done up.

COUNTY ATTORNEY: How did she seem to feel about your coming?

HALE: Why, I don't think she minded—one way or other. She didn't pay much attention. I said, "How do, Mrs. Wright, it's cold, ain't it?" And she said, "Is it?"—and went on kind of pleating at her apron. Well, I was surprised; she didn't ask me to come up to the stove, or to set down, but just sat there, not even looking at me, so I said, "I want to see John." And then she—laughed. I guess you would call it a laugh. I thought of Harry and the team outside, so I said a little sharp: "Can't I see John?" "No," she says, kind o' dull like. "Ain't he home?" says I. "Yes," says she, "he's home." "Then why can't I see him?" I asked her, out of patience. "'Cause he's dead," says she. *"Dead?"* says I. She just nodded her head, not getting a bit excited, but rockin' back and forth. "Why—where is he?" says I, not knowing what to say. She just pointed upstairs—like that [*Himself pointing to the room above*]. I got up, with the idea of going up there. I walked from there to here—then I says, "Why, what did he die of?" "He died of a rope round his neck," says she, and just went on pleatin' at her apron. Well, I went out and called Harry. I thought I might—need help. We went upstairs and there he was lyin'—

COUNTY ATTORNEY: I think I'd rather have you go into that upstairs, where you can point it all out. Just go on now with the rest of the story.

HALE: Well, my first thought was to get that rope off. It looked . . . [*Stops, his face twitches*] . . . but Harry, he went up to him, and he said, "No, he's dead all right, and we'd better not touch anything." So we went back down stairs. She was still sitting that same way. "Has anybody been notified?" I asked. "No," says she, unconcerned. "Who did this, Mrs. Wright?" said Harry. He said it businesslike—and she stopped pleatin' of her apron. "I don't know," she says. "You don't *know?"* says Harry. "No," says she. "Weren't you sleepin' in the bed with him?" says Harry. "Yes," says she, "but

I was on the inside." "Somebody slipped a rope round his neck and strangled him and you didn't wake up?" says Harry. "I didn't wake up," she said after him. We must 'a looked as if we didn't see how that could be, for after a minute she said, "I sleep sound." Harry was going to ask her more questions but I said maybe we ought to let her tell her story first to the coroner, or the sheriff, so Harry went fast as he could to Rivers' place, where there's a telephone.

COUNTY ATTORNEY: And what did Mrs. Wright do when she knew that you had gone for the coroner?

HALE: She moved from that chair to this one over here [*Pointing to a small chair in the corner*] and just sat there with her hands held together and looking down. I got a feeling that I ought to make some conversation, so I said I had come in to see if John wanted to put in a telephone, and at that she started to laugh, and then she stopped and looked at me—scared. [*The* COUNTY ATTORNEY, *who has had his notebook out, makes a note.*] I dunno, maybe it wasn't scared. I wouldn't like to say it was. Soon Harry got back, and then Dr. Lloyd came, and you, Mr. Peters, and so I guess that's all I know that you don't.

COUNTY ATTORNEY: [*Looking around*] I guess we'll go upstairs first—and then out to the barn and around there. [*To the* SHERIFF] You're convinced that there was nothing important here—nothing that would point to any motive.

SHERIFF: Nothing here but kitchen things.

[*The* COUNTY ATTORNEY, *after again looking around the kitchen, opens the door of a cupboard closet. He gets up on a chair and looks on a shelf. Pulls his hand away, sticky.*]

COUNTY ATTORNEY: Here's a nice mess.

[*The women draw nearer.*]

MRS. PETERS: [*To the other woman*] Oh, her fruit; it did freeze. [*To the* COUNTY ATTORNEY] She worried about that when it turned so cold. She said the fire'd go out and her jars would break.

SHERIFF: Well, can you beat the women! Held for murder and worryin' about her preserves.

COUNTY ATTORNEY: I guess before we're through she

may have something more serious than preserves to worry about.

HALE: Well, women are used to worrying over trifles.

[*The two women move a little closer together.*]

COUNTY ATTORNEY: [*With the gallantry of a young politician*] And yet, for all their worries, what would we do without the ladies? [*The women do not unbend. He goes to the sink, takes a dipperful of water from the pail and pouring it into a basin, washes his hands. Starts to wipe them on the roller towel, turns it for a cleaner place*] Dirty towels! [*Kicks his foot against the pans under the sink*] Not much of a housekeeper, would you say, ladies?

MRS. HALE: [*Stiffly*] There's a great deal of work to be done on a farm.

COUNTY ATTORNEY: To be sure. And yet [*With a little bow to her*] I know there are some Dickson county farmhouses which do not have such roller towels.

[*He gives it a pull to expose its full length again.*]

MRS. HALE: Those towels get dirty awful quick. Men's hands aren't always as clean as they might be.

COUNTY ATTORNEY: Ah, loyal to your sex, I see. But you and Mrs. Wright were neighbors. I suppose you were friends, too.

MRS. HALE: [*Shaking her head*] I've not seen much of her of late years. I've not been in this house—it's more than a year.

COUNTY ATTORNEY: And why was that? You didn't like her?

MRS. HALE: I liked her all well enough. Farmers' wives have their hands full, Mr. Henderson. And then—

COUNTY ATTORNEY: Yes—?

MRS. HALE: [*Looking about*] It never seemed a very cheerful place.

COUNTY ATTORNEY: No—it's not cheerful. I shouldn't say she had the homemaking instinct.

MRS. HALE: Well, I don't know as Wright had, either.

COUNTY ATTORNEY: You mean that they didn't get on very well?

MRS. HALE: No, I don't mean anything. But I don't think a place'd be any cheerfuller for John Wright's being in it.

COUNTY ATTORNEY: I'd like to talk more of that a little later. I want to get the lay of things upstairs now. [*He goes to the left, where three steps lead to a stair door.*]

SHERIFF: I suppose anything Mrs. Peters does'll be all right. She was to take in some clothes for her, you know, and a few little things. We left in such a hurry yesterday.

COUNTY ATTORNEY: Yes, but I would like to see what you take, Mrs. Peters, and keep an eye out for anything that might be of use to us.

MRS. PETERS: Yes, Mr. Henderson. [*The women listen to the men's steps on the stairs, then look about the kitchen.*]

MRS. HALE: I'd hate to have men coming into my kitchen, snooping around and criticising. [*She arranges the pans under sink which the* COUNTY ATTORNEY *had shoved out of place.*]

MRS. PETERS: Of course it's no more than their duty.

MRS. HALE: Duty's all right, but I guess that deputy sheriff that came out to make the fire might have got a little of this on. [*Gives the roller towel a pull*] Wish I'd thought of that sooner. Seems mean to talk about her for not having things slicked up when she had to come away in such a hurry.

MRS. PETERS: [*Who has gone to a small table in the left rear corner of the room, and lifted one end of a towel that covers a pan*] She had bread set. [*Stands still*]

MRS. HALE: [*Eyes fixed on a loaf of bread beside the breadbox, which is on a low shelf at the other side of the room. Moves slowly toward it*] She was going to put this in there. [*Picks up loaf, then abruptly drops it. In a manner of returning to familiar things*] It's a shame about her fruit. I wonder if it's all gone. [*Gets up on the chair and looks*] I think there's some here that's all right, Mrs. Peters. Yes—here; [*Holding it toward the window*] this is cherries, too. [*Looking again*] I declare I believe that's the only one. [*Gets down, bottle in her hand. Goes to the sink and wipes it off on the outside*] She'll feel awful bad after all her hard work in the hot weather. I remember the afternoon I put up my cherries last summer.

[*She puts the bottle on the big kitchen table, center of the room. With a sigh, is about to sit down in the rocking-chair. Before she is seated realizes what chair it is; with a slow look at it, steps back. The chair which she has touched rocks back and forth.*]

MRS. PETERS: Well, I must get those things from the front room closet. [*She goes to the door at the right, but after looking into the other room, steps back.*] You coming with me, Mrs. Hale? You could help me carry them.

[*They go in the other room; reappear,* MRS. PETERS *carrying a dress and skirt,* MRS. HALE *following with a pair of shoes.*]

MRS. PETERS: My, it's cold in there.

[*She puts the clothes on the big table, and hurries to the stove.*]

MRS. HALE: [*Examining the skirt*] Wright was close. I think maybe that's why she kept so much to herself. She didn't even belong to the Ladies Aid. I suppose she felt she couldn't do her part, and then you don't enjoy things when you feel shabby. She used to wear pretty clothes and be lively, when she was Minnie Foster, one of the town girls singing in the choir. But that— oh, that was thirty years ago. This all you was to take in?

MRS. PETERS: She said she wanted an apron. Funny thing to want, for there isn't much to get you dirty in jail, goodness knows. But I suppose just to make her feel more natural. She said they was in the top drawer in this cupboard. Yes, here. And then her little shawl that always hung behind the door. [*Opens stair door and looks*] Yes, here it is.

[*Quickly shuts door leading upstairs*]

MRS. HALE: [*Abruptly moving toward her*] Mrs. Peters?

MRS. PETERS: Yes, Mrs. Hale?

MRS. HALE: Do you think she did it?

MRS. PETERS: [*In a frightened voice*] Oh, I don't know.

MRS. HALE: Well, I don't think she did. Asking for an apron and her little shawl. Worrying about her fruit.

MRS. PETERS: [*Starts to speak, glances up, where foot-steps are heard in the room above. In a low voice*] Mr. Peters says it looks bad for her. Mr. Henderson is awful sarcastic in a speech and he'll make fun of her sayin' she didn't wake up.

MRS. HALE: Well, I guess John Wright didn't wake when they was slipping that rope under his neck.

MRS. PETERS: No, it's strange. It must have been done awful crafty and still. They say it was such a—funny way to kill a man, rigging it all up like that.

MRS. HALE: That's just what Mr. Hale said. There was a gun in the house. He says that's what he can't understand.

MRS. PETERS: Mr. Henderson said coming out that what was needed for the case was a motive; something to show anger, or—sudden feeling.

MRS. HALE: [*Who is standing by the table*] Well, I don't see any signs of anger around here. [*She puts her hand on the dish towel which lies on the table, stands looking down at table, one half of which is clean, the other half messy.*] It's wiped to here. [*Makes a move as if to finish work, then turns and looks at loaf of bread outside the breadbox. Drops towel. In that voice of coming back to familiar things*] Wonder how they are finding things upstairs. I hope she had it a little more red-up up there. You know, it seems kind of *sneaking*. Locking her up in town and then coming out here and trying to get her own house to turn against her!

MRS. PETERS: But Mrs. Hale, the law is the law.

MRS. HALE: I s'pose 'tis. [*Unbuttoning her coat*] Better loosen up your things, Mrs. Peters. You won't feel them when you go out.

[MRS. PETERS *takes off her fur tippet, goes to hang it on hook at back of room, stands looking at the under part of the small corner table.*]

MRS. PETERS: She was piecing a quilt.

[*She brings the large sewing basket and they look at the bright pieces.*]

MRS. HALE: It's log cabin pattern. Pretty, isn't it? I wonder if she was goin' to quilt it or just knot it?

[*Footsteps have been heard coming down the stairs.*

The SHERIFF *enters followed by* HALE *and the* COUNTY ATTORNEY.]

SHERIFF: They wonder if she was going to quilt it or just knot it!

[*The men laugh; the women look abashed.*]

COUNTY ATTORNEY: [*Rubbing his hands over the stove*] Frank's fire didn't do much up there, did it? Well, let's go out to the barn and get that cleared up.

[*The men go outside.*]

MRS. HALE: [*Resentfully*] I don't know as there's anything so strange, our takin' up our time with little things while we're waiting for them to get the evidence. [*She sits down at the big table smoothing out a block with decision.*] I don't see as it's anything to laugh about.

MRS. PETERS: [*Apologetically*] Of course they've got awful important things on their minds.

[*Pulls up a chair and joins* MRS. HALE *at the table*]

MRS. HALE: [*Examining another block*] Mrs. Peters, look at this one. Here, this is the one she was working on, and look at the sewing! All the rest of it has been so nice and even. And look at this! It's all over the place! Why, it looks as if she didn't know what she was about! [*After she has said this they look at each other, then start to glance back at the door. After an instant* MRS. HALE *has pulled at a knot and ripped the sewing.*]

MRS. PETERS: Oh, what are you doing, Mrs. Hale?

MRS. HALE: [*Mildly*] Just pulling out a stitch or two that's not sewed very good. [*Threading a needle*] Bad sewing always made me fidgety.

MRS. PETERS: [*Nervously*] I don't think we ought to touch things.

MRS. HALE: I'll just finish up this end. [*Suddenly stopping and leaning forward*] Mrs. Peters?

MRS. PETERS: Yes, Mrs. Hale?

MRS. HALE: What do you suppose she was so nervous about?

MRS. PETERS: Oh—I don't know. I don't know as she was nervous. I sometimes sew awful queer when I'm just tired. [MRS. HALE *starts to say something, looks at* MRS. PETERS, *then goes on sewing.*] Well, I must get these things wrapped up. They may be through sooner than we think. [*Putting apron and other things together*] I wonder where I can find a piece of paper, and string.

MRS. HALE: In that cupboard, maybe.

MRS. PETERS: [*Looking in cupboard*] Why, here's a birdcage. [*Holds it up*] Did she have a bird, Mrs. Hale?

MRS. HALE: Why, I don't know whether she did or not— I've not been here for so long. There was a man around last year selling canaries cheap, but I don't know as she took one; maybe she did. She used to sing real pretty herself.

MRS. PETERS: [*Glancing around*] Seems funny to think of a bird here. But she must have had one, or why would she have a cage? I wonder what happened to it.

MRS. HALE: I s'pose maybe the cat got it.

MRS. PETERS: No, she didn't have a cat. She's got that feeling some people have about cats—being afraid of them. My cat got in her room and she was real upset and asked me to take it out.

MRS. HALE: My sister Bessie was like that. Queer, ain't it?

MRS. PETERS: [*Examining the cage*] Why, look at this door. It's broke. One hinge is pulled apart.

MRS. HALE: [*Looking too*] Looks as if someone must have been rough with it.

MRS. PETERS: Why, yes.

[*She brings the cage forward and puts it on the table.*]

MRS. HALE: I wish if they're going to find any evidence they'd be about it. I don't like this place.

MRS. PETERS: But I'm awful glad you came with me, Mrs. Hale. It would be lonesome for me sitting here alone.

MRS. HALE: It would, wouldn't it? [*Dropping her sewing*] But I tell you what I do wish, Mrs. Peters. I wish I had come over sometimes when *she* was here. I— [*Looking around the room*]—wish I had.

MRS. PETERS: But of course you were awful busy, Mrs. Hale—your house and your children.

MRS. HALE: I could've come. I stayed away because it weren't cheerful—and that's why I ought to have come. I—I've never liked this place. Maybe because it's down in a hollow and you don't see the road. I dunno what it is, but it's a lonesome place and always was. I wish

I had come over to see Minnie Foster sometimes. I can
see now—
[*Shakes her head*]

MRS. PETERS: Well, you mustn't reproach yourself, Mrs.
Hale. Somehow we just don't see how it is with other
folks until—something comes up.

MRS. HALE: Not having children makes less work—but it
makes a quiet house, and Wright out to work all day,
and no company when he did come in. Did you know
John Wright, Mrs. Peters?

MRS. PETERS: Not to know him; I've seen him in town.
They say he was a good man.

MRS. HALE: Yes—good; he didn't drink, and kept his word
as well as most, I guess, and paid his debts. But he was
a hard man, Mrs. Peters. Just to pass the time of day
with him— [*Shivers*] Like a raw wind that gets to the
bone. [*Pauses, her eye falling on the cage*] I should
think she would 'a wanted a bird. But what do you
suppose went with it?

MRS. PETERS: I don't know, unless it got sick and died.
[*She reaches over and swings the broken door, swings
it again. Both women watch it.*]

MRS. HALE: You weren't raised round here, were you?
[MRS. PETERS *shakes her head.*] You didn't know—her?

MRS. PETERS: Not till they brought her yesterday.

MRS. HALE: She—come to think of it, she was kind of like
a bird herself—real sweet and pretty, but kind of timid
and—fluttery. How—she—did—change. [*Silence; then
as if struck by a happy thought and relieved to get
back to every day things*] Tell you what, Mrs. Peters,
why don't you take the quilt in with you? It might take
up her mind.

MRS. PETERS: Why, I think that's a real nice idea, Mrs.
Hale. There couldn't possibly be any objection to it,
could there? Now, just what would I take? I wonder if
her patches are in here—and her things.
[*They look in the sewing basket.*]

MRS. HALE: Here's some red. I expect this has got sewing
things in it. [*Brings out a fancy box*] What a pretty box.
Looks like something somebody would give you. Maybe
her scissors are in here. [*Opens box. Suddenly puts her
hand to her nose*] Why—[MRS. PETERS *bends nearer,*

then turns her face away.] There's something wrapped up in this piece of silk.

MRS. PETERS: Why, this isn't her scissors.

MRS. HALE: [*Lifting the silk*] Oh, Mrs. Peters—its—
[MRS. PETERS *bends closer.*]

MRS. PETERS: It's the bird.

MRS. HALE: [*Jumping up*] But, Mrs. Peters—look at it! Its neck! Look at its neck! It's all—other side *to*.

MRS. PETERS: Somebody—wrung—its—neck.

[*Their eyes meet. A look of growing comprehension, of horror. Steps are heard outside.* MRS. HALE *slips box under quilt pieces, and sinks into her chair. Enter* SHERIFF *and* COUNTY ATTORNEY. MRS. PETERS *rises.*]

COUNTY ATTORNEY: [*As one turning from serious things to little pleasantries*] Well, ladies, have you decided whether she was going to quilt it or knot it?

MRS. PETERS: We think she was going to—knot it.

COUNTY ATTORNEY: Well, that's interesting, I'm sure. [*Seeing the birdcage*] Has the bird flown?

MRS. HALE: [*Putting more quilt pieces over the box*] We think the—cat got it.

COUNTY ATTORNEY: [*Preoccupied*] Is there a cat?
[MRS. HALE *glances in a quick covert way at* MRS. PE-TERS.]

MRS. PETERS: Well, not *now*. They're superstitious, you know. They leave.

COUNTY ATTORNEY: [*To* SHERIFF PETERS, *continuing an interrupted conversation*] No sign at all of anyone having come from the outside. Their own rope. Now let's go up again and go over it piece by piece. [*They start upstairs.*] It would have to have been someone who knew just the—

[MRS. PETERS *sits down. The two women sit there not looking at one another, but as if peering into something and at the same time holding back. When they talk now it is in the manner of feeling their way over strange ground, as if afraid of what they are saying, but as if they can not help saying it.*]

MRS. HALE: She liked the bird. She was going to bury it in that pretty box.

MRS. PETERS: [*In a whisper*] When I was a girl—my kitten—there was a boy took a hatchet, and before my eyes—and before I could get there— [*Covers her face an instant*] If they hadn't held me back I would have— [*Catches herself, looks upstairs where steps are heard, falters weakly*]—hurt him.

MRS. HALE: [*With a slow look around her*] I wonder how it would seem never to have had any children around. [*Pause*] No, Wright wouldn't like the bird—a thing that sang. She used to sing. He killed that, too.

MRS. PETERS: [*Moving uneasily*] We don't know who killed the bird.

MRS. HALE: I knew John Wright.

MRS. PETERS: It was an awful thing was done in this house that night, Mrs. Hale. Killing a man while he slept, slipping a rope around his neck that choked the life out of him.

MRS. HALE: His neck. Choked the life out of him.

[*Her hand goes out and rests on the birdcage.*]

MRS. PETERS: [*With rising voice*] We don't know who killed him. We don't *know*.

MRS. HALE: [*Her own feeling not interrupted*] If there'd been years and years of nothing, then a bird to sing to you, it would be awful—still, after the bird was still.

MRS. PETERS: [*Something within her speaking*] I know what stillness is. When we homesteaded in Dakota, and my first baby died—after he was two years old, and me with no other then—

MRS. HALE: [*Moving*] How soon do you suppose they'll be through, looking for the evidence?

MRS. PETERS: I know what stillness is. [*Pulling herself back*] The law has got to punish crime, Mrs. Hale.

MRS. HALE: [*Not as if answering that*] I wish you'd seen Minnie Foster when she wore a white dress with blue ribbons and stood up there in the choir and sang. [*A look around the room*] Oh, I *wish* I'd come over here once in a while! That was a crime! That was a crime! Who's going to punish that?

MRS. PETERS: [*Looking upstairs*] We mustn't—take on.

MRS. HALE: I might have known she needed help! I know how things can be—for women. I tell you, it's queer, Mrs. Peters. We live close together and we live far apart. We all go through the same things—it's all just a different kind of the same thing. [*Brushes her eyes;*

noticing the bottle of fruit, reaches out for it] If I was you I wouldn't tell her her fruit was gone. Tell her it *ain't*. Tell her it's all right. Take this in to prove it to her. She—she may never know whether it was broke or not.

MRS. PETERS: [*Takes the bottle, looks about for something to wrap it in; takes petticoat from the clothes brought from the other room, very nervously begins winding this around the bottle. In a false voice*] My, it's a good thing the men couldn't hear us. Wouldn't they just laugh! Getting all stirred up over a little thing like a—dead canary. As if that could have anything to do with—with—wouldn't they *laugh!*

[*The men are heard coming down stairs.*]

MRS. HALE: [*Under her breath*] Maybe they would—maybe they wouldn't.

COUNTY ATTORNEY: No, Peters, it's all perfectly clear except a reason for doing it. But you know juries when it comes to women. If there was some definite thing. Something to show—something to make a story about—a thing that would connect up with this strange way of doing it—

[*The women's eyes meet for an instant. Enter* HALE *from outer door.*]

HALE: Well, I've got the team around. Pretty cold out there.

COUNTY ATTORNEY: I'm going to stay here a while by myself. [*To the* SHERIFF] You can send Frank out for me, can't you? I want to go over everything. I'm not satisfied that we can't do better.

SHERIFF: Do you want to see what Mrs. Peters is going to take in?

[*The* COUNTY ATTORNEY *goes to the table, picks up the apron, laughs.*]

COUNTY ATTORNEY: Oh, I guess they're not very dangerous things the ladies have picked out. [*Moves a few things about, disturbing the quilt pieces which cover the box. Steps back*] No, Mrs. Peters doesn't need supervising. For that matter, a sheriff's wife is married to the law. Ever think of it that way, Mrs. Peters?

MRS. PETERS: Not—just that way.

SHERIFF: [*Chuckling*] Married to the law. [*Moves toward

the other room] I just want you to come in here a minute, George. We ought to take a look at these windows.

COUNTY ATTORNEY: [*Scoffingly*] Oh, windows!

SHERIFF: We'll be right out, Mr. Hale.

[HALE *goes outside. The* SHERIFF *follows the* COUNTY ATTORNEY *into the other room. Then* MRS. HALE *rises, hands tight together, looking intensely at* MRS. PETERS, *whose eyes make a slow turn, finally meeting* MRS. HALE's. *A moment* MRS. HALE *holds her, then her own eyes point the way to where the box is concealed. Suddenly* MRS. PETERS *throws back quilt pieces and tries to put the box in the bag she is wearing. It is too big. She opens box, starts to take bird out, cannot touch it, goes to pieces, stands there helpless. Sound of a knob turning in the other room.* MRS. HALE *snatches the box and puts it in the pocket of her big coat. Enter* COUNTY ATTORNEY *and* SHERIFF.]

COUNTY ATTORNEY: [*Facetiously*] Well, Henry, at least we found out that she was not going to quilt it. She was going to—what is it you call it, ladies?

MRS. HALE: [*Her hand against her pocket*] We call it— knot it, Mr. Henderson.

CURTAIN

MISS LULU BETT
An American Comedy of Manners

ZONA GALE

First performed 1920

CHARACTERS

MONONA DEACON
DWIGHT HERBERT DEACON
INA DEACON
LULU BETT
BOBBY LARKIN
MRS. BETT
DIANA DEACON
NEIL CORNISH
NINIAN DEACON

TIME: *The Present*   PLACE: *The Middle Class*

The revised ending of *Miss Lulu Bett* is printed first,
with the original ending immediately following. This
replicates the order in the first published edition of the
play.

ACT I

Scene 1

The Deacon dining room: plain rose paper, oak side-board, straight chairs, a soft old brown divan, table laid for supper. Large pictures of, say, Paul and Virginia *and* Abbott Thayer's Motherhood. *A door left leads to kitchen; a door right front leads to the passage and the "other" room. Back are two windows with lace curtains, revealing shrubbery or blossoming plants; and a shelf with a clock and a photograph of* NINIAN DEACON. *Over the table is a gas burner in a glass globe. In the center of the table is a pink tulip in a pot. The stage is empty.*

[*Enter* MONONA. *She tiptoes to the table, tastes a dish or two, hides a cooky in her frock; begins a terrible little chant on miscellaneous notes. Enter* DWIGHT DEACON.]

DWIGHT: What! You don't mean you're in time for supper, baby?

MONONA: I ain't a baby.

DWIGHT: Ain't. Ain't. Ain't.

MONONA: Well, I ain't.

DWIGHT: We shall have to take you in hand, mama and I. We shall-have-to-take-you in hand.

MONONA: I ain't such a bad girl.

DWIGHT: Ain't. Ain't. Ain't.

[*Enter* INA, *door right front*]

INA: Dwightie! Have I kept you waiting?

DWIGHT: It's all right, my pet. Bear and forbear. Bear and forbear.

INA: Everything's on the table. I didn't hear Lulu call us, though. She's fearfully careless. And Dwight, she looks

169

so bad—when there's company I hate to have her
around.

[*They seat themselves.*]

DWIGHT: My dear Ina, your sister is very different from
you.

INA: Well, Lulu certainly is a trial. Come, Monona.

DWIGHT: Live and let live, my dear. We have to overlook,
you know. What have we on the festive board tonight?

INA: We have creamed salmon. On toast.

MONONA: I don't want any.

DWIGHT: *What's* this? *No* salmon?

MONONA: No.

INA: Oh now, pet! You liked it before.

MONONA: I don't want any.

DWIGHT: Just a little? A very little? What is this? Progeny
will not eat?

INA: She can eat if she will eat. The trouble is, she will
not take the time.

DWIGHT: She don't put her mind on her meals.

INA: Now, pettie, you must eat or you'll get sick.

MONONA: I don't want any.

INA: Well, pettie—then how would you like a nice egg?

MONONA: No.

INA: Some bread and milk?

MONONA: No.

[*Enter* LULU BETT. *She carries a plate of muffins.*]

INA: Lulu, Monona won't eat a thing. I should think you
might think of something to fix for her.

LULU: Can't I make her a little milk toast?

MONONA: Yes!

INA: Well now, sister. Don't toast it too much. That last
was too—and it's no use, she will *not* eat it if it's
burned.

LULU: I won't burn it on purpose.

INA: Well, see that you don't . . . Lulu! Which milk are
you going to take?

LULU: The bottle that sets in front, won't I?

INA: But that's yesterday's milk. No, take the fresh bottle
from over back. Monona must be nourished.

LULU: But then the yesterday's'll sour and I can't make
a custard pie—

DWIGHT: Kindly settle these domestic matters without bringing them to my attention at meal time.

[*Observes the tulip*]

Flowers! Who's been having flowers sent in?

INA: Ask Lulu.

DWIGHT: Suitors?

LULU: It was a quarter. There'll be five flowers.

DWIGHT: You bought it?

LULU: Yes. Five flowers. That's a nickel apiece.

DWIGHT: Yet we give you a home on the supposition that you have no money to spend, even for the necessities.

INA: Well, but, Dwightie. Lulu isn't strong enough to work. What's the use—

DWIGHT: The justice business and the dental profession do not warrant the purchase of spring flowers in my home.

INA: Well, but, Dwightie—

DWIGHT: No more. Lulu meant no harm.

INA: The back bottle, Lulu. And be as quick as you can. Remember, the back bottle. She has a terrible will, hangs on to her own ideas, and hangs on—

[*Exit* LULU.]

DWIGHT: Forbearance, my pet, forbearance. Baked potatoes. That's good—that's good. The baked potato contains more nourishment than potatoes prepared in any other way. Roasting retains it.

INA: That's what I always think.

DWIGHT: Where's your mother? Isn't she coming to supper?

INA: No. Tantrum.

DWIGHT: Oh ho, mama has a tantrum, eh? My dear Ina, your mother is getting old. She don't have as many clear-headed days as she did.

INA: Mama's mind is just as good as it ever was, sometimes.

DWIGHT: Hadn't I better call her up?

INA: You know how mama is.

[*Enter* LULU. *She takes flowerpot from table and throws it out the window. Exit* LULU.]

DWIGHT: I'd better see.

[*Goes to door and opens it*]

Mother Bett! . . . Come and have some supper. . . . Looks
to me Lulu's muffins'd go down pretty easy! Come on—
I had something funny to tell you and Ina. . . . [*Returns*]
No use. She's got a tall one on tonight, evidently.
What's the matter with her?

INA: Well, I told Lulu to put the creamed salmon on the
new blue platter, and mama thought I ought to use the
old deep dish.

DWIGHT: You reminded her that you are mistress here in
your own home? But gently, I hope?

INA: Well—I reminded her. She said if I kept on using
the best dishes I wouldn't have a cup left for my own
wake.

DWIGHT: And my little puss insisted?

INA: Why of course. I wanted to have the table look nice
for you, didn't I?

DWIGHT: My precious pussy.

INA: So then she walked off to her room. [MONONA *sings
her terrible little chant.*] Quiet, pettie, quiet!

DWIGHT: Softly, softly, *softly*, SOFTLY! . . . Well, here we
are, aren't we? I tell you people don't know what living
is if they don't belong in a little family circle.

INA: That's what I always think.

DWIGHT: Just coming home here and sort of settling
down—it's worth more than a tonic at a dollar the bottle. Look at this room. See this table. Could anything
be pleasanter?

INA: Monona! Now, it's all over both ruffles. And mama
does try so hard. . . .

DWIGHT: My dear. Can't you put your mind on the occasion?

INA: Well, but Monona *is* so messy.

DWIGHT: Women can*not* generalize. [*Clock strikes half
hour*] Curious how that clock loses. It must be fully
quarter to. It is quarter to! I'm pretty good at guessing
time.

INA: I've often noticed that.

DWIGHT: That clock is a terrible trial. Last night it was
only twenty-three after when the half hour struck.

INA: Twenty-one I thought.

DWIGHT: Twenty-three. My dear Ina, didn't I particularly
notice. It was twenty-three.

MONONA: [*Like lightning*] I want my milk toast, I want my milk toast, I want my milk toast.

INA: Do hurry, sister. She's going to get nervous.

[MONONA *chants her chant. Enter* LULU.]

LULU: I've got the toast here.

INA: Did you burn it?

LULU: Not black.

DWIGHT: There we are. Milk toast like a ku-ween. Where is our young lady daughter tonight?

INA: She's at Jenny Plow's, at a teaparty.

DWIGHT: Oh ho, teaparty. Is it?

LULU: We told you that this noon.

DWIGHT: [*Frowning at* LULU] How much is salmon the can now, Ina?

INA: How much is it, Lulu?

LULU: The large ones are forty, that used to be twenty-five. And the small ones that were ten, they're twenty-five. The butter's about all gone. Shall I wait for the butter woman or get some creamery?

DWIGHT: Not at meal time, if you please, Lulu. The conversation at my table must not deal with domestic matters.

LULU: I suppose salmon made me think of butter.

DWIGHT: There is not the remotest connection. Salmon comes from a river. Butter comes from a cow. A cow bears no relation to a river. A cow may drink from a river, she may do that, but I doubt if that was in your mind when you spoke—you're not that subtle.

LULU: No, that wasn't in my mind.

[*Enter* MOTHER BETT.]

DWIGHT: Well, Mama Bett, hungry now?

MRS. BETT: No, I'm not hungry.

INA: We put a potato in the oven for you, mama.

MRS. BETT: No, I thank you.

DWIGHT: And a muffin, Mama Bett.

MRS. BETT: No, I thank you.

LULU: Mama, can't I fix you some fresh tea?

MRS. BETT: That's right, Lulie. You're a good girl. And see that you put in enough tea so as a body can taste tea part of the way down.

INA: Sit here with us, mama.

MRS. BETT: No, I thank you. I'll stand and keep my figger.

DWIGHT: You know you look like a queen when you stand up, straight back, high head, a regular wonder for your years, you are.

MRS. BETT: Sometimes I think you try to flatter me. [*Sits. Doorbell*]

MONONA: I'll go. I'll go. Let me go.

DWIGHT: Now what can anybody be thinking of to call just at meal time. Can't I even have a quiet supper with my family without the outside world clamoring?

LULU: Maybe that's the butter woman.

DWIGHT: Lulu, no more about the butter, please.

MONONA: Come on in. Here's Bobby to see you, papa, let's feed him.

DWIGHT: Oh ho! So I'm the favored one. Then draw up to the festive board, Robert. A baked potato?

BOBBY: No, sir. I—I wanted something else.

DWIGHT: What's this? Came to see the justice about getting married, did you? Or the dentist to have your tooth pulled—eh? Same thing—eh, Ina? Ha! ha! ha!

BOBBY: I—I wondered whether—I thought if you would give me a job. . . .

DWIGHT: So that's it.

BOBBY: I thought maybe I might cut the grass or cut—cut something.

DWIGHT: My boy, every man should cut his own grass. Every man should come home at night, throw off his coat and, in his vigor, cut his own grass.

BOBBY: Yes, sir.

DWIGHT: Exercise, exercise is next to bread—next to gluten. Hold on, though—hold on. After dental hours I want to begin presently to work my garden. I have two lots. Property is a burden. Suppose you cut the grass on the one lot through the spring.

BOBBY: Good enough, sir. Can I start right in now? It isn't dark yet.

DWIGHT: That's right, that's right. Energy—it's the driving power of the nation. [*They rise.* DWIGHT *goes toward the door with* BOBBY.]

Start right in, by all means. You'll find the mower in the shed, oiled and ready. Tools always ready—that's my motto, my boy. [*Enter* DI *and* CORNISH. CORNISH *carries many favors.*] Ah ha!

DI: Where is everybody? Oh, hullo, Bobby! You came to see me?

BOBBY: Oh, hullo! No. I came to see your father.

DI: Did you? Well, there he is. Look at him.

BOBBY: You don't need to tell me where to look or what to do. Good-by. I'll find the mower, Mr. Deacon. [*Exit*]

DWIGHT: Mama! What do you s'pose? Di thought she had a beau— How are you, Cornish?

DI: Oh, papa! Why, I just hate Bobby Larkin, and the whole school knows it. Mama, wasn't Mr. Cornish nice to help carry my favors?

INA: Ah, Mr. Cornish! You see what a popular little girl we have.

CORNISH: Yes, I suppose so. That is—isn't that remarkable, Mrs. Deacon?

[*He tries to greet* LULU, *who is clearing the table.*]

DI: Oh, papa, the sweetest party—and the dearest supper and the darlingest decorations and the georgeousest— Monona, let go of me!

DWIGHT: Children, children, can't we have peace in this house?

MONONA: Ah, you'll catch it for talking so smarty.

DI: Oh, will I?

INA: Monona, don't stand listening to older people. Run around and play.

[MONONA *runs a swift circle and returns to her attitude of listener.*]

CORNISH: Pardon me—this is Miss Bett, isn't it?

LULU: I—Lulu Bett, yes.

CORNISH: I had the pleasure of meeting you the night I was here for supper.

LULU: I didn't think you'd remember.

CORNISH: Don't you think I'd remember that meat pie?

LULU: Oh, yes. The meat pie. You might remember the meat pie.

[*Exit, carrying plates*]

CORNISH: What in the dickens did I say that for?

INA: Oh, Lulu likes it. She's a wonderful cook. I don't know what we should do without her.

DWIGHT: A most exemplary woman is Lulu.

INA: That's eggsemplary, Dwightie.

DWIGHT: My darling little dictionary.

DI: Mama, Mr. Cornish and I have promised to go back to help Jenny.

INA: How nice! And Mr. Cornish, do let us see you oftener.

DWIGHT: Yes, yes, Cornish. Drop in. Any time, you know.

CORNISH: I'll be glad to come. I do get pretty lonesome evenings. [*Enter* LULU, *clearing table.*] I eat out around. I guess that's why your cooking made such an impression on me, Miss Lulu.

LULU: Yes. Yes. I s'pose it would take something like that. . . .

CORNISH: Oh, no, no! I didn't mean—you mustn't think I meant—What'd I say that for?

LULU: Don't mind. They always say that to me.
[*Exit with dishes*]

DI: Come on, Mr. Cornish. Jenny'll be waiting. Monona, let *go* of me!

MONONA: *I* don't want you!

DWIGHT: Early, darling, early! Get her back here early, Mr. Cornish.

CORNISH: Oh, I'll have her back here as soon as ever she'll come—well, ah—I mean . . . .

DI: Good-by Dwight and Ina!
[*Exit* DI *and* CORNISH.]

DWIGHT: Nice fellow, nice fellow. Don't know whether he'll make a go of his piano store, but he's studying law evenings.

INA: But we don't know anything about him, Dwight. A stranger so.

DWIGHT: On the contrary I know a great deal about him. I know that he has a little inheritance coming to him.

INA: An inheritance—really? I *thought* he was from a good family.

DWIGHT: My mercenary little pussy.

INA: Well, if he comes here so very much you know what we may expect.

DWIGHT: What may we expect?

INA: He'll fall in love with Di. And a young girl is awfully flattered when a good-looking older man pays her attention. Haven't you noticed that?

DWIGHT: How women generalize! My dear Ina, I have other matters to notice.

INA: Monona. Stop listening! Run about and play. [MONONA *runs her circle and returns.*] Well, look at that clock. It's almost your bedtime, anyway. [*Enter* LULU.]

MONONA: No.

INA: It certainly is.

MONONA: That clock's wrong. Papa said so.

INA: Mama says bedtime. In ten minutes.

MONONA: I won't go all night.

DWIGHT: Daughter, daughter, daughter . . .

MONONA: I won't go for a week. [DWIGHT *sees on clock shelf a letter.*]

INA: Oh, Dwight! It came this morning. I forgot.

LULU: I forgot too. And I laid it up there.

DWIGHT: Isn't it understood that my mail can't wait like this?

LULU: I know. I'm sorry. But you hardly ever get a letter.

DWIGHT: Of course pressing matters go to my office. Still my mail should have more careful— [*He reads.*] Now! What do you think I have to tell you?

INA: Oh, Dwightie! Something nice?

DWIGHT: That depends. I'll like it. So'll Lulu. It's company.

MONONA: I hope they bring me something decent.

INA: Oh, Dwight, who?

DWIGHT: My brother, from Oregon.

INA: Ninian coming here?

DWIGHT: Some day next week. He don't know what a charmer Lulu is or he'd come quicker.

INA: Dwight, it's been years since you've seen him.

DWIGHT: Nineteen—twenty. Must be twenty.

INA: And he's never seen me.

DWIGHT: Nor Lulu.

INA: And think where he's been. South America—Mexico—Panama and all. We must put it in the paper.

MRS. BETT: Who's coming? Why don't you say who's coming? You all act so dumb.

LULU: It's Dwight's brother, mother. His brother from Oregon.

MRS. BETT: Never heard of him.

LULU: [*Taking photograph from shelf*] That one, mother. You've dusted his picture lots of times.

MRS. BETT: That? Got to have him around long?

DWIGHT: I don't know. Wait till he sees Lulu. I expect when he sees Lulu you can't drive him away. He's going to take one look at Lulu and settle down here for life. He's going to think Lulu is—

LULU: I—think the tea must be steeped now.
[*Exit*]

DWIGHT: He's going to think Lulu is a stunner—a stunner. . . . [*The clock strikes.* MONONA *shrieks.*] Is the progeny hurt?

INA: Bedtime. Now, Monona, be mama's nice little lady. . . . Monona, quiet, pettie, quiet. . . . [LULU *enters with tea and toast.*]
Lulu, won't you take her to bed? You know Dwight and I are going to Study Club.

LULU: There, mother. Yes. I'll take her to bed. Come, Monona. And stop that noise instantly.
[MONONA *stops. As they cross* DWIGHT *spies the tulip on* LULU's *gown.*]

DWIGHT: Lulu. One moment. You *picked* the flower on the plant?

LULU: Yes. I—picked it.

DWIGHT: She buys a hothouse plant and then ruins it!

LULU: I—I—
[*She draws* MONONA *swiftly left; exeunt; the door slams.*]

DWIGHT: What a pity Lulu hasn't your manners, pettie.

MRS. BETT: What do you care? She's got yours.

DWIGHT: Mother Bett! Fare thee well.

MRS. BETT: How do you stand him? The lump!

INA: Mama dear, now drink your tea. Good-night, sweetie.

MRS. BETT: You needn't think I forgot about the platter, because I ain't. Of all the extravagant doin's, courtin' the poorhouse—
[*Exeunt* DWIGHT *and* INA. MRS. BETT *continues to look after them, her lips moving. At door appears* BOBBY.]

BOBBY: Where's Mr. Deacon?

MRS. BETT: Gone, thank the Lord!

BOBBY: I've got the grass cut.

MRS. BETT: You act like it was a trick.

BOBBY: Is—is everybody gone?

MRS. BETT: Who's this you're talkin' to?

BOBBY: Yes, well, I meant—I guess I'll go now.

[*Enter* DI.]

DI: Well, Bobby Larkin. Are you cutting grass in the dining room?

BOBBY: No, ma'am, I was not cutting grass in the dining room.

[*Enter* LULU, *collects her mother's dishes, folds cloth and watches.*]

DI: I used to think you were pretty nice, but I don't like you any more.

BOBBY: Yes you used to! Is that why you made fun of me all the time?

DI: I had to. They all were teasing me about you.

BOBBY: They were? Teasing you about me?

DI: I had to make them stop so I teased you. I never wanted to.

BOBBY: Well, I never thought it was anything like that.

DI: Of course you didn't. I—wanted to tell you.

BOBBY: You wanted—

DI: Of course I did. You must go now—they're hearing us.

BOBBY: Say—

DI: Good-night. Go the back way, Bobby—you nice thing. [*Exit* BOBBY.] Aunt Lulu, give me the cookies, please, and the apples. Mr. Cornish is on the front porch . . . mama and papa won't be home till late, will they?

LULU: I don't think so.

DI: Well, I'll see to the hall light. Don't you bother. Good-night.

LULU: Good-night, Di.

[*Exit* DI]

MRS. BETT: My land! How she wiggles and chitters.

LULU: Mother, could you hear them? Di and Bobby Larkin?

MRS. BETT: Mother hears a-plenty.

LULU: How easy she done it . . . got him right over . . . how did she do that?

MRS. BETT: Di wiggles and chitters.
LULU: It was just the other day I taught her to sew. . . .
  I wonder if Ina knows.
MRS. BETT: What's the use of you findin' fault with Inie?
  Where'd you been if she hadn't married I'd like to
  know? . . . What say? . . . eh? . . . I'm goin' to bed. . . .
  You always was jealous of Inie.
  [*Exit* MRS. BETT. LULU *crosses to shelf, takes down
  photograph of* NINIAN DEACON, *holds it, looks at it.*]

CURTAIN

Scene 2

*Same set. Late afternoon. A week later. The table is
cleared of dishes, and has an oilcloth cover.* BOBBY *is
discovered outside the window, on whose sill* DI *is sitting.*

BOBBY: So you despise me for cutting grass?
DI: No, I don't. But if you're going to be a great man why
  don't you get started at it?
BOBBY: I am started at it—inside. But it don't earn me a
  cent yet.
DI: Bobby, Bobby! I know you're great now, don't you
  ever think I don't, but I want everybody else to know.
BOBBY: Di, when you said that it sounded just like a—a
  you know.
DI: Like what?
BOBBY: Like a wife. Gee, what a word that is!
DI: Isn't it? It's ever so much more exciting word than
  husband.
  [*Enter* LULU, *followed by* MONONA. LULU *carries bowl,
  pan of apples, paring knife.* MONONA *carries basket of
  apples and a towel.* As LULU *rattles dishes,* DI *turns,
  sees* LULU. BOBBY *disappears from window.*]
DI: There's never any privacy in this house.
  [*Exit* DI.]

LULU: Hurry, Monona, I must make the pies before I get dinner. Now wipe every one.

MONONA: What for?

LULU: To make the pies.

MONONA: What do you want to make pies for?

LULU: To eat.

MONONA: What do you want to eat for?

LULU: To grow strong—and even sensible.

MONONA: It's no fun asking you a string of questions. You never get mad. Mama gets good and mad. So does papa.

LULU: Then why do you ask them questions?

MONONA: Oh, I like to get them going.

LULU: Monona!

MONONA: I told mama I didn't pass, just so I could hear her.

LULU: Why, Monona!

MONONA: Then when I told her I did pass, she did it again. When she's mad she makes awful funny faces.

LULU: You love her, don't you, Monona?

MONONA: I love her best when there's company. If there was always company, I'd always love her. Isn't she sweet before Uncle Ninian though?

LULU: I—I don't know. Monona, you mustn't talk so.

MONONA: He's been here a week and mama hasn't been cross once. Want to know what he said about you?

LULU: I—did he—did he say anything about me?

MONONA: He told papa you were the best cook he'd ever ate. Said he'd et a good many.

LULU: The cooking. It's always the cooking.

MONONA: He said some more, but I can't remember.

LULU: Monona, what else did he say?

MONONA: I don't know.

LULU: Try. . . .

MONONA: Here he is now. Ask him to his face. Hullo, Uncle Ninian! Good-by.

[*Exit* MONONA. *Enter* NINIAN.]

NINIAN: Hello, kitten! Ask him what? What do you want to ask him?

LULU: I—I think I was wondering what kind of pies you like best.

NINIAN: That's easy. I like your kind of pies best. The

best ever. Every day since I've been here I've seen you baking, Mrs. Bett.

LULU: Yes, I—bake. What did you call me then?

NINIAN: Mrs. Bett—isn't it? Every one says just Lulu, but I took it for granted. . . . Well, now—is it Mrs.? or Miss Lulu Bett?

LULU: It's Miss. . . . From choice.

NINIAN: You bet! Oh, you bet! Never doubted that.

LULU: What kind of a Mr. are you?

NINIAN: Never give myself away. Say, by George, I never thought of that before. There's no telling whether a man's married or not, by his name.

LULU: It doesn't matter.

NINIAN: Why?

LULU: Not so many people want to know.

NINIAN: Say, you're pretty good, aren't you?

LULU: If I am it never took me very far.

NINIAN: Where you been mostly?

LULU: Here. I've always been here. Fifteen years with Ina. Before that we lived in the country.

NINIAN: Never been anywhere much?

LULU: Never been anywhere at all.

NINIAN: H . . . m. Well, I want to tell you something about yourself.

LULU: About me?

NINIAN: Something that I'll bet you don't even know. It's this: I think you have it pretty hard around here.

LULU: Oh, no!

NINIAN: See here. Do you have to work like this all the time? I guess you won't mind my asking.

LULU: But I ought to work. I have a home with them. Mother too.

NINIAN: But glory! You ought to have some kind of a life of your own.

LULU: How could I do that?

NINIAN: A man don't even know what he's like till he's roamed around on his own. . . . Roamed around on his own. Course a woman don't understand that.

LULU: Why don't she? Why don't she?

NINIAN: Do you? [LULU *nods*.] I've had twenty-five years of galloping about—Brazil, Mexico, Panama.

LULU: My!

NINIAN: It's the life.

LULU: Must be. I—

NINIAN: Yes, you. Why, you've never had a thing! I guess you don't know how it seems to me, coming along—a stranger so. I don't like it.

LULU: They're very good to me.

NINIAN: Do you know why you think that? Because you've never had anybody really good to you. That's why.

LULU: But they treat me good.

NINIAN: They make a slavey of you. Regular slavey. Damned shame *I* call it.

LULU: But we have our whole living—

NINIAN: And you earn it. I been watching you ever since I've been here. Don't you ever go anywhere?

LULU: Oh, no, I don't go anywhere. I—

NINIAN: Lord! Don't you want to? Of course you do.

LULU: Of course I'd like to get clear away—or I used to want to.

NINIAN: Say—you've been a blamed fine-looking woman.

LULU: You must have been a good-looking man once yourself.

NINIAN: You're pretty good. I don't see how you do it— darned if I do.

LULU: How I do what?

NINIAN: Why come back, quick like that, with what you say. You don't look it.

LULU: It must be my grand education.

NINIAN: Education: I ain't never had it and I ain't never missed it.

LULU: Most folks are happy without an education.

NINIAN: You're not very happy, though.

LULU: Oh, no.

NINIAN: Well you ought to get up and get out of here— find—find some work you *like* to do.

LULU: But, you see, I can't do any other work—that's the trouble—women like me can't do any other work.

NINIAN: But you make this whole house go round.

LULU: If I do, nobody knows it.

NINIAN: I know it. I hadn't been in the house twenty-four hours till I knew it.

LULU: You did? You thought that. . . . Yes, well if I do I
    hate making it go round.

NINIAN: See here—couldn't you tell me a little bit about—
    what you'd *like* to do? If you had your own way?

LULU: I don't know—now.

NINIAN: What did you ever think you'd like to do?

LULU: Take care of folks that needed me. I—I mean sick
    folks or old folks or—like that. Take *care* of them. Have
    them—have them want me.

NINIAN: By George! You're a wonder.

LULU: Am I? Ask Dwight.

NINIAN: Dwight. I could knock the top of his head off the
    way he speaks to you. I'd like to see you get out of this,
    I certainly would.

LULU: I can't get out. I'll never get out—now.

NINIAN: Don't keep saying "now" like that. You—you put
    me out of business, darned if you don't.

LULU: Oh, I don't mean to feel sorry for myself—you stop
    making me feel sorry for myself!

NINIAN: I know one thing—I'm going to give Dwight
    Deacon a chunk of my mind.

LULU: Oh, no! no! no! I wouldn't want you to do that.
    Thank you.

NINIAN: Well, somebody ought to do something. See
    here—while I'm staying around you know you've got
    a friend in me, don't you?

LULU: Do I?

NINIAN: You bet you do.

LULU: Not just my cooking?

NINIAN: Oh, come now—why, I liked you the first mo-
    ment I saw you.

LULU: Honest?

NINIAN: Go on—go on. Did you like me?

LULU: Now you're just being polite.

NINIAN: Say, I wish there was some way—

LULU: Don't you bother about me.

NINIAN: I wish there was some way—
    [MONONA's *voice chants.*]
    [*Enter* MONONA.]

MONONA: You've had him long enough, Aunt Lulu—
    Can't you pay me some 'tention?

NINIAN: Come here. Give us a kiss. My stars, what a great big tall girl! Have to put a board on her head to stop this growing.

MONONA: [*Seeing diamond*] What's that?

NINIAN: That diamond came from Santa Claus. He has a jewelry shop in heaven. I have twenty others like this one. I keep the others to wear on the Sundays when the sun comes up in the west.

MONONA: Does the sun ever come up in the west?

NINIAN: Sure—on my honor. Some day I'm going to melt a diamond and eat it. Then you sparkle all over in the dark, ever after. I'm going to plant one too, some day. Then you can grow a diamond vine. Yes, on my honor.

LULU: Don't do that—don't do that.

NINIAN: What?

LULU: To her. That's lying.

NINIAN: Oh, no. That's not lying. That's just drama. Drama. Do you like going to a good show?

LULU: I've never been to any—only those that come here.

NINIAN: Think of that now. Don't you ever go to the city?

LULU: I haven't been in six years and over.

NINIAN: Well, sir, I'll tell you what I'm going to do with you. While I'm here I'm going to take you and Ina and Dwight up to the city, to see a show.

LULU: Oh, you don't want me to go.

NINIAN: Yes, sir, I'll give you one good time. Dinner and a show.

LULU: Ina and Dwight do that sometimes. I can't imagine me.

NINIAN: Well, you're coming with me. I'll look up something good. And you tell me just what you like to eat and we'll order it—

LULU: It's been years since I've eaten anything that I haven't cooked myself.

NINIAN: It has. Say, by George! why shouldn't we go to the city *tonight*.

LULU: Tonight?

NINIAN: Yes. If Dwight and Ina will. It's early yet. What do you say?

LULU: You sure you want me to go? Why—I don't know whether I've got anything I could wear.

NINIAN: Sure you have.

LULU: I—yes, I have. I could wear the waist I always thought they'd use—if I died.

NINIAN: Sure you could wear that. Just the thing. And throw some things in a bag—it'll be too late to come back tonight. Now don't you back out. . . .

LULU: Oh, the pies—

NINIAN: Forget the pies—well, no, I wouldn't say that. But hustle them up.

LULU: Oh, maybe Ina won't go. . . .

NINIAN: Leave Ina to me.

[*Exit* NINIAN.]

LULU: Mother, mother! Monona, put the rest of those apples back in the basket and carry them out.

MONONA: Yes, Aunt Lulu.

LULU: I can't get ready. They'll leave me behind. Mother! Hurry, Monona. We mustn't leave such a looking house. Mother! Monona, don't you drop those apples. [MONONA *drops them all.*]

My heavens, my pies aren't in the oven yet.

[*Enter* MRS. BETT.]

MRS. BETT: Who wants their mother?

LULU: Mother, please pick up these things for me—quick.

MRS. BETT: [*Leisurely*] What is the rush, Lulie?

LULU: Mother, Mr. Deacon—Ninian, you know—wants Ina and Dwight and me to go to the theater tonight in the city.

MRS. BETT: Does, does he? Well, you mind me, Lulie, and go on. It'll do you good.

LULU: Yes, mother. I will.

[*Exit with pies*]

MRS. BETT: No need breaking everybody's neck off, though, as I know of. Monona, get out from under my feet.

MONONA: Grandma, compared between what I am, you are nothing.

MRS. BETT: What do you mean—little ape?

MONONA: It's no fun to get you going. You're too easy, grandma dear!

[*Exit. Enter* NINIAN.]

NINIAN: All right—Dwight and Ina are game. Oh, Mrs. Bett! Won't you come to the theater with us tonight?

MRS. BETT: No. I'm fooled enough without fooling myself on purpose. But Lulie can go.

NINIAN: You don't let her go too much, do you, Mrs. Bett?

MRS. BETT: Well, I ain't never let her go to the altar if that's what you mean.

NINIAN: Don't you think she'd be better off?

MRS. BETT: Wouldn't make much difference. Why look at me. A husband, six children, four of 'em under the sod with him. And sometimes I feel as though nothin' more had happened to me than has happened to Lulie. It's all gone. For me just the same as for her. Only she ain't had the pain. [*Yawns*] What was I talkin' about just then?

NINIAN: Why—why—er, we were talking about going to the theater.

MRS. BETT: Going to the theater, are you?
[*Enter* LULU.]

NINIAN: It's all right, Miss Lulu. They'll go—both of them. Dwight is telephoning for the seats.

LULU: I was wondering why you should be so kind to me.

NINIAN: Kind? Why, this is for my own pleasure, Miss Lulu. That's what I think of mostly.

LULU: But just see. It's so wonderful. Half an hour ago I never thought I'd be going to the city now—with you all. . . .

NINIAN: I'm an impulsive cuss, you'll find, Miss Lulu.

LULU: But this is so wonderful. . . .
[*Enter* INA.]
Ina, isn't it beautiful that we're going?

INA: Oh, are you going?

NINIAN: Oh course she's going. Great snakes, why not?

INA: Only that Lulu never goes anywhere.

NINIAN: Whose fault is that?

LULU: Just habit. Pure habit.

NINIAN: Pure cussedness somewhere. Miss Lulu, now you go and get ready and Ina and I'll finish straightening up here.

LULU: Oh, I'll finish.

NINIAN: Go and get ready. I want to see that waist.

LULU: Oh, but I don't need to go yet—

NINIAN: Ina, you tell her to go—

INA: Well, but, Lulu, you aren't going to bother to change your dress, are you? You can slip something on over.

LULU: If you think this would do—

NINIAN: It will not do. Not for my party!

[*Shuts the door upon her*]

INA: How in the world did you ever get Lulu to go, Ninian? *We* never did.

NINIAN: It was very simple. I invited her.

INA: Oh, you mean—

NINIAN: I invited her. [*Doorbell rings.*] Shall I answer it?

INA: Will you please? [*Exit* NINIAN.] Mother, have you seen Di anywhere?

MRS. BETT: I ain't done nothing but see her. [*Motions to window*]

INA: [*At window*] Forevermore. That Larkin boy again. Di! Diana Deacon! Come here at once.

DI's VOICE: Yes, mama. [*At window*] Want me?

INA: I want you to stop making a spectacle of *me* before the neighborhood.

DI: Of *you!*

INA: Certainly. What will people think of me if they see you talking with Robert Larkin the whole afternoon?

DI: We weren't thinking about you, mummy.

INA: No. You never do think about me. Nobody thinks about me. And mama does try so hard—

DI: Oh, mama, I've heard you say that fifty hundred times.

INA: And what impression does it make? None. . . . Nobody listens to me. Nobody.

[*Enter* NINIAN *and* CORNISH.]

NINIAN: All right to bring him in here?

INA: Oh, Mr. Cornish! how very nice to see you.

CORNISH: Good afternoon, Mrs. Deacon. How are you, Miss Di?

NINIAN: I've just been asking Mr. Cornish if he won't join us tonight for dinner and the show.

INA: Oh, Mr. Cornish, do—we'd be so glad.

CORNISH: Why, why, if that wouldn't be—

NINIAN: You're invited, Di, you know.

DI: Me? Oh, how heavenly! Oh, but I've an engagement with Bobby—

INA: But I'm sure you'd break that to go with Uncle Ninian and Mr. Cornish.

DI: Well, I'd break it to go to the theater—

INA: Why, Di Deacon!

DI: Oh, of course to go with Uncle Ninian and Mr. Cornish.

CORNISH: This is awfully good of you. I dropped in because I got so lonesome I didn't know what else to do—that is, I mean. . . .

NINIAN: We get it. We get it.

INA: We'd love to see you any time, Mr. Cornish. Now if you'll excuse Di and me one minute.

DI: Uncle Ninian, you're a lamb.

[*Exeunt* DI *and* INA.]

MRS. BETT: I'm just about the same as I was.

CORNISH: What—er—oh, Mrs. Bett, I didn't see you.

MRS. BETT: I don't complain. But it wouldn't turn my head if some of you spoke to me once in a while. Say—can you tell me what these folks are up to?

CORNISH: Up to . . . up to?

MRS. BETT: Yes. They're all stepping round here, up to something. I don't know what.

NINIAN: Why, Mrs. Bett, we're going to the city to the theater, you know.

MRS. BETT: Well, why didn't you say so?

[*Enter* DWIGHT.]

DWIGHT: Ha! Everybody ready? Well, well, well, well. How are you, Cornish? You going too, Ina says.

CORNISH: Yes, I thought I might as well. I mean—

DWIGHT: That's right, that's right. Mama Bett. Look here!

MRS. BETT: What's that?

DWIGHT: *Ice* cream—it's *ice* cream. Who is it sits home and has *ice* cream put in her lap like a ku-ween?

MRS. BETT: Vanilly or chocolate?

DWIGHT: Chocolate, Mama Bett.

MRS. BETT: Vanilly sets better. . . . I'll put it in the ice chest—I *may* eat it.

[*Takes spoon from sideboard. Exit.* CORNISH *goes with her.*]

DWIGHT: Where's the lovely Lulu?

NINIAN: She'll be here directly.

DWIGHT: Now what I want to know, Nin, is how you've hypnotized the lovely Lulu into this thing.

NINIAN: Into going? Dwight, I'll tell you about that. I

asked her to go with us. Do you get it? I invited the woman.

DWIGHT: Ah, but with a way—with a way. She's never been anywhere like this with us. . . . Well, Nin, how does it seem to see me settled down into a respectable married citizen in my own town—eh?

NINIAN: Oh—you seem just like yourself.

DWIGHT: Yes, yes. I don't change much. Don't feel a day older than I ever did.

NINIAN: And you don't act it.

DWIGHT: Eh, you wouldn't think it to look at us, but our aunt had her hands pretty full bringing us up. Nin, we must certainly run up state and see Aunt Mollie while you're here. She isn't very well.

NINIAN: I don't know whether I'll have time or not.

DWIGHT: Nin, I love that woman. She's an angel. When I think of her I feel—I give you my word—I feel like somebody else.

[*Enter* MRS. BETT *and* CORNISH.]

NINIAN: Nice old lady.

MRS. BETT: Who's a nice old lady?

DWIGHT: You, Mama Bett! Who else but you—eh? Well, now, Nin, what about you. You've been saying mighty little about yourself. What's been happening to you, anyway?—

NINIAN: That's the question.

DWIGHT: Traveling mostly—eh?

NINIAN: Yes, traveling mostly.

DWIGHT: I thought Ina and I might get over to the other side this year, but I guess not—I guess not.

MRS. BETT: Pity not to have went while the going was good.

DWIGHT: What's that, Mama Bett? [*Enter* LULU.] Ah, the lovely Lulu. She comes, she comes! My word what a costoom. And a coif*fure*.

LULU: Thank you. How do you do, Mr. Cornish?

CORNISH: How do you do, Miss Lulu? You see they're taking me along too.

LULU: That's nice. But, Mr. Deacon, I'm afraid I can't go after all. I haven't any gloves.

NINIAN: No backing out now.

DWIGHT: Can't you wear some old gloves of Ina's?

LULU: No, no. Ina's gloves are too fat for me—I mean too—mother, how does this hat look?

MRS. BETT: You'd ought to know how it looks, Lulie. You've had it on your head for ten years, hand-running.

LULU: And I haven't any theater cape. I couldn't go with my jacket and no gloves, could I?

DWIGHT: Now why need a charmer like you care about clothes!

LULU: I wouldn't want you gentlemen to be ashamed of me.

CORNISH: Why, Miss Lulu, you look real neat.

MRS. BETT: Act as good as you look, Lulie. You mind me and go on.

[*Enter* INA.]

DWIGHT: Ha! All ready with our hat on! For a wonder, all ready with our hat on.

INA: That isn't really necessary, Dwight.

LULU: Ina, I wondered—I thought about your linen duster. Would it hurt if I wore that?

DWIGHT: The new one?

LULU: Oh no, no. The old one.

INA: Why take it, Lulu, yes, certainly. Get it, Dwightie, there in the hall.

[DWIGHT *goes.*]

CORNISH: Miss Lulu, with all the solid virtues you've got, you don't need to think for a moment of how you look.

LULU: Now you're remembering the meat pie again, aren't you?

[*Enter* DWIGHT.]

DWIGHT: Now! The festive opera cloak. Allow me! My word, what a picture! Lulu the charmer dressed for her deboo into society, eh?

NINIAN: Dwight, shut your head. I want you to understand this is Miss Lulu Bett's party—and if she says to leave you home, we'll do it.

DWIGHT: Ah, ha! An understanding between these two.

CORNISH: Well, Miss Lulu, *I* think you're just fine anyway.

LULU: Oh, thank you. Thank you. . . .

[*Enter* DI.]

INA: All ready, darling?

DI: All ready—and so excited! Isn't it exciting, Mr. Cornish?

DWIGHT: Bless me if the whole family isn't assembled. Now isn't this pleasant! Ten—let me see—twelve minutes before we need set out. Then the city and dinner—not just Lulu's cooking, but dinner! By a chef.

INA: That's sheff, Dwightie. Not cheff.

DWIGHT: [*Indicating* INA] Little crusty tonight. Pettie, your hat's just a little mite—no, over the other way.

INA: Was there anything to prevent your speaking of that before?

LULU: Ina, that hat's ever so much prettier than the old one.

INA: I never saw anything the matter with the old one.

DWIGHT: She'll be all right when we get started—out among the bright lights. Adventure—adventure is what the woman wants. I'm too tame for her.

INA: Idiot.

[*Back at window*, BOBBY LARKIN *appears.* DI *slips across to him.*]

MRS. BETT: I s'pose you all think I like being left sitting here stark alone?

NINIAN: Why, Mrs. Bett—

INA: Why, mama—

LULU: Oh, mother, I'll stay with you.

DWIGHT: Oh, look here, if she really minds staying alone I'll stay with her.

MRS. BETT: Where you going anyway?

LULU: The theater, mama.

MRS. BETT: First I've heard of it.

[MONONA *is heard chanting.*]

INA: You'll have Monona with you, mama.

[MRS. BETT *utters one note of laughter, thin and high. Enter* MONONA.]

MONONA: Where you going?

INA: The city, dear. [MONONA *cries.*] Now quiet, pettie, quiet—

MONONA: You've all got to bring me something. And I'm going to sit up and eat it, too.

MRS. BETT: Come here, you poor, neglected child.

[*Throughout the following scene* MRS. BETT *is absorbed with* MONONA, *and* DI *with* BOBBY.]

DWIGHT: What's Lulu the charmer so still for, eh?

LULU: I was thinking how nice it is to be going off with you all like this.

DWIGHT: Such a moment advertises to the single the joys of family life as Ina and I live it.

INA: It's curious that you've never married, Ninian.

NINIAN: Don't say it like that. Maybe I have. Or maybe I will.

DWIGHT: She wants everybody to marry but she wishes she hadn't.

INA: Do you *have* to be so foolish?

DWIGHT: Hi—better get started before she makes a scene. It's too early yet, though. Well—Lulu, you dance on the table.

INA: Why, Dwight?

DWIGHT: Got to amuse ourselves somehow. They'll begin to read the funeral service over us.

NINIAN: Why not the wedding service?

DWIGHT: Ha, ha, ha!

NINIAN: I shouldn't object. Should you, Miss Lulu?

LULU: I—I don't know it so I can't say it.

NINIAN: I can say it.

DWIGHT: Where'd you learn it?

NINIAN: Goes like this: I, Ninian, take thee, Lulu, to be my wedded wife.

DWIGHT: Lulu don't dare say that.

NINIAN: Show him, Miss Lulu.

LULU: I, Lulu, take thee, Ninian, to be my wedded husband.

NINIAN: You will?

LULU: I will. There—I guess I can join in like the rest of you.

NINIAN: And I will. There, by Jove! have we entertained the company, or haven't we?

INA: Oh, honestly—I don't think you ought to—holy things so—what's the matter, Dwightie?

DWIGHT: Say, by George, you know, a civil wedding is binding in this state.

NINIAN: A civil wedding—oh, well—

DWIGHT: But I happen to be a magistrate.

INA: Why, Dwightie—why, Dwightie. . . .

CORNISH: Mr. Deacon, this can't be possible.

DWIGHT: I tell you, what these two have said is all that they have to say according to law. And there don't have to be witnesses—say!

LULU: Don't . . . don't . . . don't let Dwight scare you.

NINIAN: Scare me! why, I think it's a good job done if you ask me.

[*Their eyes meet in silence.*]

INA: Mercy, sister!

DWIGHT: Oh, well—I should say we can have it set aside up in the city and no one will be the wiser.

NINIAN: Set aside nothing. I'd like to see it stand.

INA: Ninian, are you serious?

NINIAN: Of course I'm serious.

INA: Lulu. You hear him? What are you going to say to that?

LULU: He isn't in earnest.

NINIAN: I am in earnest—hope to die.

LULU: Oh, no, no!

NINIAN: You come with me. We'll have it done over again somewhere if you say so.

LULU: Why—why—that couldn't be. . . .

NINIAN: Why couldn't it be—why couldn't it?

LULU: How could you want me?

NINIAN: Didn't I tell you I liked you from the first minute I saw you?

LULU: Yes. Yes, you did. But—no, no. I couldn't let you—

NINIAN: Never mind that. Would *you* be willing to go with me? Would you?

LULU: But you—you said you wanted—oh, maybe you're just doing this because—

NINIAN: Lulu. Never mind any of that. Would *you* be willing to go with me?

LULU: Oh, if I thought—

NINIAN: Good girl—

INA: Why, Lulu. Why, Dwight. It can't be legal.

DWIGHT: Why? Because it's your sister? I've married dozens of couples this way. Dozens.

NINIAN: Good enough—eh, Lulu?

LULU: It's—it's all right, I guess.

DWIGHT: Well, I'll be dished.

CORNISH: Well, by Jerusalem. . . .

INA: Sister!

NINIAN: I was going to make a trip south this month on my way home from here. Suppose we make sure of this thing and start right off. You'd like that, wouldn't you? Going to Savannah?

LULU: Yes, I'd like that.

NINIAN: Then that's checked off.

DWIGHT: I suppose we call off our trip to the city tonight then.

NINIAN: Call off nothing. Come along. Give us a send-off. You can shoot our trunks after us, can't you? All right, Miss Lulu—er—er, Mrs. Lulu?

LULU: If you won't be ashamed of me.

NINIAN: I can buy you some things in the city tomorrow.

LULU: Oh . . .

INA: Oh, mama, mama! Did you hear? Di! Aunt Lulu's married.

DI: Married? Aunt Lulu?

INA: Just now. Right here. By papa.

DI: Oh, to Mr. Cornish?

CORNISH: No, Miss Di. Don't you worry.

INA: To Ninian, mama. They've just been married—Lulu and Ninian.

MRS. BETT: Who's going to do your work?

LULU: Oh, mother dearest—I don't know who will. I ought not to have done this. Well, of course, I didn't do it—

MRS. BETT: I knew well enough you were all keeping something from me.

INA: But, mama! It was so sudden—

LULU: I never planned to do it, mother—not like this—

MRS. BETT: Well, Inie, I should think Lulie might have had a little more consideration to her than this.

[*At the window, behind the curtain,* DI *has just kissed* BOBBY *good-by.*]

LULU: Mother dearest, tell me it's all right.

MRS. BETT: This is what comes of going to the theater.

LULU: Mother—

DWIGHT: Come on, everybody, if we're going to make that train.

NINIAN: Yes. Let's get out of this.

CORNISH: Come, Miss Di.

INA: Oh, I'm so *flustrated!*

DWIGHT: Come, come, come, all! On to the festive city!

MONONA: [*Dancing stiffly up and down*] I was to a wedding! I was to a wedding!

NINIAN: Good-by, Mama Bett!

LULU: Mother, mother! Don't forget the two pies!

CURTAIN

ACT II

Scene 1

Side porch, wicker furnished. At the back are two windows, attractively curtained and revealing shaded lamps; between the windows a door, of good lines, set in white clapboards. The porch is raised but a step or two. Low greenery, and a path leading off sharply left. It is evening, a month after LULU's *marriage.*

[*Discover* INA, DWIGHT, MRS. BETT *and* MONONA.]

INA: Dwight dear, the screen has never been put on that back window.

DWIGHT: Now, why can't my puss remind me of that in the morning instead of the only time I have to take my ease with my family.

INA: But, Dwight, in the mornings you are so busy—

DWIGHT: What an argumentative puss you are. By Jove! look at that rambler rosebush. It's got to be sprayed.

INA: You've said that every night for a week, Dwight. . . .

DWIGHT: Don't exaggerate like that, Ina. It's bad for Monona.

INA: Dwight, look, quick. There go our new neighbors. They have a limousine—Perhaps I have been a little slow about calling. Look at them, Dwight!

DWIGHT: My dear Ina, I see them. Do you want me to pat them on the back?

INA: Well, I think you might be interested. [MONONA *chants softly.*]
Dwight, I wonder if Monona really has a musical gift.

DWIGHT: She's a most unusual child. Do you know it? [*Enter* DI, *from house.*]

INA: Oh, they both are. Where are *you* going, I'd like to know?

DI: Mama, I have to go down to the liberry.

INA: It seems to me you have to go to the library every evening. Dwight, do you think she ought to go?

DWIGHT: Diana, is it necessary that you go?

DI: Well, everybody else goes, and—

INA: I will not have you downtown in the evenings.

DI: But you let me go last night.

INA: All the better reason why you should *not* go tonight.

MONONA: Mama, let me go with her.

INA: Very well, Di, you may go and take your sister.

MONONA: Goody, goody! last time you wouldn't let me go.

INA: That's why mama's going to let you go tonight.

DWIGHT: I thought you said the child must go to bed half an hour earlier because she wouldn't eat her egg.

INA: Yes, that's so, I did. Monona, you can't go.

MONONA: But I didn't want my egg—honest I didn't.

INA: Makes no difference. You must eat or you'll get sick. Mama's going to teach you to eat. Go on, Di, to the library if it's necessary.

DWIGHT: I suppose Bobby Larkin has to go to the library tonight, eh?

INA: Dwight, I wouldn't joke her about him. Scold her about him, the way you did this morning.

DI: But papa was cross about something else this morning. And tonight he isn't. Good-by, Dwight and Ina!

[*Exit* DI.]

MONONA: I hate the whole family.

MRS. BETT: Well, I should think she would.

INA: Why, mama! Why, Pettie Deacon!

[MONONA *weeps silently*.]

DWIGHT: [*To* INA] Say no more, my dear. It's best to over-look. Show a sweet spirit. . . .

MRS. BETT: About as much like a father and mother as a cat and dog.

DWIGHT: We've got to learn—

MRS. BETT: Performin' like a pair of weathercocks.

[*Both talking at once*]

DWIGHT: Mother Bett! Are you talking, or am I?

MRS. BETT: I am. But you don't seem to know it.

DWIGHT: Let us talk, pussy, and she'll simmer down. Ah—nothing new from the bride and groom?

INA: No, Dwight. And it's been a week since Lulu wrote. She said he'd bought her a new red dress—and a hat. Isn't it too funny—to think of Lulu—

DWIGHT: I don't understand why they plan to go straight to Oregon without coming here first.

INA: It isn't a bit fair to mama, going off that way. Leaving her own mother—why, she may never see mama again.

MRS. BETT: Oh I'm going to last on quite a while yet.

DWIGHT: Of course you are, Mama Bett. You're my best girl. That reminds me, Ina, we must run up to visit Aunt Mollie. We ought to run up there next week. She isn't well.

INA: Let's do that. Dear me, I wish Lulu was here to leave in charge. I certainly do miss Lulu—lots of ways.

MRS. BETT: 'Specially when it comes mealtime.

INA: Is that somebody coming here?

DWIGHT: Looks like it—yes, so it is. Some caller, as usual. [*Enter* LULU.] Well, if it isn't Miss Lulu Bett.

INA: Why, sister!

MRS. BETT: Lulie. Lulie. Lulie.

LULU: How did you know?

INA: Know what?

LULU: That it isn't Lulu Deacon.

DWIGHT: What's this?

INA: Isn't Lulu Deacon. What are you talking?

LULU: Didn't he write to you?

DWIGHT: Not a word. All we've had we had from you— the last from Savannah, Georgia.

LULU: Savannah, Georgia . . .

DWIGHT: Well, but he's here with you, isn't he?

INA: Where is he? Isn't he here?

LULU: Must be most to Oregon by this time.

DWIGHT: Oregon?

LULU: You see, he had another wife.

INA: Another wife!

DWIGHT: Why, he had not.

LULU: Yes, another wife. He hasn't seen her for fifteen years and he thinks she's dead. But he isn't sure.

DWIGHT: Nonsense. Why of course she's dead if he thinks so.

LULU: I had to be sure.

INA: Monona! Go upstairs to bed at once.

MONONA: It's only quarter of.

INA: Do as mama tells you.

MONONA: But—

INA: Monona!

[*She goes, kissing them all good-night and taking her time about it. Everything is suspended while she kisses them and departs, walking slowly backward.*]

MRS. BETT: Married? Lulie, was your husband married?

LULU: Yes, my husband was married, mother.

INA: Mercy, think of anything like that in our family.

DWIGHT: Well, go on—go on. Tell us about it.

LULU: We were going to Oregon. First down to New Orleans and then out to California and up the coast. . . . Well, then at Savannah, Georgia, he said he thought I better know first. So then he told me.

DWIGHT: Yes—well, what did he say?

LULU: Cora Waters. Cora Waters. She married him down in San Diego eighteen years ago. She went to South America with him.

DWIGHT: Well, he never let us know of it, if she did.

LULU: No. She married him just before he went. Then in South America, after two years, she ran away. That's all he knows.

DWIGHT: That's a pretty story.

LULU: He says if she was alive she'd be after him for a divorce. And she never has been so he thinks she must be dead. The trouble is he wasn't sure. And I had to be sure.

INA: Well, but mercy! Couldn't he find out now?

LULU: It might take a long time and I didn't want to stay and not know.

INA: Well then why didn't he say so here?

LULU: He would have. But you know how sudden everything was. He said he thought about telling us right here that afternoon when—when it happened but of course that'd been hard, wouldn't it? And then he felt so sure she was dead.

INA: Why did he tell you at all then?

DWIGHT: Yes. Why indeed?

LULU: I thought that just at first but only just at first. Of course that wouldn't have been right. And then you see he gave me my choice.

DWIGHT: Gave you your choice?

LULU: Yes. About going on and taking the chances. He gave me my choice when he told me, there in Savannah, Georgia.

DWIGHT: What made him conclude by then that you ought to be told?

LULU: Why, he'd got to thinking about it. [*A silence*] The only thing, as long as it happened I kind of wish he hadn't told me till we got to Oregon.

INA: Lulu! Oh, you poor poor thing. . . .

[MRS. BETT *suddenly joins* INA *in tears, rocking her body.*]

LULU: Don't, mother. Oh, Ina, don't. . . . He felt bad too.

DWIGHT: He! He must have.

INA: It's you. It's you. *My* sister!

LULU: I never thought of it making you both feel bad. I knew it would make Dwight feel bad. I mean, it was his brother—

INA: Thank goodness! nobody need know about it.

LULU: Oh, yes. People will have to know.

DWIGHT: I do not see the necessity.

LULU: Why, what would they think?

DWIGHT: What difference does it make what they think?

LULU: Why, I shouldn't like—you see they might—why, Dwight, I think we'll have to tell them.

DWIGHT: You do. You think the disgrace of bigamy in this family is something the whole town will have to know about.

LULU: Say. I never thought about it being that.

DWIGHT: What did you think it was? And whose disgrace is it, pray?

LULU: Mine. And Ninian's.

DWIGHT: Ninian's. Well, he's gone. But you're here. And I'm here—and my family. Folks'll feel sorry for you. But the disgrace, that would reflect on me.

LULU: But if we don't tell what'll they think?

DWIGHT: They'll think what they always think when a wife leaves her husband. They'll think you couldn't get along. That's all.

LULU: I should hate that. I wouldn't want them to think I hadn' been a good wife to Ninian.

DWIGHT: Wife? You never were his wife. That's just the point.

LULU: Oh!

DWIGHT: Don't you realize the position he's in? . . . See here—do you intend—Are you going to sue Ninian?

LULU: Oh! no! no! no!

INA: Why, Lulu, any one would think you loved him.

LULU: I do love him. And he loved me. Don't you think I know? He loved me.

INA: Lulu.

LULU: I love him—I do, and I'm not ashamed to tell you.

MRS. BETT: Lulie, Lulie, was his other wife—was she *there?*

LULU: No, no, mother. She wasn't there.

MRS. BETT: Then it ain't so bad. I was afraid maybe she turned you out.

LULU: No, no. It wasn't that bad, mother.

DWIGHT: In fact I simply will not have it, Lulu. You expect, I take it, to make your home with us in the future on the old terms.

LULU: Well—

DWIGHT: I mean did Ninian give you any money?

LULU: No. He didn't give me any money—only enough to get home on. And I kept my suit and the other dress—why! I wouldn't have taken any money.

DWIGHT: That means that you will have to continue to live here on the old terms and of course I'm quite willing that you should. Let me tell you, however, that this is on condition—on condition that this disgraceful business is kept to ourselves.

INA: Truly, Lulu, wouldn't that be best? They'll talk anyway. But this way they'll only talk about you and the other way it'll be about all of us.

LULU: But the other way would be the truth.

DWIGHT: My dear Lulu, are you sure of that?

LULU: Sure?

DWIGHT: Yes. Did he give you any proofs?

LULU: Proofs?

DWIGHT: Letters—documents of any sort? Any sort of assurance that he was speaking the truth?

LULU: Why—no. Proofs—no. He told me.

DWIGHT: He told you!

LULU: That was hard enough to have to do. It was terrible for him to have to do. What proofs—

DWIGHT: I may as well tell you that I myself have no idea that Ninian told you the truth. He was always imagining things, inventing things—you must have seen that. I know him pretty well—have been in touch with him more or less the whole time. In short I haven't the least idea he was ever married before.

LULU: I never thought of that.

DWIGHT: Look here—hadn't you and he had some little tiff when he told you?

LULU: No—no! Not once. He was very good to me. This dress—and my shoes—and my hat. And another dress, too. [*She takes off her hat.*] He liked the red wing—I wanted black—oh, Dwight! He did tell me the truth!

DWIGHT: As long as there's any doubt about it—and I feel the gravest doubts—I desire that you should keep silent and protect my family from this scandal. I have taken you into my confidence about these doubts for your own profit.

LULU: My own profit!

[*Moves toward the door*]

INA: Lulu—you see! We just couldn't have this known about Dwight's own brother, could we now?

DWIGHT: You have it in your own hands to repay me, Lulu, for anything that you feel I may have done for you in the past. You also have it in your hands to decide whether your home here continues. This is not a pleasant position for me to find myself in. In fact it is distinctly unpleasant I may say. But you see for yourself. [LULU *goes into the house.*]

MRS. BETT: Wasn't she married when she thought she was?

INA: Mama, do please remember Monona. Yes—Dwight thinks now she's married all right and that it was all right, all the time.

MRS. BETT: Well, I hope so, for pity sakes.

MONONA'S VOICE: [*From upstairs*] Mama! Come on and hear me say my prayers, why don't you?

DARKNESS

Scene 2

INA *seated*. MONONA *jumping on and off the porch, chanting.*

[*Enter* DWIGHT.]

DWIGHT: Ah, this is great . . . no place like home after all, is there?

INA: Now, Monona, sit down and be quiet. You've played enough for one day.
[*Enter* MRS. BETT.]

MONONA: How do you know I have?

DWIGHT: Ah, Mama Bett. Coming out to enjoy the evening air?

MRS. BETT: No, I thank you.

DWIGHT: Well, well, well, let's see what's new in the great press of our country. . . .
[*They are now seated in the approximate positions assumed at the opening of* Scene 1.]

INA: Dwight dear, nothing has been done about that screen for the back window.

DWIGHT: Now why couldn't my puss have reminded me of that this morning instead of waiting for the only time I have to take my ease with my family.

INA: But Dwightie, in the mornings you're so busy—

DWIGHT: You are argumentative, pussy—you certainly are. And you ought to curb it. For that matter I haven't sprayed that rambler rosebush.

INA: Every single night for a month you've spoken of spraying that rosebush.

DWIGHT: Ina, will you cease your exaggerations on Monona's account if not on mine. Exaggeration, my pet, is one of the worst of female faults. Exaggeration—

INA: Look, Dwight! our new neighbors have got a dog. Great big brute of a thing. He's going to tear up every towel I spread on our grass.... [*Enter* DI, *from the house.*] Now, Di, where are you going?

DI: Mama, I have to go down to the liberry.

INA: Now, Di—

DI: You let me go last night.

MONONA: Mama, I can go, can't I? Because you wouldn't let me go last night.

INA: No, Monona, you may *not* go.

MONONA: Oh, why not?

INA: Because mama says so. Isn't that enough?

MRS. BETT: Anybody'd think you was the king—layin' down the law an' layin' down the law an' layin' down— Where's Lulie?

DI: Mama, isn't Uncle Ninian coming back?

INA: Hush.... No. Now don't ask mama any more questions.

DI: But supposing people ask me. What'll I say?

INA: Don't say anything at all about Aunt Lulu.

DI: But, mama, what has she done?

INA: Di! Don't you think mama knows best?

DI: [*Softly*] No, I don't.... Well anyway Aunt Lulu's got on a perfectly beautiful dress tonight....

INA: And you know, Dwight, Lulu's clothes give me the funniest feeling. As if Lulu was wearing things bought for her by some one that wasn't—that was—

DWIGHT: By her husband who has left her.

DI: Is that what it is, papa?

DWIGHT: That's what it is, my little girl.

DI: Well, I think it's a shame. And I think Uncle Ninian is a slunge.

INA: Di Deacon!

DI: I do! And I'd be ashamed to think anything else. I'd like to tell everybody.

DWIGHT: There's no need for secrecy now.

INA: Dwight, really—do you think we ought—

DWIGHT: No need whatever for secrecy. The truth is Lulu's husband has tired of her and sent her home. We may as well face it.

INA: But, Dwight—how awful for Lulu....

DWIGHT: Lulu has us to stand by her.

[*Enter* LULU.]

LULU: That sounds good. That I have you to stand by me.

DWIGHT: My dear Lulu, the family bond is the strongest bond in the world. Family. Tribe. The—er—pack. Standing up for the family honor, the family reputation is the highest nobility. [*Exit* DI *by degrees left.*] I tell you of all history the most beautiful product is the family tie. Of it are born family consideration—

INA: Why, you don't look like yourself . . . is it your hair, Lulu? You look so strange. . . .

LULU: Don't you like it? Ninian liked it.

DWIGHT: In that case I think you'd show more modesty if you arranged your hair in the old way.

LULU: Yes, you would think so. Dwight, I want you to give me Ninian's Oregon address.

DWIGHT: You want what?

LULU: Ninian's Oregon address. It's a funny thing but I haven't it.

DWIGHT: It would seem that you have no particular need for that particular address.

LULU: Yes I have. I want it. You have it haven't you, Dwight?

DWIGHT: Certainly I have it.

LULU: Won't you please write it down for me?
[*She offers him tablet.*]

DWIGHT: My dear Lulu, now why revive anything? No good can come by—

LULU: But why shouldn't I have his address?

DWIGHT: If everything is over between you why should you?

LULU: But you say he's still my husband.

DWIGHT: If my brother has shown his inclination as plainly as I judge that he has it is certainly not my place to put you in touch with him again.

LULU: I don't know whose place it is. But I've got to know more—I've got to know more, Dwight. This afternoon I went to the post office to ask for his address—it seemed so strange to be doing that, after all that's been—They didn't know his address—I could see how they wondered at my asking. And I knew how the others wondered—Mis' Martin, Mis' Curtis, Mis' Grove.

"Where you hiding that handsome husband of yours?"
they said. All I could say was that he isn't here. Dwight!
I won't live like that. I want to know the truth. You
give me Ninian's address.

DWIGHT: My dear Lulu! My *dear* Lulu! You are not the
one to write to him. Have you no delicacy?

LULU: So much delicacy that I want to be sure whether
I'm married or not.

DWIGHT: Then I myself will take this up with my brother.
I will write to him about it.

LULU: Here's everything—if you're going to write him,
do it now.

DWIGHT: My dear Lulu! don't be absurd.

LULU: Ina! Help me! If this was Dwight—and they didn't
know whether he had another wife or not and you
wanted to ask him and you didn't know where he was—
oh, don't you see? Help me.

INA: Well of course. I see it all, Lulu. And yet—why not
let Dwight do it in his own way? Wouldn't that be better?

LULU: Mother!

MRS. BETT: Lulie. Set down. Set down, why don't you?

LULU: Dwight, you write that letter to Ninian. And you
make him tell you so that you'll understand. I know he
spoke the truth. But I want you to know.

DWIGHT: M—m. And then I suppose as soon as you have
the proofs you're going to tell it all over town.

LULU: I'm going to tell it all over town just as it is—unless
you write to him.

INA: Lulu! Oh, you wouldn't!

LULU: I would. I will.

DWIGHT: And get turned out of the house as you would
be?

INA: Dwight. Oh, you wouldn't!

DWIGHT: I would. I will. Lulu knows it.

LULU: I shall tell what I know and then leave your house
anyway unless you get Ninian's word. And you're going
to write to him now.

DWIGHT: You would leave your mother? And leave Ina?

LULU: Leave everything.

INA: Oh, Dwight! We can't get along without Lulu.

DWIGHT: Isn't this like a couple of women? . . . Rather than let you in for a show of temper, Lulu, I'd do anything.

[*Writes*]

MONONA: [*Behind* INA] Mama, can I write Uncle Ninian a little letter, too?

INA: For pity sakes, aren't you in bed yet?

MONONA: It's only quarter of.

INA: Well you may go to bed *now* because you have sat there listening. How often must mama tell you not to listen to grown people.

MONONA: Do they always say something bad?

INA: Monona, you are to go up to bed at once.

[*She makes her leisurely rounds for kisses.*]

MONONA: Papa, it's your turn to hear me say my prayers tonight.

DWIGHT: Very well, pettie. When you're ready call me. [*Exit* MONONA.] There, Lulu. The deed is done. Now I hope you're satisfied.

[*Places the letter in his pocket*]

LULU: I want you to give me the letter to mail, please.

DWIGHT: Why this haste, sister mine? I'll mail it in the morning.

LULU: I'll mail it now. Now.

DWIGHT: I may take a little stroll before bedtime—I'll mail it then. There's nothing like a brisk walk to induce sound restful sleep.

LULU: I'll mail the letter now.

DWIGHT: I suppose I'll have to humor your sister, Ina. Purely on your account you understand.

[*Hands the letter*]

INA: Oh, Dwight, how good you are!

LULU: There's—there's one thing more I want to speak about. If—if you and Ina go to your Aunt Mollie's then Ninian's letter might come while you're away.

DWIGHT: Conceivably. Letters do come while a man's away.

LULU: Yes. And I thought if you wouldn't mind if I opened it—

DWIGHT: Opened it? Opened *my* letter?

LULU: Yes, you see it'll be about me mostly. You wouldn't mind if I did open it?

DWIGHT: But you say you know what will be in it, *Miss* Bett?

LULU: I did know till you—I've got to see that letter, Dwight.

DWIGHT: And so you shall. But not until I show it to you. My dear Lulu, you know how I hate having my mail interfered with. You shall see the letter all in good time when Ina and I return.

LULU: You wouldn't want to let me—just see what he says?

DWIGHT: I prefer always to open my own letters.

LULU: Very well, Dwight.

[*She moves away, right.*]

INA: And Lulu, I meant to ask you: Don't you think it might be better if you—if you kept out of sight for a few days?

LULU: Why?

INA: Why set people wondering till we have to?

LULU: They don't have to wonder as far as I'm concerned. [*Exit*]

MRS. BETT: I'm going through the kitchen to set with Grandma Gates. She always says my visits are like a dose of medicine.

[*Exit* MRS. BETT.]

INA: It certainly has changed Lulu—a man coming into her life. She never spoke to me like that before.

DWIGHT: I saw she wasn't herself. I'd do anything to avoid having a scene—you know that. . . . You do know that, don't you?

INA: But I really think you ought to have written to Ninian. It's—it's not a nice position for Lulu.

DWIGHT: Nice! But whom has she got to blame for it?

INA: Why, Ninian.

DWIGHT: Herself! To tell you the truth, I was perfectly amazed at the way she snapped him up here that afternoon.

INA: Why but, Dwight—

DWIGHT: Brazen. Oh, it was brazen.

INA: It was just fun in the first place.

DWIGHT: But no really nice woman—

INA: Dwightie—what did you say in the letter?

DWIGHT: What did I say? I said, I said: "DEAR BROTHER,

I take it that the first wife story was devised to relieve you of a distasteful situation. Kindly confirm. Family well as usual. Business fair." Covers it, don't it?

INA: Oh, Dwightie—how complete that is.

DWIGHT: I'm pretty good at writing brief concise letters— that say the whole thing, eh?

INA: I've often noticed that. . . .

DWIGHT: My precious pussy. . . . Oh, how unlike Lulu you are!

[*Right.* DI *and* BOBBY *appear, walking very slowly and very near.* DWIGHT *rises, holds out his arms.*]

INA: Poor dear foolish Lulu! Oh, Dwight—what if it was Di in Lulu's place?

DWIGHT: Such a thing couldn't happen to Di. Di was born with ladylike feelings.

[*They enter the house.* INA *extinguishes a lamp.* DWIGHT *turns down the hall gas. Pause.* DI *and* BOBBY *come to the veranda.*]

DI: Bobby dear! You don't kiss me as if you really wanted to kiss me tonight. . . .

DARKNESS

Scene 3

The Same. Evening, a week later. Stage flooded with moonlight, house lighted. At the piano, just inside the window, LULU *and* CORNISH *are finishing a song together,* LULU *accompanying.*

> How sweet the happy evening's close,
> 'Tis the hour of sweet repose—
> > Good-night.

> The summer wind has sunk to rest,
> The moon serenely bright
> Unfolds her calm and gentle ray,
> Softly now she seems to say,
> > Good-night.

[*As they sing,* DI *slips into the house, unseen.*]

CORNISH: Why, Miss Lulu, you're quite a musician.

LULU: Oh, no. I've never played in front of anybody—
[*They come to the porch.*] I don't know what Ina and
Dwight would say if they heard me.

CORNISH: What a pretty dress that is, Miss Lulu!

LULU: I made this from one of Ina's old ones since she's
been gone. I don't know what Ina and Dwight are going
to say about this dress, made like this, when they get
home.

CORNISH: When are they coming back?

LULU: Any time now. They've been gone most a week.
Do you know I never had but one compliment before
that wasn't for my cooking.

CORNISH: You haven't!

LULU: He told me I done up my hair nice. That was after
I took notice how the ladies in Savannah, Georgia, done
up theirs.

CORNISH: I guess you can do most anything you set your
hand to, Miss Lulu: Look after Miss Di and sing and
play and cook—

LULU: Yes, cook. But I can't earn anything. I'd like to
earn something.

CORNISH: You would! Why, you have it fine here, I
thought.

LULU: Oh, fine, yes. Dwight gives me what I have. And
I do their work.

CORNISH: I see. I never thought of that. . . .
[*Pause*]

LULU: You're wondering why I didn't stay with *him!*

CORNISH: Oh, no.

LULU: Yes you are! The whole town's wondering. They're
all talking about me.

CORNISH: Well, Miss Lulu, you know it don't make any
difference to your friends what people say.

LULU: But they don't know the truth. You see, he had
another wife.

CORNISH: Lord sakes!

LULU: Dwight thinks it isn't true. He thinks—he didn't
have another wife. . . . You see, Dwight thinks he didn't
want me.

CORNISH: But—your husband—I mean, why doesn't he write to Mr. Deacon and tell him the truth—

LULU: He has written. The letter's in there on the piano.

CORNISH: What'd he say?

LULU: Dwight doesn't like me to touch his mail. I'll have to wait till he comes back.

CORNISH: Lord sakes! ... You—you—you're too nice a girl to get a deal like this. Darned if you aren't.

LULU: Oh, no.

CORNISH: Yes you are, too! And there ain't a thing I can do.

LULU: It's a good deal to have somebody to talk to. . . .

CORNISH: Sure it is.

LULU: ... Cora Waters. Cora Waters, of San Diego, California. And she never heard of me.

CORNISH: No. She never did, did she? Ain't life the darn—

[*Enter* MRS. BETT.]

MRS. BETT: I got Monona into bed. And it's no fool of a job neither.

LULU: Did you, mother? Come and sit down.

MRS. BETT: Yes. She went to bed with a full set of doll dishes. . . . Ain't it nice with the folks all gone? . . . I don't hear any more playin' and singin'. It sounded real good.

LULU: We sung all I knew how to play, mama.

MRS. BETT: I use' to play on the melodeon.

CORNISH: Well, well, well.

MRS. BETT: That was when I was first married. We had a little log house in a clearing in York State. I was seventeen—and he was nineteen. While he was chopping I use' to sit on a log with my sewing. Jenny was born in that house. I was alone at the time. I was alone with her when she died, too. She was sixteen—little bits of hands she had—[*Yawns. Rises, wanders toward door*] Can't we have some more playin' and singin'?

LULU: After a little while, mama—dear.

MRS. BETT: It went kind of nice—that last tune you sung. [*Hums the air. Enters house.*]

CORNISH: I must be going along too, Miss Lulu.

LULU: I can't think why Di doesn't come. She ought not to be out like this without telling me—

[MRS. BETT *appears beside the piano, lifts and examines the letters lying there.*]

CORNISH: Well, don't you mind on my account. I've enjoyed every minute I've been here.

LULU: Mother! Those are Dwight's letters—don't you touch them.

MRS. BETT: I ain't hurting them or him neither.

[*Disappears, the letters in her hand*]

CORNISH: Good-night, Miss Lulu. If there was anything I could do at any time you'd let me know, wouldn't you?

LULU: Oh, thank you.

CORNISH: I've had an awful nice time, singing, and listening to you talk—well of course—I mean the supper was just fine! And so was the music.

LULU: Oh, no.

[MRS. BETT *appears at the door with a letter.*]

MRS. BETT: Lulie. I guess you didn't notice. This one's from Ninian.

LULU: Mother—

MRS. BETT: I opened it—why of course I did. It's from Ninian. [*Holds out unfolded letter and an old newspaper clipping*] The paper's awful old—years back, looks like. See. Says "Corie Waters, music hall singer—married last night to Ninian Deacon"— Say, Lulie, that must be her.

LULU: Yes, that's her. That's her—Cora Waters. . . . Oh, then he *was* married to her just like he said!

CORNISH: Oh, Miss Lulu! I'm so sorry!

LULU: No, no. Because he wanted me! He didn't say that just to get rid of me!

CORNISH: Oh, that way . . . I see. . . .

LULU: I'm so thankful it wasn't that.

MRS. BETT: Then everything's all right once more. Ain't that nice!

LULU: I'm so thankful it wasn't that..

CORNISH: Yes, I can understand that. Well, I—I guess I ought to be going now, Miss Lulu. . . . Why, it *is* Miss Lulu Bett, isn't it?

LULU: [*Abstractedly, with the paper*] Yes—yes—good-night, Mr. Cornish, Good-night.

CORNISH: Good-night, Miss Lulu. . . . I wonder if you would let me tell you something.

LULU: Why—

CORNISH: I guess I don't amount to much. I'll never be a lawyer. I'm no good at business and everything I say sounds wrong to me. And yet I do believe I do know enough not to bully a woman—not to make her unhappy, maybe even—I could make her a little happy. Miss Lulu, I hate to see you looking and talking so sad. Do you think we could possibly arrange—

LULU: Oh!

CORNISH: I guess maybe you've heard something about a little something I'm supposed to inherit. Well, I got it. Of course, it's only five hundred dollars. We could get that little Warden house and furnish up the parlor with pianos—that is, if you could ever think of marrying me.

LULU: Don't say that—don't say that!

MRS. BETT: Better take him, Lulie. A girl ought to take any young man that will propose in front of her mother!

CORNISH: Of course if you loved him very much then I'd ought not to be talking this way to you.

LULU: You see Ninian was the first person who was ever kind to me. Nobody ever wanted me, nobody ever even thought of me. Then he came. It might have been somebody else. It might have been you. But it happened to be Ninian and I do love him.

CORNISH: I see. I guess you'll forgive me for what I said.

LULU: Of course.

CORNISH: Miss Lulu, if that five hundred could be of any use to you, I wish you'd take it.

LULU: Oh, thank you, thank you, I couldn't.

CORNISH: Well, I guess I'll be stepping along. If you should want me, I'm always there. I guess you know that.

[*Exit*]

MRS. BETT: Better burn that up. I wouldn't have it round.

LULU: But mother! Mother dear, try to understand. This

means that Ninian told the truth. He wasn't just trying to get rid of me.

MRS. BETT: Did he want you to stay with him?

LULU: I don't know. But I think he did. Anyway, now I know the truth about him.

MRS. BETT: Well, I wouldn't want anybody else to know. Here, let me have it and burn it up.

LULU: Mama, mama! Aren't you glad for me that now I can prove Ninian wasn't just making up a story so I'd go away?

MRS. BETT: [*Clearly and beautifully*] Oh, Lulu! My little girl! Is that what they said about you? Mother knows it wasn't like that. Mother knows he loved you. . . . How still it is here! Where's Inie?

LULU: They've gone away, you know. . . .

MRS. BETT: Well, I guess I'll step over to Grandma Gates's a spell. See how her rheumatism is. I'll be back before long—I'll be back. . . .

[*Exit. For a moment* LULU *breaks down and sobs. Rises to lay* DWIGHT's *letter through the window on piano. Slight sound. She listens. Enter* DI *from house. She is carrying a traveling bag.*]

LULU: Di! Why, Di! What does this mean? Where were you going? Why, mama won't like your carrying her nice new satchel. . . .

DI: Aunt Lulu—the idea. What right have you to interfere with me like this?

LULU: Di, you must explain to me what this means. . . . Di, where can you be going with a satchel this time of the night? Di Deacon, are you running away with somebody?

DI: You have no right to ask me questions, Aunt Lulu.

LULU: Di, you're going off with Bobby Larkin. Aren't you? Aren't you?

DI: If I am it's entirely our own affair.

LULU: Why, Di. If you and Bobby want to be married why not let us get you up a nice wedding here at home—

DI: Aunt Lulu, you're a funny person to be telling *me* what to do.

LULU: I love you just as much as if I was married happy, in a home.

DI: Well, you aren't. And I'm going to do just as I think best. Bobby and I are the ones most concerned in this, Aunt Lulu.

LULU: But—but getting married is for your whole life!

DI: Yours wasn't.

LULU: Di, my dear little girl, you must wait at least till mama and papa get home.

DI: That's likely. They say I'm not to be married till I'm twenty-one.

LULU: Well, but how young that is.

DI: It is to you. It isn't young to me, remember, Aunt Lulu.

LULU: But this is wrong—it is wrong!

DI: There's nothing wrong about getting married if you stay married.

LULU: Well, then it can't be wrong to let your mother and father know.

DI: It isn't. But they'd treat me wrong. Mama'd cry and say I was disgracing *her*. And papa—first he'd scold me and then he'd joke me about it. He'd joke me about it every day for weeks, every morning at breakfast, every night here on the porch—he'd joke me.

LULU: Why, Di! Do you feel that way, too?

DI: You don't know what it is to be laughed at or paid no attention to, everything you say.

LULU: Don't I? Don't I? Is that why you're going?

DI: Well, it's one reason.

LULU: But, Di, do you love Bobby Larkin?

DI: Well . . . I could love almost anybody real nice that was nice to me.

LULU: Di . . . Di . . .

DI: It's true. [BOBBY *enters*.] You ought to know that. . . . You did it. Mama said so.

LULU: Don't you think that I don't know. . . .

DI: Oh, Bobby, she's trying to stop us! But she can't do it—I've told her so—

BOBBY: She don't have to stop us. We're stopped.

DI: What do you mean?

BOBBY: We're minors.

DI: Well, gracious—you didn't have to tell them that.

BOBBY: No. They knew *I* was.

DI: But, silly. Why didn't you tell them you're not.

BOBBY: But I am.

DI: For pity sakes—don't you know how to do anything?

BOBBY: What would you have me do, I'd like to know?

DI: Why tell them we're both—whatever it is they want us to be. We look it. We know we're responsible—that's all they care for. Well, you are a funny. . . .

BOBBY: You wanted me to lie?

DI: Oh! don't make out you never told a fib.

BOBBY: Well, but this—why, Di—about a thing like this. . . .

DI: I never heard of a lover flatting out like that!

BOBBY: Anyhow, there's nothing to do now. The cat's out. I've told our ages. We've got to have our folks in on it.

DI: Is that all you can think of?

BOBBY: What else is there to think of?

DI: Why, let's go to Bainbridge or Holt and tell them we're of age and be married there.

LULU: Di, wherever you go I'll go with you. I won't let you out of my sight.

DI: Bobby, why don't you answer her?

BOBBY: But I'm not going to Bainbridge or Holt or any town and lie, to get you or any other girl.

DI: You're about as much like a man in a story as—as papa is.

[*Enter* DWIGHT *and* INA.]

DWIGHT: What's this? What's this about papa?

INA: Well, what's all this going on here?

LULU: Why, Ina!

DI: Oh, mama! I—I didn't know you were coming so soon. Hello, dear! Hello, papa! Here's—here's Bobby. . . .

DWIGHT: What an unexpected pleasure, *Master* Bobby.

BOBBY: Good-evening, Mrs. Deacon. Good-evening, Mr. Deacon.

DWIGHT: And Lulu. Is it Lulu? Is this lovely houri our Lulu? Is this Miss Lulu Bett? Or is this Lulu something else by now? You can't tell what Lulu'll do when you leave her alone at home. Ina—our festive ball gown!

LULU: Ina, I made it out of that old muslin of yours, you know. I thought you wouldn't care—

INA: Oh, that! I was going to use it for Di but it doesn't matter. You are welcome to it, Lulu. Little youthful for anything but home wear, isn't it?

DWIGHT: It looks like a wedding gown. Why are you wearing a wedding gown—eh, Lulu?

INA: Di Deacon, what have you got mama's new bag for?

DI: I haven't done anything to the bag, mama.

INA: Well, but what are you doing with it here?

DI: Oh, nothing! Did you—did you have a good time?

INA: Yes, we did—but I can't see.... Dwight, look at Di with my new black satchel.

DWIGHT: What is this, Diana?

DI: Well, I'm—I'm not going to use it for anything.

INA: I wish somebody would explain what is going on here. Lulu, can't you explain?

DWIGHT: Aha! Now, if Lulu is going to explain that's something like it. When Lulu begins to explain we get imagination going.

LULU: Di and I have a little secret. Can't we have a little secret if we want one?

DWIGHT: Upon my word, she has a beautiful secret. I don't know about your secrets, Lulu.

[*Enter* MRS. BETT.]

MRS. BETT: Hello, Inie.

INA: Oh, mother dear....

DWIGHT: Well, Mother Bett....

MRS. BETT: That you, Dwight? [*To* BOBBY] ... Don't you help me. I guess I can help myself yet awhile. [*Climbs the two steps. To* DI.] Made up your mind to come home, did you? [*Seats herself*] I got a joke. Grandma Gates says it's all over town they wouldn't give Di and Bobby Larkin a license to get married.

[*Single note of laughter, thin and high*]

DWIGHT: What nonsense!

INA: Is it nonsense? Haven't I been trying to find out where the new black bag went? Di! Look at mama....

DI: Listen to that, Bobby. Listen!

INA: That won't do, Di. You can't deceive mama, and don't you try.

BOBBY: Mrs. Deacon, I—

DWIGHT: Diana!

DI: Yes, papa.

DWIGHT: Answer your mother. Answer *me*. Is there anything in this absurd tale?

DI: No, papa.

DWIGHT: Nothing whatever?

DI: No, papa.

DWIGHT: Can you imagine how such a ridiculous story started?

DI: No, papa.

DWIGHT: Very well. Now we know where we are. If anybody hears this report repeated, send them to *me*.

INA: Well, but that satchel—

DWIGHT: One moment. Lulu will of course verify what the child has said.

LULU: If you cannot settle this with Di, you cannot settle it with me.

DWIGHT: A shifty answer. You're a bird at misrepresenting facts. . . .

LULU: Oh! . . .

DWIGHT: Lulu, the bird!

LULU: Lulu, the dove to put up with you.
[*Exit*]

INA: Bobby wanted to say something. . . .

BOBBY: No, Mrs. Deacon. I have nothing—more to say. I'll—I'll go now.

DWIGHT: Good-night, Robert.
[INA *and* DWIGHT *transfer bags and wraps to the house.*]

BOBBY: Good-night, Mr. Deacon. Good-by, Di.
[DI *follows* BOBBY, *right.*]

DI: Bobby, come back, you hate a lie—but what else could I do?

BOBBY: What else could you do? I'd rather they never let us see each other again than to lose you in the way I've lost you now.

DI: Bobby!

BOBBY: It's true. We mustn't talk about it.

DI: Bobby! I'll go back and tell them all.

BOBBY: You can't go back. Not out of a thing like that. Good-by, Di.
[*Exit. Enter* DWIGHT *and* INA.]

DI: If you have any fear that I may elope with Bobby Larkin, let it rest. I shall never marry him if he asks me fifty times a day.

INA: Really, darling?

DI: Really and truly, and he knows it, too.

DWIGHT: A-ha! The lovelorn maiden all forlorn makes up her mind not to be so lorn as she thought she was. How does it seem not to be in love with him, Di— eh?

DI: Papa, if you make fun of me any more I'll—I'll let the first train of cars I can find run over me. . . .

[*Sobs as she runs to house*]

MRS. BETT: Wait, darling! Tell grandma! Did Bobby have another wife too?

[*Exeunt* MRS. BETT *and* DI.]

INA: Di, I'd be ashamed, when papa's so good to you. Oh, my! what parents have to put up with. . . .

DWIGHT: Bear and forbear, pettie—bear and forbear. . . . By the way, Lulu, haven't I some mail somewhere about?

LULU: Yes, there's a letter there. I'll get it for you.

[*She reaches through the window.*]

DWIGHT: A-ha! An epistle from my dear brother Ninian.

INA: Oh, from Ninian, Dwight?

DWIGHT: From Ninian—the husband of Miss Lulu Bett . . . You opened the letter? . . . Your sister has been opening my mail.

INA: But, Dwight, if it's from Ninian—

DWIGHT: It is my mail.

INA: Well, what does he say?

DWIGHT: I shall read the letter in my own time. My present concern is the disregard for my wishes. What excuse have you to offer?

LULU: None.

INA: Dwight, she knows what's in it and we don't. Hurry up.

DWIGHT: She is an ungrateful woman.

[*Opens the letter, with the clipping*]

INA: [*Over his shoulder*] Ah! . . . Dwight, then he was . . .

DWIGHT: M—m—m—m. So after having been absent with my brother for a month you find that you were not married to him.

LULU: You see, Dwight, he told the truth. He did have another wife. He didn't just leave me.

DWIGHT: But this seems to me to make you considerably worse off than if he had.

LULU: Oh, no! No! If he hadn't—hadn't liked me, he wouldn't have told me about her. You see that, don't you?

DWIGHT: That your apology? . . . Look here, Lulu! This is a bad business. The less you say about it the better for all our sakes. You see that, don't you?

LULU: See that? Why, no. I wanted you to write to him so I could tell the truth. You said I mustn't tell the truth till I had the proofs.

DWIGHT: Tell whom?

LULU: Tell everybody. I want them to know.

DWIGHT: Then you care nothing for our feelings in this matter?

LULU: Your feelings?

DWIGHT: How this will reflect on us—it's nothing to you that we have a brother who's a bigamist?

LULU: But it's me—it's me.

DWIGHT: You! You're completely out of it. You've nothing more to say about it whatever. Just let it be as it is . . . drop it. That's all I suggest.

LULU: I want people to know the truth.

DWIGHT: But it's nobody's business but our business . . . for all our sakes let us drop this matter. . . . Now I tell you, Lulu—here are three of us. Our interests are the same in this thing—only Ninian is our relative and he's nothing to you now. Is he?

LULU: Why—

DWIGHT: Let's have a vote. Your snap judgment is to tell this disgraceful fact broadcast. Mine is, least said soonest mended. What do you say, Ina?

INA: Oh, goodness—if we get mixed up in a scandal like this we'll never get away from it. Why, I wouldn't have people know of it for worlds.

DWIGHT: Exactly. Ina has stated it exactly. Lulu, I think you should be reconciled.

INA: My poor poor sister! Oh, Dwight! when I think of it—what have I done, what have *we* done—that I should have a good kind loving husband—be so protected, so loved, when other women . . . Darling! You *know* how sorry I am—we all are—

LULU: Then give me the only thing I've got—that's my pride. My pride that he didn't want to get rid of me.

DWIGHT: What about my pride? Do you think I want everybody to know that my brother did a thing like that?

LULU: You can't help that.

DWIGHT: But I want you to help it. I want you to promise me that you won't shame us like this before all our friends.

LULU: You want me to promise what?

DWIGHT: I want you,—I ask you to promise me that you will keep this with us—a family secret.

LULU: No! No! I won't do it! I won't do it! I won't do it!

DWIGHT: You refuse to do this small thing for us?

LULU: Can't you understand anything? I've lived here all my life—on your money. I've not been strong enough to work they say—well, but I've been strong enough to be a hired girl in your house—and I've been glad to pay for my keep. . . . But there wasn't a thing about it that I liked. Nothing about being here that I liked. . . . Well, then I got a little something, same as other folks. I thought I was married and I went off on the train and he bought me things and I saw different towns. And then it was all a mistake. I didn't have any of it. I came back here and went into your kitchen again—I don't know why I came back. I suppose it's because I'm most thirty-four and new things ain't so easy any more—but what have I got or what'll I ever have? And now you want to put on to me having folks look at me and think he run off and left me and having them all wonder. I can't stand it. I can't stand it. I can't. . . .

DWIGHT: You'd rather they'd know he fooled you when he had another wife?

LULU: Yes. Because he wanted me. How do I know— maybe he wanted me only just because he was lonesome, the way I was. I don't care why. And I won't have folks think he went and left me.

DWIGHT: That is wicked vanity.

LULU: That's the truth. Well, why can't they know the truth?

DWIGHT: And bring disgrace on us all?

LULU: It's me—It's me—

DWIGHT: You—you—you—you're always thinking of yourself.

LULU: Who else thinks of me. And who do you think of— who do you think of, Dwight? I'll tell you that, because I know you better than any one else in the world knows you—better even than Ina. And I know that you'd sac- rifice Ina, Di, mother, Monona, Ninian—everybody, just to your own idea of who you are. You're one of the men who can smother a whole family and not even know you're doing it.

DWIGHT: You listen to me. It's Ninian I'm thinking about.

LULU: Ninian. . . .

DWIGHT: Yes, yes . . . Ninian! . . . Of course if you don't care what happens to him, it doesn't matter.

LULU: What do you mean?

DWIGHT: If you don't love him any more. . . .

LULU: You know I love him. I'll always love him.

DWIGHT: That's likely. A woman doesn't send the man she loves to prison.

LULU: I send him to prison! Why, he's brought me the only happiness I've ever had. . . .

DWIGHT: But prison is just where he'll go and you'll be the one to send him there.

LULU: Oh! That couldn't be. . . . That couldn't be. . . .

DWIGHT: Don't you realize that bigamy is a crime? If you tell this thing he'll go to prison . . . nothing can save him.

LULU: I never thought of that. . . .

DWIGHT: It's time you did think. Now will you promise to keep this with us, a family secret?

LULU: Yes. I promise.

DWIGHT: You will? . . .

LULU: Yes . . . I will.

DWIGHT: A . . . h. You'll be happy some day to think you've done this for us, Lulu.

LULU: I s'pose so. . . .

INA: This makes up for everything. My sweet self-sacri- ficing sister!

LULU: Oh, stop that!

INA: Oh, the pity of it . . . the pity of it! . . .

LULU: Don't you go around pitying me! I'll have you know I'm glad the whole thing happened.

CURTAIN

ACT III

Revised version

The Deacons' side porch. Discover MRS. BETT, *tidying the porch and singing. It is the following morning.*

[*Enter* LULU *with bag.*]

MRS. BETT: Where you going now, for pity sakes?

LULU: Mother. Now, mother darling, listen and try to understand.

MRS. BETT: Well, I am listening, Lulie.

LULU: Mother, I can't stay here. I can't stay here any longer. I've got to get clear away from Dwight and Ina.

MRS. BETT: You want to live somewhere else, Lulie?

LULU: I can't live here and have people think Ninian left me. I can't tell the truth and bring disgrace on Ninian. And I can't stay here in Dwight's kitchen a day longer. Oh, mother! I wish you could see—

MRS. BETT: Why, Lulie, I do see that.

LULU: You do, mother?

MRS. BETT: I've often wondered why you didn't go before.

LULU: Oh, mother, you dear—

MRS. BETT: You needn't think because I'm old I don't know a thing or two.

LULU: You want me to go?

MRS. BETT: It's all I can do for you now, Lulie. Just to want you to go. I'm old and I'm weak and I can't keep care of you like when you was little.

LULU: Oh, mother, I'm so glad!

MRS. BETT: I ain't exactly glad—

225

LULU: Dearest, I mean I was so afraid you wouldn't understand—

MRS. BETT: Why wouldn't I understand, I'd like to know? You speak like I didn't have a brain in my skull.

LULU: No, dear, but—

MRS. BETT: You mind me, Lulie, and go on. Go on. . . . Say, scat's sake, you can't go. You ain't got any money.

LULU: Yes, mother, I have. I've got twelve dollars.

MRS. BETT: And I ain't got much. Only enough to bury me nice.

LULU: Don't you worry, mother. I'll be all right. I'll get work.

MRS. BETT: Mother wants to help you. Here, Lulie, you take my funeral fifty. Joke on Dwight to make him bury me.

LULU: Oh, no, mother, I couldn't.

MRS. BETT: You mind me, Lulie. Do as mother tells you.

LULU: Mother, dearest! Oh, I wish I could take you with me!

MRS. BETT: You needn't to worry about me. If I get lonesome I can give Dwight the dickens.

LULU: Good-by—dear—good-by. I'll go the back way, they won't see me.

[LULU *kisses her and turns away left.*]

MRS. BETT: Lulie. Mother loves you. You know that, don't you?

LULU: Dearest, yes—yes, I do know.

[*She goes.* MRS. BETT *trembles, turns, sees her dust-cloth, goes on working and begins to hum. Enter* DWIGHT.]

DWIGHT: Ready for breakfast, Mama Bett?

MRS. BETT: No, I ain't ready.

DWIGHT: Neither is the breakfast. Lulu must be having the tantrum.

MRS. BETT: I s'pose you think that's funny.

DWIGHT: Lulu ought to think of you—old folks ought to have regular meals—

MRS. BETT: Old? Old? Me, old?

DWIGHT: Well, you're hungry. That's what makes you so cross, Mama Bett.

MRS. BETT: All you think of is food, anyhow.

DWIGHT: Who has a better right? Who provides the food we eat?

MRS. BETT: That's all you're good for.

DWIGHT: Well, I may not amount to much in this old world of ours but I flatter myself I'm a good provider.

MRS. BETT: If I was going to brag I'd brag original.

DWIGHT: You mustn't talk like that. You know you're my best girl.

MRS. BETT: Don't you best-girl me.

DWIGHT: There, there, there . . .

MRS. BETT: Now look at you. Walking all over me like I wasn't here—like I wasn't nowhere.

DWIGHT: Now, Mama Bett, you're havin' the tantrum.

MRS. BETT: Am I? All right then I am. What you going to do about it? How you going to stop me?

DWIGHT: Now, now, now, now. . .

[*Enter* INA.]

INA: Dwight, I can't think what's happened to Lulu. Breakfast isn't even started.

DWIGHT: Lulu must be having a rendezvous.

[*Grandma snorts.*]

INA: That's randevoo, Dwightie. Not rendezvous.

DWIGHT: You two are pretty particular, seems to me.

MRS. BETT: Oh, no! We ain't used to the best.

[DI *is at the door.*]

DI: Hello, family! What's the matter with breakfast?

MRS. BETT: There ain't any.

INA: Di, let's you and I get breakfast just to show Aunt Lulu that we can.

MRS. BETT: Say if you two are going to get breakfast, I'll go over to Grandma Gates for a snack.

[*Enter* MONONA.]

MONONA: What do you s'pose? Aunt Lulu's trunk is locked and strapped in her room.

INA: Monona, stop imagining things.

MONONA: Well, it is. And I saw her going down the walk with her satchel when I was washing me.

DWIGHT: Lulu must be completely out of her mind.

MRS. BETT: First time I've known her to show good sense in years.

INA: Why, mama!

DWIGHT: Mother Bett, do you know where Lulu is?

MRS. BETT: Mother knows a-plenty.

INA: Mama, what do you mean?

MRS. BETT: I know all about Lulie being gone. She went this morning. I told her to go.

INA: Why, mama! How can you talk so! When Dwight has been so good to you and Lulu . . .

MRS. BETT: Good, yes, he's give us a pillow and a baked potato—

DWIGHT: So! You and Lulu presume to upset the arrangement of my household without one word to me.

MRS. BETT: Upset, upset—You cockroach! . . .

INA: Monona! Stop listening. Now run away and play. Di, you go and begin breakfast.

DI: Yes, mummy.

MONONA: Aw, let me stay.

INA: [*Exeunt* DI *and* MONONA.] Go at once, children. Mother, you ought not to use such language before young people.

MRS. BETT: Don't you think they're fooled. What do you suppose Di was going to run away with Bobby Larkin for, only to get away from you.

DWIGHT: Mother Bett!

MRS. BETT: What do you suppose Lulu married Ninian for—only to get shed of both of you.

INA: Oh please, please, somebody think a little bit of me. Dwight, do go after Lulu—go to the depot—she couldn't get away before the 8:37.

DWIGHT: My dear Ina, my dignity—

INA: Oh, please do go!

DWIGHT: Oh, my heavens! what a house full of women—

INA: Dwight, we can't get along without Lulu.

DWIGHT: Upsetting things about my ears . . .
    [*Exit*]

INA: Mama, I do think it's too bad of you—oh! now I'll try to get some breakfast.
    [*Exit*]

MRS. BETT: Going to try to, he-e!
    [*Enter* MONONA.]

MONONA: Oh, grandma isn't it fun with so much going on!

MRS. BETT: What's that, you little ape?

MONONA: Oh, I just love it! Everybody makes such funny faces.

MRS. BETT: Some people are born with funny faces. Monona, ain't you ever going to grow up?

MONONA: Grandma, I am grown up.

MRS. BETT: You don't act like it.

MONONA: Well, grown folks don't neither.

MRS. BETT: Sh-hh-hhh, stop talking back to me.

MONONA: Everybody shushes me. If I don't talk, how'll they know I'm there?

MRS. BETT: I guess they could bear up if they didn't know you was there.

MONONA: I'd better get in, or I'll catch it.

[MONONA *sings a silly song.*]

MRS. BETT: [*Rocking in rhythm with the song*] Scot's sake, what am I doing! Them wicked words.

[*Enter* DI.]

DI: Monona, mama wants you.

MONONA: I'd better go or I'll catch it. I'll catch it anyway—

[*Exit. Enter* NINIAN.]

DI: Uncle Ninian! Well it's just about time you showed up.

NINIAN: You're right, Di. But I came as soon as I could.

DI: You might as well know. I think you're a perfect slunge.

MRS. BETT: Land sakes!

NINIAN: Mrs. Bett.

MRS. BETT: Don't you come near me! Don't you speak to me! You whited centipede!

NINIAN: That's what I expected and that's what I deserve.

MRS. BETT: Move on! Move on!

NINIAN: Let me tell you something first, Mother Bett.

MRS. BETT: Don't you "mother" me.

NINIAN: Yes, that's just what I mean, *Mother* Bett. I've found that the woman I married died in Rio years ago. Here's a letter from the consul.

MRS. BETT: Dead? Ain't that nice! But what ailed you all the time? A man with any get-up-and-get would have known that all along.

NINIAN: I'm not excusing myself any, Mother Bett.

MRS. BETT: Well, perhaps you're as good as you know

how to be. Anyway, your mother's responsible for a good deal without counting you.

NINIAN: Mother Bett, where is Lulu?

MRS. BETT: Who, Lulie? Oh, she's run away.

NINIAN: What do you say?

MRS. BETT: She's gone off on the train this morning. I told her to go.

NINIAN: Mother Bett, Mother Bett—where has she gone?

MRS. BETT: Gone to call her soul her own, I guess.

NINIAN: But Mother Bett, where did Lulu go?

MRS. BETT: She might be at the depot.

NINIAN: Can I catch her?

MRS. BETT: You can catch her if ye can run in them white—mittens.

NINIAN: Run? Watch me.

[*Exit running*]

DI: Oh! Grandma, isn't it just too romantic?

MRS. BETT: What do you mean—rheumatic?

[*Enter* MONONA.]

MONONA: Breakfast's ready, grandma.

MRS. BETT: Breakfast! I wouldn't know coffee from flap-jacks.

MONONA: I've been catching it all morning and I didn't do a thing.

MRS. BETT: What's that, little ape?

MONONA: Grandma, honestly, do you see why because Aunt Lulu ran away the whole family should pick on me?

MRS. BETT: Come here, you poor neglected child!

MONONA: Mama's getting breakfast and she's burned all over and she's so cross—m-m-m. Why here she comes now!

MRS. BETT: Who?

DI: Aunt Lulu!

[*Enter* LULU.]

LULU: Mother—

MONONA: Oh, goody—now they'll pick on you instead of me.

MRS. BETT: [*Softly*] Monona! You run down the road as tight as you can and catch your Uncle Ninian quick—Sh-sh-sh—

MONONA: Uncle Ninian! Oh—oh!

[*Exit*]

LULU: Mother—what do you think I've heard?

MRS. BETT: Land knows! my head's whirlin'. Who found you?

LULU: Found me?

MRS. BETT: I can count up to 'leven in this house that's went after you or went after them that went after them—oh land! . . .

LULU: Mother, the station agent said to me just now when I went to buy my ticket, he said, "You just missed your husband. He went hurrying up the street." I couldn't go till I knew.

DI: Why, Aunt Lulu, haven't you heard—

MRS. BETT: Sh-h-h-h—Leave it burst.

[*Enter* DWIGHT.]

DWIGHT: So . . . after making me traipse all over town for you and before breakfast. . . . What is the meaning of this, Lulu? Answer me.

MRS. BETT: Sit down, Dwight. Take off your hat why don't you?

[*Enter* INA.]

INA: Forevermore.

LULU: Were you looking for me, Dwight?

DWIGHT: What about our breakfast, may I ask?

LULU: Haven't you had your breakfast, Dwight? I had mine in the bakery.

MRS. BETT: In the bakery! On expense!

INA: Lulu, where have you been?

LULU: How good of you to miss me!

INA: Lulu, you don't act like yourself.

LULU: That's the way I heard the women talk in Savannah, Georgia. "So good of you to miss me."

DWIGHT: Lulu, let's have no more of this nonsense. . . .

LULU: Whose nonsense, Dwight? I've left your home for good and all. I'm going somewhere else to work.

INA: Why, Lulu, what will people think of Dwight and me if we let you do that?

DWIGHT: So you thought better of the promise you made to us last evening not to tell our affairs broadcast.

LULU: Your affairs? No, Dwight, you can tell them anything you like when I'm gone.

INA: How am I ever going to keep house without you?
Dwight, you've simply got to make her stay. When I
think of what I went through while she was away ...
everything boils over, and what I don't expect to
b-b-boil b-b-burns. Sister, how can you be so cruel
when Dwight and I—

DWIGHT: Patience, patience, pettie ... Lulu, I ask you to
stay here where you belong.

LULU: No, Dwight, I'm through.

DWIGHT: So, sister mine, have you found some other man
willing to run away with you?

LULU: That will do, Dwight. You've pretended so long
you can't be honest with yourself, any of the time. Your
whole life is a lie.

MRS. BETT: Save your breath, Lulie.

[*Enter* MONONA *with* NINIAN.]

DWIGHT: At least, Miss Lulu Bett, neither Ina nor I ever
had to lie about our marriage.

MONONA: Here he is, grandma.

LULU: Oh ...

NINIAN: What's that your saying, Dwight?

INA: Forevermore!

LULU: Ninian ...

NINIAN: Lulu ... So I didn't miss you.

DWIGHT: Ha! ha! ... The happy bridegroom comes at
last. What's the meaning of this, Ninian?

NINIAN: I'll bet he's made life beautiful for you since you
got back. Anything more to say, Dwight?

DWIGHT: Yes, Lulu was planning to run away. ... I was
telling her she'd better stay here at home where she'd
have us to stand by her.

NINIAN: Yes, I've heard how you stood by her. You're a
magnificent protector, you are!

DWIGHT: Look here, Nin, don't you feel that you have to
sacrifice yourself. Lulu is well enough off here.

INA: She was quite happy until you came, Ninian.

NINIAN: You hypocrites!

MRS. BETT: Hypocrites! He-e!

INA: Children, stop listening to older people.

DI: Oh, mama! ...

MONONA: [*Crying*] Oh ... Let me stay!

INA: Children! . . . [*Exeunt* DI *and* MONONA.] Ninian, how can you say such things to us!

NINIAN: Lulu has suffered as much from you as she has from me.

MRS. BETT: That's right, Ninian. Plain talk won't hurt nobody around here.

NINIAN: Lulu, can you forgive me?

LULU: But Cora Waters . . . what of her?

DWIGHT: Yes, what about your other wife?

NINIAN: I haven't any other wife—just Lulu.

MRS. BETT: Cora Waters is dead. I knew it all along.

LULU: Ninian, is it true?

NINIAN: Yes, it's true.

MRS. BETT: He's confided in his mother. He told me all about it.

NINIAN: Will you come back to me, Lulu?

MRS. BETT: Better take him, Lulie. You can have that fifty to furnish up the parlor.

LULU: Oh, mother! I wish we could have you with us.

NINIAN: Do you forgive me?

LULU: I forgave you in Savannah, Georgia.

CURTAIN

ACT III

As originally produced December 27, 1920

The piano store: empty, bare, three or four upright pianos with bright plush spreads and plush-covered stools. Back, a dark green sateen curtain. It is the following morning.

[*Discover* CORNISH *at a little table, on which is opened a large black book. Enter* MONONA, *carrying basket of parcels.*]

MONONA: Oh, Mr. Cornish . . .

CORNISH: Hello, there Monona! How's everything?

MONONA: Everything's perfectly awful up to our house.

CORNISH: Miss Lulu's all right, I hope?

MONONA: Aunt Lulu is—

CORNISH: There! I knew it. I knew this thing was going to wind up in a fit of sickness—

MONONA: Sick . . . No. She's gone.

CORNISH: Gone! Miss Lulu gone?

MONONA: Run away.

CORNISH: Oh, with who?

MONONA: Nobody, I guess. She skipped out of the house early this morning. It was me saw her going down the walk with her bag. It was me told everybody. It was me found her trunk packed and locked in her room. That's all.

CORNISH: This is terrible, terrible—and your people not home yet?

MONONA: I should say they are. Came last night.

CORNISH: But what are they doing to find her?

MONONA: Papa said he wouldn't do a thing. Mamma's

234

been getting breakfast and she's burned all over, and she's so cross—m-m!

CORNISH: Yes, but aren't they trying to find Lulu—your Aunt Lulu—

MONONA: Grandma says she knows she's dead. Probably she's drowned in the river and they'll get her out with her hair all stringy—

CORNISH: See here. I think I'll come up to your house. I'll put a little notice on my door—

MONONA: I better go now. I'll catch it anyhow. I've been catching it all the morning and I didn't do a thing. Mr. Cornish, honestly, do you see why, because Aunt Lulu ran away, the whole family should pick on me?

CORNISH: Well, we must all help as much as we can, Monona—

MONONA: Up to our house, honestly, you'd think I was the one that had done it. And I may!

[*Exit, running*]

CORNISH: I'll be right there, as soon as I can lock up.

[*He disappears behind the green curtain. Pause. Enter* LULU.]

LULU: Mr. Cornish. Mr. Cornish.

[CORNISH *appears.*]

CORNISH: Well!

LULU: Well!

CORNISH: You're out early.

LULU: Oh, no!

CORNISH: My, but I'm glad to see you. Won't you sit down?

LULU: I can only stay a minute. Wasn't that Monona just went out of here?

CORNISH: Yes, that was Monona.

LULU: Did she say anything about me?

CORNISH: She—she said you'd run away. She—she must have been mistaken.

LULU: No, she wasn't. I have.

CORNISH: Why, Miss Lulu!

LULU: Or I'm going on the 10:10. My bag's in the bakery. I had my breakfast in the bakery. . . . I've left them for good.

CORNISH: Then I suppose he cut up like a hyena over that letter being opened.

LULU: Oh, he forgave me that.

CORNISH: Forgave you!

LULU: Overlooked it, rather.

CORNISH: Anyway he's convinced now about that other Mrs. Ninian Deacon?

LULU: Yes, but you mustn't say anything about that, please, ever.

CORNISH: Even now? Well, I'll be jumped up. *Even now?* Then—I guess I see why you're going.

LULU: It isn't only that. I'm going . . . I'm *going!*

CORNISH: I see. Would—would you tell me where?

LULU: Maybe. After a while.

CORNISH: I do want you to. Because I—I think you're a brick.

LULU: Oh, no!

CORNISH: Yes, you are. By George! you don't find very many *married* women with as good sense as you've got. That is, I mean—

LULU: All right. I know. Thank you.

CORNISH: You've been a jewel in their home—I know that. They're going to miss you no end.

LULU: They'll miss my cooking.

CORNISH: They'll miss more than that. I've watched you there. . . .

LULU: You have?

CORNISH: You made the whole place go.

LULU: You don't mean just the cooking?

CORNISH: No.

LULU: I never had but one compliment before that wasn't for my cooking. He told me I done up my hair nice. . . . That was after I took notice how the ladies in Savannah, Georgia, done up theirs.

CORNISH: Well, well, well! . . .

LULU: I must go now. I wanted to say good-by to you. . . .

CORNISH: I hate to have you go. I—I hate to have you go.

LULU: Oh, well!

CORNISH: Look here, I wish—I wish you weren't going.

LULU: Do you? Good-by.

CORNISH: Can't I come to the depot with you?

LULU: You can't leave the store alone.

CORNISH: Yes. I'll put a little notice on the door. . . .

LULU: No. That would be bad for the business. Good-by.

CORNISH: Good-by, Miss Lulu! Good-by, good-by, good-by! . . .

LULU: There's something else. I'm going to tell you—I don't care what Dwight says. [*Takes letter from her handbag*] As long as I told you the other part, I'm going to tell you this.

CORNISH: I want to know everything you'll let me know.

LULU: See—at the office this morning was this. It's from Ninian.

CORNISH: Well, I should think he'd better write.

LULU: Nobody must know. It was bad enough for the family before, but now . . . here it is:

". . . just want you to know you're actually rid of me. I've heard from her, in Brazil. She ran out of money and thought of me, and her lawyer wrote to me. . . ."
. . . He incloses the lawyer's letter.

"I've never been any good—Dwight would tell you that if his pride would let him tell the truth once in a while. But there isn't anything in my life makes me feel as bad as this. . . ."
. . . well, that part doesn't matter. But you see. He didn't lie to get rid of me—and she was alive just as he thought she might be!

CORNISH: And you're free now.

LULU: That's so—I am. I hadn't thought of that. . . . It's late. Now I'm really going. Good-by.

CORNISH: Don't say good-by.

LULU: It's nearly train time.

CORNISH: Don't you go. . . . Do you think you could possibly stay here with me?

LULU: Oh! . . .

CORNISH: I haven't got anything. I guess maybe you've heard something about a little something I'm supposed to inherit. Well, it's only five hundred dollars. . . . That little Warden house—it don't cost much—you'd be surprised. Rent, I mean. I can get it now. I went and looked at it the other day but then I didn't think . . . well, I mean, it don't cost near as much as this store. We could furnish up the parlor with pianos . . . that is, if you could ever think of such a thing as marrying me.

LULU: But—you *know!* Why, don't the disgrace—

CORNISH: What disgrace?

LULU: Oh, you—you—

CORNISH: There's only this about that. Of course, if you loved him very much then I ought not to be talking this way to you. But I didn't think—

LULU: You didn't think what?

CORNISH: That you did care so very much about him. I don't know why.

LULU: I wanted somebody of my own. That's the reason I done what I done. I know that now.

CORNISH: I figured that way. . . . Look here, I ought to tell you. I'm not—I'm awful lonesome myself. This is no place to live. Look—look here. [*He draws the green curtain revealing the mean little cot and washstand.*] I guess living so is one reason why I want to get married. I want some kind of a home.

LULU: Of course.

CORNISH: I ain't never lived what you might say private.

LULU: I've lived too private.

[*Pause*]

CORNISH: Then there's another thing. I—I don't believe I'm ever going to be able to do anything with the law.

LULU: I don't see how anybody does.

CORNISH: And I'm not much good in a business way. Sometimes I think that I may never be able to make any money.

LULU: Lots of men don't.

CORNISH: Well, there it is. I'm no good at business. I'll never be a lawyer. And—and everything I say sounds wrong to me. And yet I do believe that I'd know enough not to bully a woman. Not to make her unhappy. Maybe—even, I could make her a little happy.

LULU: Lots of men do.

[*Voices. Enter* INA, DWIGHT *and* MRS. BETT.]

INA: Oh, Dwight! she's still here.

DWIGHT: So this is where we find our Lulu!

LULU: Did you want me, Dwight?

INA: Want you? Why, Lulu! are you crazy? Of course we want you. Why aren't you home?

[*Nursing her wrist, which is bandaged, with the other hand, which is bandaged, too*]

MRS. BETT: Lulie, Lulie, we thought you'd gone off again.

LULU: Mother, darling . . .

DWIGHT: Here am I kept home from the office, trying my best to take your place. You're a most important personage, Miss Lulu Bett.

LULU: What did you want of me?

INA: Want of you? Why, my goodness . . .

DWIGHT: If you had tasted bacon fried as the bacon was fried which I have tasted this day—

INA: Oh, Dwight, that's not funny!

DWIGHT: No. And the muffins were not funny either. Yes they were!

LULU: How good of you to miss me!

INA: Lulu, you don't act like yourself.

LULU: That was the way I heard the women talk in Savannah, Georgia. "So good of you to miss me."

DWIGHT: Lulu, what does this mean? No more of this nonsense.

LULU: Whose nonsense, Dwight?

DWIGHT: We know that your trunk is locked and strapped in your room and you were seen going down the street with a bag. You have flown here, presumably to discuss your situation with an outsider. Is this fair to us?

LULU: What do you want me to do, Dwight?

INA: Do? Why, we want you to come home.

LULU: Home!

DWIGHT: Also to explain your amazing behavior.

CORNISH: May I do that, Miss Lulu?

LULU: No—no thank you. I think I'd like to speak for myself. Dwight, I've left your home for good and all.

INA: Sister . . .

MRS. BETT: Lulie . . . Lulie! . . .

DWIGHT: Ah-ha! You have thought better of the promise you made to Ina and me last evening not to tell our affairs broadcast.

LULU: I've thought no better of it—and no worse. I couldn't. But I've been thinking of something else. Of you, Dwight.

DWIGHT: Ah—I'm flattered.

LULU: . . . Let it go at that. . . . In any case, I've left your home.

INA: But where are you going?

LULU: I meant to go somewhere else and work.

INA: Go somewhere else and work. Cook? Lulu, have you

no consideration for Dwight and me at all? What would people think if we let you do that. . . .

DWIGHT: Patience, patience, pettie. Let's have no more of this, Lulu. I imagine you're not quite well. Come home with us, now, there's a good girl.

LULU: No, Dwight.

INA: Lulu, I simply can't keep house without you. When I think of going through with what I went through this summer while you were away. . . . Everything b-boils over and what I don't expect to b-boil b-burns. . . . [Sobs] Dwightie, you've got to make her stay.

DWIGHT: Pettie—control yourself. . . . Lulu, I ask you, I implore you, to come back home with us.

CORNISH: Miss Lulu . . .

LULU: Yes?

CORNISH: May I tell them?

LULU: What is there to tell them?

CORNISH: I think Miss Lulu and I are going to—arrange.

LULU: O but not yet—not yet.

DWIGHT: What—you? You and Cornish? I should think not. How can you?

LULU: Cora Waters is alive. Ninian's heard from her. There's her lawyer's letter.

INA: Forevermore!

MRS. BETT: What you talking—what you talking. I want to know but I ain't got something in my head. . . . Lulie, you ain't going to get married again, are you—after waiting so long?

DWIGHT: Don't be disturbed, Mother Bett. She wasn't married that first time. No marriage about it.

INA: Dwight! If Lulu marries Mr. Cornish, then everybody'll have to know about Ninian and his other wife.

LULU: That's so. You would have to tell, wouldn't you? I never thought of that. Well—you can get used to the idea while I'm gone.

DWIGHT: Gone?

INA: Gone where?

MRS. BETT: Where you goin' now, for pity sakes?

LULU: Away. I thought I wanted somebody of my own. Well, maybe it was just myself.

DWIGHT: What ridiculous talk is this?

CORNISH: Lulu—couldn't you stay with me—

LULU: Sometime, maybe. I don't know. But first I want to see out of my own eyes. For the first time in my life. Good-by, mother.

MRS. BETT: Lulie, Lulie . . .

LULU: [*At the door*] Good-by. Good-by, all of you. I'm going I don't know where—to work at I don't know what. But I'm going from choice!

[*Exit.* CORNISH *follows her.*]

MRS. BETT: Who's going to do your work now, I'd like to know?

CURTAIN

MACHINAL

SOPHIE TREADWELL

First performed 1928

CHARACTERS

YOUNG WOMAN
TELEPHONE GIRL
STENOGRAPHER
FILING CLERK
ADDING CLERK
MOTHER
HUSBAND
BELLBOY
NURSE
DOCTOR
YOUNG MAN
GIRL
MAN
BOY
MAN
ANOTHER MAN
WAITER
JUDGE
LAWYER FOR DEFENSE
LAWYER FOR PROSECUTION
COURT REPORTER
BAILIFF
REPORTER
SECOND REPORTER
THIRD REPORTER
JAILER
MATRON
PRIEST

THE PLOT is the story of a woman who murders her husband—an ordinary young woman, any woman.

THE PLAN is to tell this story by showing the different phases of life that the woman comes in contact with, and in none of which she finds any place, any peace. The woman is essentially soft, tender, and the life around her is essentially hard, mechanized. Business, home, marriage, having a child, seeking pleasure—all are difficult for her—mechanical, nerve nagging. Only in an illicit love does she find anything with life in it for her, and when she loses this, the desperate effort to win free to it again is her undoing.

The story is told in nine scenes. In the dialogue of these scenes there is the attempt to catch the rhythm of our common city speech, its brassy sound, its trick of repetition, etc.

Then there is, also, the use of many different sounds chosen primarily for their inherent emotional effect (steel riveting, a priest chanting, a Negro singing, jazz band, etc.), but contributing also to the creation of a background, an atmosphere.

THE HOPE is to create a stage production that will have "style," and at the same time, by the story's own innate drama, by the directness of its telling, by the variety and quick changingness of its scenes, and the excitement of its sounds, to create an interesting play.

SCENICALLY this play is planned to be handled in two basic sets (or in one set with two backs)

The first division—(the first Four Episodes)—needs an entrance at one side, and a back having a door and a large window. The door gives, in

Episode 1—to Vice President's office.
Episode 2—to hall.
Episode 3—to bathroom.
Episode 4—to corridor.

And the window shows, in

Episode 1—An opposite office.
Episode 2—An inner apartment court.
Episode 3—Window of a dance casino opposite.
Episode 4—Steel girders.

(Of these, only the casino window is important. Sky could be used for the others.)

The second division—(the last Five Episodes)—has the same side entrance, but the back has only one opening—for a small window (barred).

Episode 5, window is masked by electric piano.
Episode 6, window is disclosed (sidewalk outside).
Episode 7, window is curtained.
Episode 8, window is masked by Judge's bench.
Episode 9, window is disclosed (sky outside).

There is a change of furniture, and props for each episode—(only essential things, full of character).

For Episode 9, the room is closed in from the sides, and there is a place with bars and a door in it, put straight across stage down front (back far enough to leave a clear passageway in front of it).

LIGHTING concentrated and intense.—Light and shadow—bright light and darkness.—This darkness, already in the scene, grows and blacks out the light for dark stage when the scene changes are made.

OFFSTAGE VOICES: Characters in the Background Heard, but Unseen:

A Janitor
A Baby
A Boy and a Girl
A Husband and Wife
A Husband and Wife

A Radio Announcer
A Negro Singer

MECHANICAL OFFSTAGE SOUNDS
A small jazz band
A hand organ
Steel riveting
Telegraph instruments
Aeroplane engine

MECHANICAL ONSTAGE SOUNDS
Office Machines (Typewriters, telephones, etc.)
Electric piano.

CHARACTERS: In the Background Seen, Not Heard
(Seen, off the main set; i.e., through a window or door)
Couples of men and women dancing
A Woman in a bathrobe
A Woman in a wheel chair
A Nurse with a covered basin
A Nurse with a tray
The feet of men and women passing in the street

EPISODE ONE

To Business

SCENE:
   an office:
   a switchboard,
   filing cabinet,
   adding machine,
   typewriter and table,
   manifold machine.

SOUNDS:
   office machines:
   typewriters,
   adding machine,
   manifold,
   telephone bells,
   buzzers.

CHARACTERS AND THEIR MACHINES:
   A YOUNG WOMAN *(typewriter)*,
   A STENOGRAPHER *(typewriter)*,
   A FILING CLERK *(filing cabinet and manifold)*,
   An ADDING CLERK *(adding machine)*,
      TELEPHONE OPERATOR *(switchboard)*,
      JONES.

BEFORE THE CURTAIN:
   Sounds of machines going. They continue throughout the scene, and accompany the YOUNG WOMAN's *thoughts after the scene is blacked out.*

AT THE RISE OF THE CURTAIN:
   All the machines are disclosed, and all the characters with the exception of the YOUNG WOMAN.

Of these characters, the YOUNG WOMAN, *going any day to any business. Ordinary. The confusion of her own inner thoughts, emotions, desires, dreams cuts her off from any actual adjustment to the routine of work. She gets through this routine with a very small surface of her consciousness. She is not homely and she is not pretty. She is preoccupied with herself—with her person. She has well kept hands, and a trick of constantly arranging her hair over her ears.*

The STENOGRAPHER *is the faded, efficient woman office worker. Drying, dried.*

The ADDING CLERK *is her male counterpart.*

The FILING CLERK *is a boy not grown, callow adolescence.*

The TELEPHONE GIRL, *young, cheap and amorous.*

Lights come up on office scene. Two desks right and left. Telephone booth back right center. Filing cabinet back of center. Adding machine back left center.

ADDING CLERK: [*In the monotonous voice of his monotonous thoughts; at his adding machine*] 2490, 28, 76, 123, 36842, 1, ¼, 37, 804, 23½, 982.
FILING CLERK: [*In the same way—at his filing desk*] Accounts—A. Bonds—B. Contracts—C. Data—D. Earnings—E.
STENOGRAPHER: [*In the same way—left*] Dear Sir—in re—your letter—recent date—will state—
TELEPHONE GIRL: Hello—Hello—George H. Jones Company good morning—hello hello—George H. Jones Company good morning—hello.
FILING CLERK: Market—M. Notes—N. Output—O. Profits—P.—! [*Suddenly*] What's the matter with Q?

TELEPHONE GIRL: Matter with it—Mr. J.—Mr. K. wants you—What you mean matter? Matter with what?

FILING CLERK: Matter with Q.

TELEPHONE GIRL: Well—what is? Spring 1726?

FILING CLERK: I'm asking yuh—

TELEPHONE GIRL: WELL?

FILING CLERK: Nothing filed with it—

TELEPHONE GIRL: Well?

FILING CLERK: Look at A. Look at B. What's the matter with Q?

TELEPHONE GIRL: Ain't popular. Hello—Hello—George H. Jones Company.

FILING CLERK: Hot dog! Why ain't it?

ADDING CLERK: Has it personality?

STENOGRAPHER: Has it Halitosis?

TELEPHONE GIRL: Has it got it?

FILING CLERK: Hot dog!

TELEPHONE GIRL: What number do you want? [*Recognizing but not pleased*] Oh—hello—sure I know who it is—tonight? Uh, uh—[*Negative, but each with a different inflection*]—you heard me—No!

FILING CLERK: Don't you like him?

STENOGRAPHER: She likes 'em all.

TELEPHONE GIRL: I do not!

STENOGRAPHER: Well—pretty near all!

TELEPHONE GIRL: What number do you want? Wrong number. Hello—hello—George H. Jones Company. Hello, hello—

STENOGRAPHER: Memorandum—attention Mr. Smith— at a conference of—

ADDING CLERK: 125—83¾—22—908—34—¼—28593—

FILING CLERK: Report—R, Sales—S, Trade—T.

TELEPHONE GIRL: Shh—! Yes, Mr. J.—? No—Miss A. ain't in yet—I'll tell her, Mr. J.—just the minute she gets in.

STENOGRAPHER: She's late again, huh?

TELEPHONE GIRL: Out with her sweetie last night, huh?

FILING CLERK: Hot dog.

ADDING CLERK: She ain't got a sweetie.

STENOGRAPHER: How do you know?

ADDING CLERK: I know.

FILING CLERK: Hot dog.

ADDING CLERK: She lives alone with her mother.

TELEPHONE GIRL: Spring 1876? Hello—Spring 1876. Spring! Hello, Spring 1876? 1876! Wrong number! Hello! Hello!

STENOGRAPHER: Director's meeting semiannual report card.

FILING CLERK: Shipments—Sales—Schedules—S.

ADDING CLERK: She doesn't belong in an office.

TELEPHONE GIRL: Who does?

STENOGRAPHER: I do!

ADDING CLERK: You said it!

FILING CLERK: Hot dog!

TELEPHONE GIRL: Hello—hello—George H. Jones Company—hello—hello—

STENOGRAPHER: I'm efficient. She's inefficient.

FILING CLERK: She's inefficient.

TELEPHONE GIRL: She's got J. going.

STENOGRAPHER: Going?

TELEPHONE GIRL: Going and coming.

FILING CLERK: Hot dog.

[Enter JONES.]

JONES: Good morning, everybody.

TELEPHONE GIRL: Good morning.

FILING CLERK: Good morning.

ADDING CLERK: Good morning.

STENOGRAPHER: Good morning, Mr. J.

JONES: Miss A. isn't in yet?

TELEPHONE GIRL: Not yet, Mr. J.

FILING CLERK: Not yet.

ADDING CLERK: Not yet.

STENOGRAPHER: She's late.

JONES: I just wanted her to take a letter.

STENOGRAPHER: I'll take the letter.

JONES: One thing at a time and that done well.

ADDING CLERK: [Yessing] Done well.

STENOGRAPHER: I'll finish it later.

JONES: Hew to the line.

ADDING CLERK: Hew to the line.

STENOGRAPHER: Then I'll hurry.

JONES: Haste makes waste.

ADDING CLERK: Waste.

STENOGRAPHER: But if you're in a hurry.

JONES: I'm never in a hurry—That's how I get ahead! [*Laughs. They all laugh.*] First know you're right—then go ahead.

ADDING CLERK: Ahead.

JONES: [*To* TELEPHONE GIRL] When Miss A. comes in tell her I want her to take a letter. [*Turns to go in—then*] It's important.

TELEPHONE GIRL: [*Making a note*] Miss A.—important.

JONES: [*Starts up—then*] And I don't want to be disturbed.

TELEPHONE GIRL: You're in conference?

JONES: I'm in conference. [*Turns—then*] Unless its A.B.—of course.

TELEPHONE GIRL: Of course—A.B.

JONES: [*Starts—turns again; attempts to be facetious*] Tell Miss A. the early bird catches the worm. [*Exit* JONES.]

TELEPHONE GIRL: The early worm gets caught.

ADDING CLERK: He's caught.

TELEPHONE GIRL: Hooked.

ADDING CLERK: In the pan.

FILING CLERK: Hot dog.

STENOGRAPHER: We beg leave to announce— [*Enter* YOUNG WOMAN. *Goes behind telephone booth to desk right.*]

STENOGRAPHER: You're late!

FILING CLERK: You're late.

ADDING CLERK: You're late.

STENOGRAPHER: And yesterday!

FILING CLERK: The day before.

ADDING CLERK: And the day before.

STENOGRAPHER: You'll lose your job.

YOUNG WOMAN: No!

STENOGRAPHER: No? [*Workers exchange glances.*]

YOUNG WOMAN: I can't!

STENOGRAPHER: Can't? [*Same business*]

FILING CLERK: Rent — bills — installments — miscellaneous.

ADDING CLERK: A dollar ten—ninety-five—3.40—35—12.60.

STENOGRAPHER: Then why are you late?

YOUNG WOMAN: Why?

STENOGRAPHER: Excuse!

ADDING CLERK: Excuse!

FILING CLERK: Excuse.

TELEPHONE GIRL: Excuse it, please.

STENOGRAPHER: Why?

YOUNG WOMAN: The subway?

TELEPHONE GIRL: Long distance?

FILING CLERK: Old stuff!

ADDING CLERK: That stall!

STENOGRAPHER: Stalled?

YOUNG WOMAN: No—

STENOGRAPHER: What?

YOUNG WOMAN: I had to get out!

ADDING CLERK: Out!

FILING CLERK: Out?

STENOGRAPHER: Out where?

YOUNG WOMAN: In the air!

STENOGRAPHER: Air?

YOUNG WOMAN: All those bodies pressing.

FILING CLERK: Hot dog!

YOUNG WOMAN: I thought I would faint! I had to get out in the air!

FILING CLERK: Give her the air.

ADDING CLERK: Free air—

STENOGRAPHER: Hot air.

YOUNG WOMAN: Like I'm dying.

STENOGRAPHER: Same thing yesterday. [*Pause*] And the day before.

YOUNG WOMAN: Yes—what am I going to do?

ADDING CLERK: Take a taxi!

[*They laugh.*]

FILING CLERK: Call a cop!

TELEPHONE GIRL: Mr. J. wants you.

YOUNG WOMAN: Me?

TELEPHONE GIRL: You!

YOUNG WOMAN: [*Rises*] Mr. J.!

STENOGRAPHER: Mr. J.

TELEPHONE GIRL: He's bellowing for you!

[YOUNG WOMAN *gives last pat to her hair—goes off into door—back.*]

STENOGRAPHER: [*After her*] Get it just right.

FILING CLERK: She's always doing that to her hair.

TELEPHONE GIRL: It gives a line—it gives a line—

FILING CLERK: Hot dog.

ADDING CLERK: She artistic.

STENOGRAPHER: She's inefficient.

FILING CLERK: She's inefficient.

STENOGRAPHER: Mr. J. knows she's inefficient.

ADDING CLERK: 46-23-84-2-2-2-1,492—678.

TELEPHONE GIRL: Hello—hello—George H. Jones Company—hello—Mr. Jones? He's in conference.

STENOGRAPHER: [*Sarcastic*] Conference!

ADDING CLERK: Conference.

FILING CLERK: Hot dog!

TELEPHONE GIRL: Do you think he'll marry her?

ADDING CLERK: If she'll have him.

STENOGRAPHER: If she'll have him!

FILING CLERK: Do you think she'll have him?

TELEPHONE GIRL: How much does he get?

ADDING CLERK: Plenty—5,000—10,000—15,000—20,000—25,000.

STENOGRAPHER: And plenty put away.

ADDING CLERK: Gas Preferred—4's—steel—5's—oil—6's.

FILING CLERK: Hot dog.

STENOGRAPHER: Will she have him? Will she have him? This agreement entered into—party of the first part—party of the second part—will he have her?

TELEPHONE GIRL: Well, I'd hate to get into bed with him. [*Familiar melting voice*] Hello—humhum—hum—hum—hold the line a minute—will you—hum hum. [*Professional voice*] Hell, hello—A.B., just a minute, Mr. A.B.—Mr. J.? Mr. A.B.—go ahead, Mr. A.B. [*Melting voice*] We were interrupted—huh—huh—huh-huhuh—hum—hum.

[*Enter* YOUNG WOMAN—*she goes to her chair, sits with folded hands.*]

FILING CLERK: That's all you ever say to a guy—

STENOGRAPHER: Hum—hum—or uh huh—[*Negative*]

TELEPHONE GIRL: That's all you have to. [*To phone*] Hum—hum—hum hum—hum hum—

STENOGRAPHER: Mostly hum hum.

ADDING CLERK: You've said it!

FILING CLERK: Hot dog.

TELEPHONE GIRL: Hum hum huh hum humhumhum—tonight? She's got a date—she told me last night—hum-humhuh—hum—all right. [*Disconnects*] Too bad—my boy friend's got a friend—but my girl friend's got a date.

YOUNG WOMAN: You have a good time.

TELEPHONE GIRL: Big time.

STENOGRAPHER: Small time.

ADDING CLERK: A big time on the small time.

TELEPHONE GIRL: I'd ask you, kid, but you'd be up to your neck!

STENOGRAPHER: Neckers!

ADDING CLERK: Petters!

FILING CLERK: Sweet papas.

TELEPHONE GIRL: Want to come?

YOUNG WOMAN: Can't.

TELEPHONE GIRL: Date?

YOUNG WOMAN: My mother.

STENOGRAPHER: Worries?

TELEPHONE GIRL: Nags—hello—George H. Jones Company—Oh hello—

[YOUNG WOMAN *sits before her machine—hands in lap, looking at them.*]

STENOGRAPHER: Why don't you get to work?

YOUNG WOMAN: [*Dreaming*] What?

ADDING CLERK: Work!

YOUNG WOMAN: Can't.

STENOGRAPHER: Can't?

YOUNG WOMAN: My machine's out of order.

STENOGRAPHER: Well, fix it!

YOUNG WOMAN: I can't—got to get somebody.

STENOGRAPHER: Somebody! Somebody! Always somebody! Here, sort the mail, then!

YOUNG WOMAN: [*Rises*] All right.

STENOGRAPHER: And hurry! You're late.

YOUNG WOMAN: [*Sorting letters*] George H. Jones & Company—George H. Jones Inc. George H. Jones—

STENOGRAPHER: You're always late.

ADDING CLERK: You'll lose your job.

YOUNG WOMAN: [*Hurrying*] George H. Jones—George H. Jones Personal—

TELEPHONE GIRL: Don't let 'em get your goat, kid—tell 'em where to get off.

YOUNG WOMAN: What?

TELEPHONE GIRL: Ain't it all set?

YOUNG WOMAN: What?

TELEPHONE GIRL: You and Mr. J.

STENOGRAPHER: You and the boss.

FILING CLERK: You and the big chief.

ADDING CLERK: You and the big cheese.

YOUNG WOMAN: Did he tell you?

TELEPHONE GIRL: I told you!

ADDING CLERK: I told you!

STENOGRAPHER: I don't believe it.

ADDING CLERK: 5,000—10,000—15,000.

FILING CLERK: Hot dog.

YOUNG WOMAN: No—it isn't so.

STENOGRAPHER: Isn't it?

YOUNG WOMAN: No.

TELEPHONE GIRL: Not yet.

ADDING CLERK: But soon.

FILING CLERK: Hot dog.

[*Enter* JONES.]

TELEPHONE GIRL: [*Busy*] George H. Jones Company— Hello—Hello.

STENOGRAPHER: Awaiting your answer—

ADDING CLERK: 5,000—10,000—15,000—

JONES: [*Crossing to* YOUNG WOMAN—*puts hand on her shoulder, all stop and stare*] That letter done?

YOUNG WOMAN: No. [*She pulls away.*]

JONES: What's the matter?

STENOGRAPHER: She hasn't started.

JONES: O.K.—want to make some changes.

YOUNG WOMAN: My machine's out of order.

JONES: O.K.—use the one in my room.

YOUNG WOMAN: I'm sorting the mail.

STENOGRAPHER: [*Sarcastic*] One thing at a time!

JONES: [*Retreating—goes back center*] O.K. [*To* YOUNG WOMAN] When you're finished.

[*Starts back to his room*]

STENOGRAPHER: Haste makes waste.

JONES: [*At door*] O.K.—don't hurry.

[*Exits*]

STENOGRAPHER: Hew to the line!

TELEPHONE GIRL: He's hewing.

FILING CLERK: Hot dog.

TELEPHONE GIRL: Why did you flinch, kid?

YOUNG WOMAN: Flinch?

TELEPHONE GIRL: Did he pinch?

YOUNG WOMAN: No!

TELEPHONE GIRL: Then what?

YOUNG WOMAN: Nothing!—Just his hand.

TELEPHONE GIRL: Oh—just his hand—[*Shakes her head thoughtfully*] Uhhuh. [*Negative*] Uhhuh. [*Decisively*] No! Tell him no.

STENOGRAPHER: If she does she'll lose her job.

ADDING CLERK: Fired.

FILING CLERK: The sack!

TELEPHONE GIRL: [*On the defensive*] And if she doesn't?

ADDING CLERK: She'll come to work in a taxi!

TELEPHONE GIRL: Work?

FILING CLERK: No work.

STENOGRAPHER: No worry.

ADDING CLERK: Breakfast in bed.

STENOGRAPHER: [*Sarcastic*] Did Madame ring?

FILING CLERK: Lunch in bed!

TELEPHONE GIRL: A double bed! [*In phone*] Yes, Mr. J. [*To* YOUNG WOMAN] J. wants you.

YOUNG WOMAN: [*Starts to get to her feet—but doesn't*] I can't—I'm not ready—in a minute. [*Sits staring ahead of her*]

ADDING CLERK: 5,000—10,000—15,000—

FILING CLERK: Profits—plans—purchase—

STENOGRAPHER: Call your attention our prices are fixed.

TELEPHONE GIRL: Hello—hello—George H. Jones Company—hello—hello—

YOUNG WOMAN: [*Thinking her thoughts aloud—to the subdued accompaniment of the office sounds and voices*] Marry me—wants to marry me—George H. Jones—George H. Jones and Company—Mrs. George H. Jones—Mrs. George H. Jones. Dear Madame—marry—do you take this man to be your wedded husband—I do—to love honor and to love—kisses—no—I can't—George H. Jones—How would you like to marry me—What do you say—Why Mr. Jones I—let me look at your little hands—you have such pretty little hands—let me hold your pretty little hands—George H. Jones—Fat hands—flabby hands—don't touch me—please—fat hands are never weary—please don't—married—all girls—most girls—married—babies—a baby—curls— little curls all over its head—George H. Jones— straight—thin—bald—don't touch me—please—no— can't—must—somebody—something—no rest—must rest—no rest—must rest—no rest—late today—yester-day—before—late—subway—air—pressing—bodies pressing—bodies—trembling—air—stop—air—late— job—no job—fired—late—alarm clock—alarm clock— alarm clock—hurry—job—ma—nag—nag—nag—ma— hurry—job—no job—no money—installments due—no money — money — George H. Jones — money — Mrs. George H. Jones—money—no work—no worry—free!— rest—sleep till nine—sleep till ten—sleep till noon— now you take a good rest this morning—don't get up till you want to—thank you—oh thank you—oh don't!— please don't touch me—I want to rest—no rest—earn— got to earn—married—earn—no—yes—earn—all girls— most girls—ma—pa—ma—all women—most women— I can't—must—maybe—must—somebody—something —ma—pa—ma—can I, ma? Tell me, ma—something— somebody.

[*The scene blacks out. The sounds of the office machines continue until the scene lights into Episode Two—and the office sounds become the sound of a radio, offstage.*]

EPISODE TWO

At Home

SCENE:
  a kitchen:
  table,
  chairs,
  plates and food,
  garbage can,
  a pair of rubber gloves.
  The door at the back now opens on a
  hall—the window, on an apartment
  house court.

SOUNDS:
  buzzer,
  radio (voice of announcer; music and singer)

CHARACTERS:
  YOUNG WOMAN,
  MOTHER

OUTSIDE VOICES: *characters heard, but not seen:*
  a JANITOR,
  a BABY,
  a MOTHER *and a* SMALL BOY,
  a YOUNG BOY *and* YOUNG GIRL,
  a HUSBAND *and a* WIFE,
  another HUSBAND *and a* WIFE.

AT RISE:
  YOUNG WOMAN *and* MOTHER *eating—radio offstage—
    radio stops.*

YOUNG WOMAN: Ma—I want to talk to you.

MOTHER: Aren't you eating a potato?

YOUNG WOMAN: No.

MOTHER: Why not?

YOUNG WOMAN: I don't want one.

MOTHER: That's no reason. Here! Take one.

YOUNG WOMAN: I don't want it.

MOTHER: Potatoes go with stew—here!

YOUNG WOMAN: Ma, I don't want it!

MOTHER: Want it! Take it!

YOUNG WOMAN: But I—oh, all right. [*Takes it—then*] Ma, I want to ask you something.

MOTHER: Eat your potato.

YOUNG WOMAN: [*Takes a bite—then*] Ma, there's something I want to ask you—something important.

MOTHER: Is it mealy?

YOUNG WOMAN: S'all right. Ma—tell me.

MOTHER: Three pounds for a quarter.

YOUNG WOMAN: Ma—tell me—
[*Buzzer*]

MOTHER: [*Her dull voice brightening*] There's the garbage. [*Goes to door—or dumbwaiter—opens it. Stop radio.*]

JANITOR'S VOICE: [*Offstage*] Garbage.

MOTHER: [*Pleased—busy*] All right. [*Gets garbage can—puts it out.* YOUNG WOMAN *walks up and down.*] What's the matter now?

YOUNG WOMAN: Nothing.

MOTHER: That jumping up from the table every night the garbage is collected! You act like you're crazy.

YOUNG WOMAN: Ma, do all women—

MOTHER: I suppose you think you're too nice for anything so common! Well, let me tell you, my lady, that it's a very important part of life.

YOUNG WOMAN: I know, but, Ma, if you—

MOTHER: If it weren't for garbage cans where would we be? Where would we all be? Living in filth—that's what! Filth! I should think you'd be glad! I should think you'd be grateful!

YOUNG WOMAN: Oh, Ma!

MOTHER: Well, are you?

YOUNG WOMAN: Am I what?

MOTHER: Glad! Grateful.

YOUNG WOMAN: Yes!

MOTHER: You don't act like it!

YOUNG WOMAN: Oh, Ma, don't talk!

MOTHER: You just said you wanted to talk.

YOUNG WOMAN: Well now—I want to think. I got to think.

MOTHER: Aren't you going to finish your potato?

YOUNG WOMAN: Oh, Ma!

MOTHER: Is there anything the matter with it?

YOUNG WOMAN: No—

MOTHER: Then why don't you finish it?

YOUNG WOMAN: Because I don't want it.

MOTHER: Why don't you?

YOUNG WOMAN: Oh, Ma! Let me alone!

MOTHER: Well, you've got to eat! If you don't eat—

YOUNG WOMAN: Ma! Don't nag!

MOTHER: Nag! Just because I try to look out for you—
nag! Just because I try to care for you—nag! Why, you
haven't sense enough to eat! What would become of
you I'd like to know—if I didn't nag!
[Offstage—a sound of window opening—all these offstage sounds come in through the court window at the
back.]

WOMAN'S VOICE: Johnny—Johnny—come in now!

A SMALL BOY'S VOICE: Oh, Ma!

WOMAN'S VOICE: It's getting cold.

A SMALL BOY'S VOICE: Oh, Ma!

WOMAN'S VOICE: You heard me! [Sound of window slam-
ming]

YOUNG WOMAN: I'm grown up, Ma.

MOTHER: Grown up! What do you mean by that?

YOUNG WOMAN: Nothing much—I guess. [Offstage sound
of baby crying. MOTHER rises, clatters dishes.] Let's
not do the dishes right away, Ma. Let's talk—I gotta.

MOTHER: Well, I can't talk with dirty dishes around—you
may be able to but— [Clattering—clattering]

YOUNG WOMAN: Ma! Listen! Listen!—There's a man wants
to marry me.

MOTHER: [Stops clattering—sits] What man?

YOUNG WOMAN: He says he fell in love with my hands.

MOTHER: In love! Is that beginning again! I thought you
were over that!

[*Offstage* BOY'S VOICE—*whistles*—GIRL'S VOICE *answers.*]

BOY'S VOICE: Come on out.

GIRL'S VOICE: Can't.

BOY'S VOICE: Nobody'll see you.

GIRL'S VOICE: I can't.

BOY'S VOICE: It's dark now—come on.

GIRL'S VOICE: Well—just for a minute.

BOY'S VOICE: Meet you round the corner.

YOUNG WOMAN: I got to get married, Ma.

MOTHER: What do you mean?

YOUNG WOMAN: I gotta.

MOTHER: You haven't got in trouble, have you?

YOUNG WOMAN: Don't talk like that!

MOTHER: Well, you say you got to get married—what do you mean?

YOUNG WOMAN: Nothing.

MOTHER: Answer me!

YOUNG WOMAN: All women get married, don't they?

MOTHER: Nonsense!

YOUNG WOMAN: You got married, didn't you?

MOTHER: Yes, I did!

[*Offstage voices*]

WOMAN'S VOICE: Where you going?

MAN'S VOICE: Out.

WOMAN'S VOICE: You were out last night.

MAN'S VOICE: Was I?

WOMAN'S VOICE: You're always going out.

MAN'S VOICE: Am I?

WOMAN'S VOICE: Where are you going?

MAN'S VOICE: Out.

[*End of offstage voices*]

MOTHER: Who is he? Where did you come to know him?

YOUNG WOMAN: In the office.

MOTHER: In the office!

YOUNG WOMAN: It's Mr. J.

MOTHER: Mr. J.?

YOUNG WOMAN: The Vice-President.

MOTHER: Vice-President! His income must be—Does he know you've got a mother to support?

YOUNG WOMAN: Yes.

MOTHER: What does he say?

YOUNG WOMAN: All right.

MOTHER: How soon you going to marry him?

YOUNG WOMAN: I'm not going to.

MOTHER: Not going to!

YOUNG WOMAN: No! I'm not going to.

MOTHER: But you just said—

YOUNG WOMAN: I'm not going to.

MOTHER: Are you crazy?

YOUNG WOMAN: I can't, Ma! I can't!

MOTHER: Why can't you?

YOUNG WOMAN: I don't love him.

MOTHER: Love!—what does that amount to! Will it clothe you? Will it feed you? Will it pay the bills?

YOUNG WOMAN: No! But it's real just the same!

MOTHER: Real!

YOUNG WOMAN: If it isn't—what can you count on in life?

MOTHER: I'll tell you what you can count on! You can count that you've got to eat and sleep and get up and put clothes on your back and take 'em off again—that you got to get old—and that you got to die. That's what you can count on! All the rest is in your head!

YOUNG WOMAN: But, Ma—didn't you love Pa?

MOTHER: I suppose I did—I don't know—I've forgotten—what difference does it make—now?

YOUNG WOMAN: But then!—oh Ma, tell me!

MOTHER: Tell you what?

YOUNG WOMAN: About all that—love!

[Offstage voices]

WIFE'S VOICE: Don't.

HUSBAND'S VOICE: What's the matter—don't you want me to kiss you?

WIFE'S VOICE: Not like that.

HUSBAND'S VOICE: Like what?

WIFE'S VOICE: That silly kiss!

HUSBAND'S VOICE: Silly kiss?

WIFE'S VOICE: You look so silly—oh I know what's coming when you look like that—and kiss me like that—don't—go away—

[End of offstage voices]

MOTHER: He's a decent man, isn't he?

YOUNG WOMAN: I don't know. How should I know—yet.

MOTHER: He's a Vice-President—of course he's decent.

YOUNG WOMAN: I don't care whether he's decent or not.
I won't marry him.

MOTHER: But you just said you wanted to marry—

YOUNG WOMAN: Not him.

MOTHER: Who?

YOUNG WOMAN: I don't know—I don't know—I haven't
found him yet!

MOTHER: You talk like you're crazy!

YOUNG WOMAN: Oh, Ma—tell me!

MOTHER: Tell you what?

YOUNG WOMAN: Tell me—[*Words suddenly pouring out*]
Your skin oughtn't to curl—ought it—when he just
comes near you—ought it? That's wrong, ain't it? You
don't get over that, do you—ever, do you or do you?
How is it, Ma—do you?

MOTHER: Do you what?

YOUNG WOMAN: Do you get used to it—so after a while
it doesn't matter? Or don't you? Does it always matter?
You ought to be in love, oughtn't you, Ma? You must
be in love, mustn't you, Ma? That changes everything,
doesn't it—or does it? Maybe if you just like a person
it's all right—is it? When he puts a hand on me, my
blood turns cold. But your blood oughtn't to run cold,
ought it? His hands are—his hands are—fat, Ma—don't
you see—his hands are fat—and they sort of press—and
they're fat—don't you see?—Don't you see?

MOTHER: [*Stares at her bewildered*] See what?

YOUNG WOMAN: [*Rushing on*] I've always thought I'd find
somebody—somebody young—and—and attractive—
with wavy hair—wavy hair—I always think of children
with curls—little curls all over their head—somebody
young—and attractive—that I'd like—that I'd love—
But I haven't found anybody like that yet—I haven't
found anybody—I've hardly known anybody—you'd
never let me go with anybody and—

MOTHER: Are you throwing it up to me that—

YOUNG WOMAN: No—let me finish, Ma! No—let me finish! I just mean I've never found anybody—anybody—
nobody's ever asked me—till now—he's the only man
that's ever asked me—And I suppose I got to marry
somebody—all girls do—

MOTHER: Nonsense.

YOUNG WOMAN: But, I can't go on like this, Ma—I don't know why—but I can't—it's like I'm all tight inside—sometimes I feel like I'm stifling!—You don't know—stifling. [*Walks up and down*] I can't go on like this much longer—going to work—coming home—going to work—coming home—I can't— Sometimes in the subway I think I'm going to die—sometimes even in the office if something don't happen—I got to do something—I don't know—it's like I'm all tight inside.

MOTHER: You're crazy.

YOUNG WOMAN: Oh, Ma!

MOTHER: You're crazy!

YOUNG WOMAN: Ma—if you tell me that again I'll kill you! I'll kill you!

MOTHER: If that isn't crazy!

YOUNG WOMAN: I'll kill you— Maybe I am crazy— I don't know. Sometimes I think I am—the thoughts that go on in my mind—sometimes I think I am—I can't help it if I am— I do the best I can—I do the best I can and I'm nearly crazy! [MOTHER *rises and sits.*] Go away! Go away! You don't know anything about anything! And you haven't got any pity—no pity—you just take it for granted that I go to work every day—and come home every night and bring my money every week—you just take it for granted—you'd let me go on forever—and never feel any pity—

[*Offstage radio—a voice singing a sentimental mother song or popular home song.* MOTHER *begins to cry—crosses to chair left—sits.*]

YOUNG WOMAN: Oh Ma—forgive me! Forgive me!

MOTHER: My own child! To be spoken to like that by my own child!

YOUNG WOMAN: I didn't mean it, Ma—I didn't mean it! [*She goes to her mother—crosses to left.*]

MOTHER: [*Clinging to her hand*] You're all I've got in the world—and you don't want me—you want to kill me.

YOUNG WOMAN: No—no, I don't, Ma! I just said that!

MOTHER: I've worked for you and slaved for you!

YOUNG WOMAN: I know, Ma.

MOTHER: I brought you into the world.

YOUNG WOMAN: I know, Ma.

MOTHER: You're flesh of my flesh and—

YOUNG WOMAN: I know, Ma, I know.

MOTHER: And—

YOUNG WOMAN: You rest, now, Ma—you rest—

MOTHER: [*Struggling*] I got to do the dishes.

YOUNG WOMAN: I'll do the dishes— You listen to the music, Ma—I'll do the dishes.

[MA *sits.* YOUNG WOMAN *crosses to behind screen. Takes a pair of rubber gloves and begins to put them on. The* MOTHER *sees them—they irritate her—there is a return of her characteristic mood.*]

MOTHER: Those gloves! I've been washing dishes for forty years and I never wore gloves! But my lady's hands! My lady's hands!

YOUNG WOMAN: Sometimes you talk to me like you're jealous, Ma.

MOTHER: Jealous?

YOUNG WOMAN: It's my hands got me a husband.

MOTHER: A husband? So you're going to marry him now!

YOUNG WOMAN: I suppose so.

MOTHER: If you ain't the craziest—

[*The scene blacks out. In the darkness, the mother song goes into jazz—very faint—as the scene lights into*]

EPISODE THREE

Honeymoon

SCENE:
  hotel bedroom:
  bed,
  chair,
  mirror.
  The door at the back now opens on a bathroom; the window, on a dancing casino opposite.

SOUNDS:
  a small jazz band (violin, piano, saxophone—very dim, at first, then louder).

CHARACTERS:
  YOUNG WOMAN,
  HUSBAND,
  BELLBOY

OFFSTAGE:
  *seen but not heard—*MEN *and* WOMEN *dancing in couples.*

AT RISE:
  set dark.

BELLBOY, HUSBAND, *and* YOUNG WOMAN *enter.* BELLBOY *carries luggage. He switches on light by door. Stop music.*

HUSBAND: Well, here we are.
  [*Throws hat on bed;* BELLBOY *puts luggage down,*

*crosses to window; raises shade three inches; opens
window three inches. Sounds of jazz music louder.
Offstage.*]

BELLBOY: [*Comes to man for tip*] Anything else, Sir?
[*Receives tip. Exits*]

HUSBAND: Well, here we are.

YOUNG WOMAN: Yes, here we are.

HUSBAND: Aren't you going to take your hat off—stay a
while? [YOUNG WOMAN *looks around as though looking for a way out, then takes off her hat, pulls the hair
automatically around her ears.*] This is all right, isn't
it? Huh? Huh?

YOUNG WOMAN: It's very nice.

HUSBAND: Twelve bucks a day! They know how to soak
you in these pleasure resorts. Twelve bucks! [*Music*]
Well—we'll get our money's worth out of it all right.
[*Goes toward bathroom*] I'm going to wash up. [*Stops
at door*] Don't you want to wash up? [YOUNG WOMAN
shakes head "No."] I do! It was a long trip! I want to
wash up! [*Goes off—closes door; sings in bathroom.*
YOUNG WOMAN *goes to window—raises shade—sees
the dancers going round and round in couples. Music
is louder. Re-enter* HUSBAND.] Say, pull that blind
down! They can see in!

YOUNG WOMAN: I thought you said there'd be a view of
the ocean!

HUSBAND: Sure there is.

YOUNG WOMAN: I just see people—dancing.

HUSBAND: The ocean's beyond.

YOUNG WOMAN: [*Desperately*] I was counting on seeing
it!

HUSBAND: You'll see it tomorrow—what's eating you?
We'll take in the boardwalk—Don't you want to wash
up?

YOUNG WOMAN: No!

HUSBAND: It was a long trip. Sure you don't? [YOUNG
WOMAN *shakes her head "No."* HUSBAND *takes off his
coat—puts it over chair.*] Better make yourself at home.
I'm going to. [*She stares at him—moves away from the
window.*] Say, pull down that blind!
[*Crosses to chair down left—sits*]

YOUNG WOMAN: It's close—don't you think it's close?

HUSBAND: Well—you don't want people looking in, do you? [*Laughs*] Huh—huh?

YOUNG WOMAN: No.

HUSBAND: [*Laughs*] I guess not. Huh? [*Takes off shoes.* YOUNG WOMAN *leaves the window, and crosses down to the bed.*] Say—you look a little white around the gills! What's the matter?

YOUNG WOMAN: Nothing.

HUSBAND: You look like you're scared.

YOUNG WOMAN: No.

HUSBAND: Nothing to be scared of. You're with your husband, you know. [*Takes her to chair, left*]

YOUNG WOMAN: I know.

HUSBAND: Happy?

YOUNG WOMAN: Yes.

HUSBAND: [*Sitting*] Then come here and give us a kiss. [*He puts her on his knee.*] That's the girlie. [*He bends her head down, and kisses her along the back of her neck.*] Like that? [*She tries to get to her feet.*] Say— stay there! What you moving for? —You know—you got to learn to relax, little girl— [*Dancers go off. Dim lights. Pinches her above knee*] Say, what you got under there?

YOUNG WOMAN: Nothing.

HUSBAND: Nothing! [*Laughs*] That's a good one! Nothing, huh? Huh? That reminds me of the story of the pullman porter and the—what's the matter—did I tell you that one?

[*Music dims off and out.*]

YOUNG WOMAN: I don't know.

HUSBAND: The pullman porter and the tart?

YOUNG WOMAN: No.

HUSBAND: It's a good one—well—the train was just pulling out and the tart—

YOUNG WOMAN: You did tell that one!

HUSBAND: About the—

YOUNG WOMAN: Yes! Yes! I remember now!

HUSBAND: About the—

YOUNG WOMAN: Yes!

HUSBAND: All right—if I did. You're sure it was the one about the—

YOUNG WOMAN: I'm sure.

HUSBAND: When he asked her what she had underneath her seat and she said—

YOUNG WOMAN: Yes! Yes! That one!

HUSBAND: All right— But I don't believe I did. [*She tries to get up again, as he holds her.*] You know you have got something under there—what is it?

YOUNG WOMAN: Nothing—just—just my garter.

HUSBAND: Your garter! Your garter! Say did I tell you the one about—

YOUNG WOMAN: Yes! Yes!

HUSBAND: [*With dignity*] How do you know which one I meant?

YOUNG WOMAN: You told me them all!

HUSBAND: [*Pulling her back to his knee*] No, I didn't! Not by a jugful! I got a lot of 'em up my sleeve yet—that's part of what I owe my success to—my ability to spring a good story— You know—you got to learn to relax, little girl—haven't you?

YOUNG WOMAN: Yes.

HUSBAND: That's one of the biggest things to learn in life. That's part of what I owe my success to. Now you go and get those heavy things off—and relax.

YOUNG WOMAN: They're not heavy.

HUSBAND: You haven't got much on—have you? But you'll feel better with 'em off. [*Gets up*] Want me to help you?

YOUNG WOMAN: No.

HUSBAND: I'm your husband, you know.

YOUNG WOMAN: I know.

HUSBAND: You aren't afraid of your husband, are you?

YOUNG WOMAN: No—of course not—but I thought maybe—can't we go out for a little while?

HUSBAND: Out? What for?

YOUNG WOMAN: Fresh air—walk—talk.

HUSBAND: We can talk here—I'll tell you all about myself. Go along now. [YOUNG WOMAN *goes toward bathroom door—gets bag.*] Where are you going?

YOUNG WOMAN: In here.

HUSBAND: I thought you'd want to wash up.

YOUNG WOMAN: I just want to—get ready.

HUSBAND: You don't have to go in there to take your clothes off!

YOUNG WOMAN: I want to.

HUSBAND: What for?

YOUNG WOMAN: I always do.

HUSBAND: What?

YOUNG WOMAN: Undress by myself.

HUSBAND: You've never been married till now—have you? [*Laughs*] Or have you been putting something over on me?

YOUNG WOMAN: No.

HUSBAND: I understand—kind of modest—huh? Huh?

YOUNG WOMAN: Yes.

HUSBAND: I understand women— [*Indulgently*] Go along. [*She goes off—starts to close door.* YOUNG WOMAN *exits.*] Don't close the door—thought you wanted to talk. [*He looks around the room with satisfaction—after a pause—rises—takes off his collar.*] You're awful quiet—what are you doing in there?

YOUNG WOMAN: Just—getting ready—

HUSBAND: [*Still in his mood of satisfaction*] I'm going to enjoy life from now on— I haven't had such an easy time of it. I got where I am by hard work and self denial—now I'm going to enjoy life—I'm going to make up for all I missed—aren't you about ready?

YOUNG WOMAN: Not yet.

HUSBAND: Next year maybe we'll go to Paris. You can buy a lot of that French underwear—and Switzerland— all my life I've wanted a Swiss watch—that I bought right there— I coulda' got a Swiss watch here, but I always wanted one that I bought right there— Isn't that funny—huh? Isn't it? Huh? Huh?

YOUNG WOMAN: Yes.

HUSBAND: All my life I've wanted a Swiss watch that I bought right there. All my life I've counted on having that some day—more than anything—except one thing— you know what?

YOUNG WOMAN: No.

HUSBAND: Guess.

YOUNG WOMAN: I can't.

HUSBAND: Then I'm coming in and tell you.

YOUNG WOMAN: No! Please! Please don't.

HUSBAND: Well hurry up then! I thought you women

didn't wear much of anything these days—huh? Huh?
I'm coming in!

YOUNG WOMAN: No—no! Just a minute!

HUSBAND: All right. Just a minute!

[YOUNG WOMAN *is silent.*]

HUSBAND: [*Laughs and takes out watch*] 13—14— I'm
counting the seconds on you—that's what you said,
didn't you—just a minute! —49—50—51—52—53—

[*Enter* YOUNG WOMAN.]

YOUNG WOMAN: [*At the door*] Here I am.

[*She wears a little white gown that hangs very straight.
She is very still, but her eyes are wide with a curious,
helpless, animal terror.*]

HUSBAND: [*Starts toward her—stops. The room is in
shadow except for one dim light by the bed. Sound of
girl weeping*] You crying? [*Sound of weeping*] What
you crying for?

[*Crosses to her*]

YOUNG WOMAN: [*Crying out*] Ma! Ma! I want my mother!

HUSBAND: I thought you were glad to get away from her.

YOUNG WOMAN: I want her now—I want somebody.

HUSBAND: You got me, haven't you?

YOUNG WOMAN: Somebody—somebody—

HUSBAND: There's nothing to cry about. There's nothing
to cry about.

[*The scene blacks out. The music continues until the
lights go up for Episode Four. Rhythm of the music is
gradually replaced by the sound of steel riveting for
Episode Four.*]

EPISODE FOUR

Maternal

SCENE:
   a room in a hospital:
   bed,
   chair.
   The door in the back now opens on a corridor;
   the window on a tall building going up.

SOUNDS:
   outside window—riveting.

CHARACTERS IN THE SCENE:
   YOUNG WOMAN,
   DOCTORS,
   NURSES,
   HUSBAND.

CHARACTERS SEEN BUT NOT HEARD:
   WOMAN IN WHEEL CHAIR,
   WOMAN IN BATHROBE,
   STRETCHER WAGON,
   NURSE WITH TRAY,
   NURSE WITH COVERED BASIN.

AT RISE:
   YOUNG WOMAN *lies still in bed. The door is open. In the corridor, a stretcher wagon goes by.*

[*Enter* NURSE.]
NURSE: How are you feeling today? [*No response from*

274

YOUNG WOMAN] Better? [*No response*] No pain? [*No response*]. NURSE *takes her watch in one hand,* YOUNG WOMAN's *wrist in the other—stands, then goes to chart at foot of bed—writes.*] You're getting along fine. [*No response*] Such a sweet baby you have, too. [*No response*] Aren't you glad it's a girl? [YOUNG WOMAN *makes sign with her head "No."*] You're not! Oh, my! That's no way to talk! Men want boys—women ought to want girls. [*No response*] Maybe you didn't want either, eh? [YOUNG WOMAN *signs "No." Riveting machine*] You'll feel different when it begins to nurse. You'll just love it then. Your milk hasn't come yet—has it? [*Sign—"No"*] It will! [*Sign—"No"*] Oh, you don't know Doctor! [*Goes to door—turns*] Anything else you want? [YOUNG WOMAN *points to window.*] Draft? [*Sign—"No"*] The noise? [YOUNG WOMAN *signs "Yes."*] Oh, that can't be helped. Hospital's got to have a new wing. We're the biggest Maternity Hospital in the world. I'll close the window, though. [YOUNG WOMAN *signs "No."*] No?

YOUNG WOMAN: [*Whispers*] I smell everything then.

NURSE: [*Starting out the door—riveting machine*] Here's your man!

[*Enter* HUSBAND *with large bouquet. Crosses to bed.*]

HUSBAND: Well, how are we today?

[YOUNG WOMAN—*no response*]

NURSE: She's getting stronger!

HUSBAND: Of course she is!

NURSE: [*Taking flowers*] See what your husband brought you.

HUSBAND: Better put 'em in water right away. [*Exit* NURSE.] Everything OK? [YOUNG WOMAN *signs "No."*] Now see here, my dear, you've got to brace up, you know! And—and face things! Everybody's got to brace up and face things! That's what makes the world go round. I know all you've been through but— [YOUNG WOMAN *signs "No."*] Oh, yes I do! I know all about it! I was right outside all the time! [YOUNG WOMAN *makes violent gesture of "No." Ignoring*] Oh yes! But you've got to brace up now! Make an effort! Pull yourself together! Start the uphill climb! Oh I've been down—but

I haven't stayed down. I've been licked but I haven't stayed licked! I've pulled myself up by my own boot-straps, and that's what you've got to do! Will power! That's what conquers! Look at me! Now you've got to brace up! Face the music! Stand the gaff! Take life by the horns! Look it in the face! —Having a baby's natural! Perfectly natural thing—why should—

[YOUNG WOMAN *chokes—points wildly to door. Enter* NURSE *with flowers in a vase.*]

NURSE: What's the matter?

HUSBAND: She's got that gagging again—like she had the last time I was here.

[YOUNG WOMAN *gestures him out.*]

NURSE: Better go, sir.

HUSBAND: [*At door*] I'll be back.

[YOUNG WOMAN *gasping and gesturing*]

NURSE: She needs rest.

HUSBAND: Tomorrow then. I'll be back tomorrow—to-morrow and every day—goodbye.

[*Exits*]

NURSE: You got a mighty nice husband, I guess you know that? [*Writes on chart*] Gagging.

[*Corridor life*—WOMAN IN BATHROBE *passes door. Enter* DOCTOR, YOUNG DOCTOR, NURSE *wheeling surgeon's wagon with bottles, instruments, etc.*]

DOCTOR: How's the little lady today?

[*Crosses to bed*]

NURSE: She's better, Doctor.

DOCTOR: Of course she's better! She's all right—aren't you? [YOUNG WOMAN *does not respond.*] What's the matter? Can't you talk?

[*Drops her hand—takes chart*]

NURSE: She's a little weak yet, Doctor.

DOCTOR: [*At chart*] Milk hasn't come yet?

NURSE: No, Doctor.

DOCTOR: Put the child to breast. [YOUNG WOMAN—"No—no!"—*Riveting machine*] No? Don't you want to nurse your baby? [YOUNG WOMAN *signs "No."*] Why not? [*No response*] These modern neurotic women, eh, Doctor? What are we going to do with 'em? [YOUNG DOCTOR *laughs.* NURSE *smiles.*] Bring the baby!

YOUNG WOMAN: No!

DOCTOR: Well—that's strong enough. I thought you were too weak to talk—that's better. You don't want your baby?

YOUNG WOMAN: No.

DOCTOR: What do you want?

YOUNG WOMAN: Let alone—let alone.

DOCTOR: Bring the baby.

NURSE: Yes, Doctor—she's behaved very badly every time, Doctor—very upset—maybe we better not.

DOCTOR: I decide what we better and better not here, Nurse!

NURSE: Yes, Doctor.

DOCTOR: Bring the baby.

NURSE: Yes, Doctor.

DOCTOR: [*With chart*] Gagging—you mean nausea.

NURSE: Yes, Doctor but—

DOCTOR: No buts, nurse.

NURSE: Yes, Doctor.

DOCTOR: Nausea!—Change her diet!— What is her diet?

NURSE: Liquids.

DOCTOR: Give her solids.

NURSE: Yes, Doctor. She says she can't swallow solids.

DOCTOR: Give her solids.

NURSE: Yes, Doctor.

[*Starts to go—riveting machine*]

DOCTOR: Wait—I'll change her medicine. [*Takes pad and writes prescription in Latin. Hands it to* NURSE] After meals. [*To door*] Bring her baby.

[*Exit* DOCTOR, *followed by* YOUNG DOCTOR *and* NURSE *with surgeon's wagon.*]

NURSE: Yes, Doctor.

[*Exits*]

YOUNG WOMAN: [*Alone*] Let me alone—let me alone—let me alone—I've submitted to enough—I won't submit to any more—crawl off—crawl off in the dark—Vixen crawled under the bed—way back in the corner under the bed—they were all drowned—puppies don't go to heaven—heaven—golden stairs—long stairs—long—too long—long golden stairs—climb those golden stairs—stairs—stairs—climb—tired—too tired—dead—no mat-

ter—nothing matters—dead—stairs—long stairs—all the
dead going up—going up to be in heaven—heaven—
golden stairs—all the children coming down—coming
down to be born—dead going up—children coming
down—going up—coming down—going up—coming
down—going up—coming down—going up—stop—
stop—no—no traffic cop—no—no traffic cop in heaven—
traffic cop—traffic cop—can't you give us a smile—
tired—too tired—no matter—it doesn't matter—St. Peter—St. Peter at the gate—you can't come in—no matter—it doesn't matter—I'll rest—I'll lie down—down—
all written down—down in a big book—no matter—it
doesn't matter— I'll lie down—it weighs me—it's over
me—it weighs—weighs—it's heavy—it's a heavy book—
no matter—lie still—don't move—can't move—rest—
forget—they say you forget—a girl—aren't you glad it's
a girl—a little girl—with no hair—none—little curls all
over his head—a little bald girl—curls—curls all over
his head—what kind of hair has God? no matter—it
doesn't matter—everybody loves God—they've got to—
got to—got to love God—God is love—even if he's bad
they got to love him—even if he's got fat hands—fat
hands—no no—he wouldn't be God—His hands make
you well—He lays on his hands—well—and happy—
no matter—doesn't matter—far—too far—tired—too tired
Vixen crawled off under bed—eight—there were eight—
a woman crawled off under the bed—a woman has
one—two three four—one two three four—one two
three four—two plus two is four—two times two is
four—two times four is eight Vixen had eight—one two
three four five six seven eight—eight—Puffie had
eight—all drowned—drowned—drowned in blood—
blood— oh God! God—God never had one—Mary had
one—in a manger—the lowly manger—God's on a high
throne—far—too far—no matter—it doesn't matter—
God Mary Mary God Mary—Virgin Mary—Mary had
one—the Holy Ghost—the Holy Ghost—George H.
Jones—oh don't—please don't! Let me rest—now I can
rest—the weight is gone—inside the weight is gone—
it's only outside—outside—all around—weight—I'm
under it—Vixen crawled under the bed—there were

eight—I'll not submit any more—I'll not submit—I'll not submit—

[*The scene blacks out. The sound of riveting continues until it goes into the sound of an electric piano and the scene lights up for Episode Five.*]

EPISODE FIVE

Prohibited

SCENE:
  bar:
  bottles,
  tables,
  chairs,
  electric piano.

SOUND:
  electric piano.

CHARACTERS:
  MAN *behind the bar,*
  POLICEMAN *at bar,*
  WAITER.
  At Table 1: a MAN *and a* WOMAN
  At Table 2: a MAN *and a* BOY
  At Table 3: TWO MEN *waiting for* TWO GIRLS, *who are*
     TELEPHONE GIRL *of Episode One and* YOUNG WOMAN.

AT RISE:
  Everyone except the GIRLS *on. Of the characters, the*
  MAN *and* WOMAN *at Table 1 are an ordinary man and*
  woman. THE MAN *at Table 2 is a middle-aged fairy; the*
  BOY *is young, untouched. At Table 3, 1st* MAN *is pleas-*
  ing, common, vigorous. He has coarse wavy hair. 2ND
  MAN *is an ordinary salesman type.*

1ST MAN: [*At Table 3*] I'm going to beat it.
2ND MAN: Oh, for the love of Mike.
1ST MAN: They ain't going to show.

2ND MAN: Sure they'll show.

1ST MAN: How do you know they'll show?

2ND MAN: I tell you you can't keep that baby away from me—just got to— [*Snaps fingers*]—She comes running.

1ST MAN: Looks like it.

2ND MAN: [*To* WAITER—*makes sign* "2," *with his fingers*] The same.

[WAITER *goes to the bar.*]

MAN: [*At Table* 2] Oh, I'm sorry I brought you here.

BOY: Why?

MAN: This Purgatory of noise! I brought you here to give you pleasure—let you taste pleasure. This sherry they have here is bottled—heaven. Wait till you taste it.

BOY: But I don't drink.

MAN: Drink! This isn't drink! Real amontillado is sunshine and orange groves—it's the Mediterranean and blue moonlight and—love? Have you ever been in love?

BOY: No.

MAN: Never in love with—a woman?

BOY: No—not really.

MAN: What do you mean—really?

BOY: Just—that.

MAN: Ah! [*Makes sign to* WAITER] Two—you know what I want—Two.

[WAITER *goes to the bar.*]

MAN: [*At Table* 1] Well, are you going through with it, or ain't you?

WOMAN: That's what I want to do—go through with it.

MAN: But you can't.

WOMAN: Why can't I?

MAN: How can yuh? [*Silence*] It's nothing—most women don't think anything about it—they just—Bert told me a doctor to go to—gave me the address—

WOMAN: Don't talk about it!

MAN: Got to talk about it—you got to get out of this. [*Silence*—MAN *makes sign to* WAITER.] What you having?

WOMAN: Nothing—I don't want anything. I had enough.

MAN: Do you good. The same?

WOMAN: I suppose so.

MAN: [*Makes sign "2" to* WAITER] The same.

[WAITER *goes to the bar.*]

1ST MAN: [*At Table 3*] I'm going to beat it.

2ND MAN: Oh say, listen! I'm counting on you to take the other one off my hands.

1ST MAN: I'm going to beat it.

2ND MAN: For the love of Mike have a heart! Listen—as a favor to me—I got to be home by six—I promised my wife—sure. That don't leave me no time at all if we got to hang around—entertain some dame. You got to take her off my hands.

1ST MAN: Maybe she won't fall for me.

2ND MAN: Sure she'll fall for you! They all fall for you— even my wife likes you—tries to kid herself it's your brave exploits, but I know what it is—sure she'll fall for you.

[*Enter two girls—*TELEPHONE GIRL *and* YOUNG WOMAN.]

GIRL: [*Coming to Table*] Hello—

2ND MAN: [*Grouch*] Good night.

GIRL: Good night? What's eatin' yuh?

2ND MAN: [*Same*] Nothin's eatin' me—thought somethin' musta swallowed you.

GIRL: Why?

2ND MAN: You're late!

GIRL: [*Unimpressed*] Oh—[*Brushing it aside*]—Mrs. Jones—Mr. Smith.

2ND MAN: Meet my friend, Mr. Roe. [*They all sit. To the* WAITER] The same, and two more.

[WAITER *goes.*]

GIRL: So we kept you waiting, did we?

2ND MAN: Only about an hour.

YOUNG WOMAN: Was it that long?

2ND MAN: We been here that long—ain't we, Dick?

1ST MAN: Just about, Harry.

2ND MAN: For the love of God what delayed yuh?

GIRL: Tell Helen that one.

2ND MAN: [*To* YOUNG WOMAN] The old Irish woman that
went to her first race? Bet on the skate that came in
last—she went up to the jockey and asked him, "For
the love of God, what delayed yuh?"
[*All laugh.*]

YOUNG WOMAN: Why, that's kinda funny!

2ND MAN: Kinda!—What do you mean kinda?

YOUNG WOMAN: I just mean there are not many of 'em
that are funny at all.

2ND MAN: Not if you haven't heard the funny ones.

YOUNG WOMAN: Oh I've heard 'em all.

1ST MAN: Not a laugh in a carload, eh?

GIRL: Got a cigarette?

2ND MAN: [*With package*] One of these?

GIRL: [*Taking one*] Uhhuh.
[*He offers the package to* YOUNG WOMAN.]

YOUNG WOMAN: [*Taking one*] Uhhuh.

2ND MAN: [*To* 1ST MAN] One of these?

1ST MAN: [*Showing his own package*] Thanks—I like
these. [*He lights* YOUNG WOMAN's *cigarette.*]

2ND MAN: [*Lighting* GIRL's *cigarette*] Well—baby—how
they comin', huh?

GIRL: Couldn't be better.

2ND MAN: How's every little thing?

GIRL: Just great.

2ND MAN: Miss me?

GIRL: I'll say so—when did you get in?

2ND MAN: Just a coupla hours ago.

GIRL: Miss me?

2ND MAN: Did I? You don't know the half of it.

YOUNG WOMAN: [*Interrupting restlessly*] Can we dance
here?

2ND MAN: Not here.

YOUNG WOMAN: Where do we go from here?

2ND MAN: Where do we go from here! You just got here!

1ST MAN: What's the hurry?

2ND MAN: What's the rush?

YOUNG WOMAN: I don't know.

GIRL: Helen wants to dance.

YOUNG WOMAN: I just want to keep moving.

1ST MAN: [*Smiling*] You want to keep moving, huh?

2ND MAN: You must be one of those restless babies! Where do we go from here!

YOUNG WOMAN: It's only some days—I want to keep moving.

1ST MAN: You want to keep moving, huh? [*He is staring at her smilingly.*]

YOUNG WOMAN: [*Nods*] Uhhuh.

1ST MAN: [*Quietly*] Stick around a while.

2ND MAN: Where do we go from here! Say, what kind of a crowd do you run with, anyway?

GIRL: Helen don't run with any crowd—do you, Helen?

YOUNG WOMAN: [*Embarrassed*] No.

1ST MAN: Well, I'm not a crowd—run with me.

2ND MAN: [*Gratified*] All set, huh?—Dick was about ready to beat it.

1ST MAN: That's before I met the little lady.

[WAITER *serves drinks.*]

1ST MAN: Here's how.

2ND MAN: Here's to you.

GIRL: Here's looking at you.

YOUNG WOMAN: Here's—happy days.

[*They all drink.*]

1ST MAN: That's good stuff!

2ND MAN: Off a boat.

1ST MAN: Off a boat?

2ND MAN: They get all their stuff here—off a boat.

GIRL: That's what *they* say.

2ND MAN: No! Sure! Sure they do! Sure!

GIRL: It's all right with me.

2ND MAN: But they do! Sure!

GIRL: I believe you, darling!

2ND MAN: Did you miss me?

GIRL: Uhhuh. [*Affirmative*]

2ND MAN: Any other daddies?

GIRL: Uhhuh. [*Negative*]

2ND MAN: Love any daddy but daddy?

GIRL: Uhhuh. [*Negative*]

2ND MAN: Let's beat it!

GIRL: [*A little self-conscious before* YOUNG WOMAN] We just got here.

2ND MAN: Don't I know it—Come on!

GIRL: But—[*Indicates* YOUNG WOMAN]

2ND MAN: [*Not understanding*] They're all set—aren't you?

1ST MAN: [*To* YOUNG WOMAN] Are we?
[*She doesn't answer.*]

2ND MAN: I got to be out to the house by six—come on—[*Rising—to* GIRL] Come on, kid—let's us beat it! [GIRL *indicates* YOUNG WOMAN.] [*Now understanding—very elaborate*] Business is business, you know! I got a lot to do yet this afternoon—thought you might go along with me—help me out—how about it?

GIRL: [*Rising, her dignity preserved*] Sure—I'll go along with you—help you out.
[*Both rise.*]

2ND MAN: All right with you folks?

1ST MAN: All right with me.

2ND MAN: All right with you? [*To* YOUNG WOMAN]

YOUNG WOMAN: All right with me.

2ND MAN: Come on, kid. [*They rise.*] Where's the damage?

1ST MAN: Go on!

2ND MAN: No!

1ST MAN: Go on!

2ND MAN: I'll match you.

YOUNG WOMAN: Heads win!

GIRL: Heads I win—tails you lose.

2ND MAN: [*Impatiently*] He's matching me.

1ST MAN: Am I matching you or you matching me?

2ND MAN: I'm matching you. [*They match.*] You're stung!

1ST MAN: [*Contentedly*] Not so you can notice it. [*Smiles at* YOUNG WOMAN]

GIRL: That's for you, Helen.

2ND MAN: She ain't dumb! Come on.

GIRL: [*To* 1ST MAN]. You be nice to her now. She's very fastidious.—Goodbye.
[*Exit* 2ND MAN *and* GIRL.]

YOUNG WOMAN: I know what business is like.

1ST MAN: You do—do yuh?

YOUNG WOMAN: I used to be a business girl myself before—

1ST MAN: Before what?

YOUNG WOMAN: Before I quit.

1ST MAN: What did you quit for?

YOUNG WOMAN: I just quit.

1ST MAN: You're married, huh?

YOUNG WOMAN: Yes—I am.

1ST MAN: All right with me.

YOUNG WOMAN: Some men don't seem to like a woman
after she's married—

[WAITER *comes to the table.*]

1ST MAN: What's the difference?

YOUNG WOMAN: Depends on the man, I guess.

1ST MAN: Depends on the woman, I guess. [*To* WAITER,
makes sign of "2"] The same.

[WAITER *goes to the bar.*]

MAN: [*At Table 1*] It don't amount to nothing. God! Most
women just—

WOMAN: I know—I know—I know.

MAN: They don't think nothing of it. They just—

WOMAN: I know—I know—I know.

[*Re-enter* 2ND MAN *and* GIRL. *They go to Table* 3.]

2ND MAN: Say, I forgot—I want you to do something for
me, will yuh?

1ST MAN: Sure—what is it?

2ND MAN: I want you to telephone me out home tomorrow—and ask me to come into town—will yuh?

1ST MAN: Sure—why not?

2ND MAN: You know—business—get me?

1ST MAN: I get you.

2ND MAN: I've worked the telegraph gag to death—and
my wife likes you.

1ST MAN: What's your number?

2ND MAN: I'll write it down for you.
[*Writes*]

1ST MAN: How is your wife?

2ND MAN: She's fine.

1ST MAN: And the kid?

2ND MAN: Great. [*Hands him the card. To girl*] Come on,
kid. [*Turns back to* YOUNG WOMAN] Get this bird to
tell you about himself.

GIRL: Keep him from it.

2ND MAN: Get him to tell you how he killed a couple a spig down in Mexico.

GIRL: You been in Mexico?

2ND MAN: He just came up from there.

GIRL: Can you teach us the tango?

YOUNG WOMAN: You killed a man?

2ND MAN: Two of 'em! With a bottle! Get him to tell you— with a bottle. Come on, kid. Goodbye.

[*Exit* 2ND MAN *and* GIRL.]

YOUNG WOMAN: Why did you?

1ST MAN: What?

YOUNG WOMAN: Kill 'em?

1ST MAN: To get free.

YOUNG WOMAN: Oh.

MAN: [*At Table* 2] You really must taste this—just taste it. It's a real amontillado, you know.

BOY: Where do they get it here?

MAN: It's always down the side streets one finds the real pleasures, don't you think?

BOY: I don't know.

MAN: Learn. Come, taste this! Amontillado! Or don't you like amontillado?

BOY: I don't know. I never had any before.

MAN: Your first taste! How I envy you! Come, taste it! Taste it! And die.

[BOY *tastes wine—finds it disappointing.*]

MAN: [*Gilding it*] Poe was a lover of amontillado. He returns to it continually, you remember—or are you a lover of Poe?

BOY: I've read a lot of him.

MAN: But are you a lover?

1ST MAN: [*At Table* 3] There were a bunch of bandidos— bandits, you know, took me into the hills—holding me there—what was I to do? I got the two birds that guarded me drunk one night, and then I filled the empty bottle with small stones—and let 'em have it!

YOUNG WOMAN: Oh!

1ST MAN: I had to get free, didn't I? I let 'em have it—
YOUNG WOMAN: Oh—then what did you do?
1ST MAN: Then I beat it.
YOUNG WOMAN: Where to—?
1ST MAN: Right here. [*Pause*] Glad?
YOUNG WOMAN: [*Nods*] Yes.
1ST MAN: [*Makes sign to* WAITER *of* "2"] The same.
   [WAITER *goes to bar.*]

MAN: [*At Table 1*] You're just scared because this is the
   first time and—
WOMAN: I'm not scared.
MAN: Then what are you for Christ's sake?
WOMAN: I'm not scared. I want it—I want to have it—that
   ain't being scared, is it?
MAN: It's being goofy.
WOMAN: I don't care.
MAN: What about your folks?
WOMAN: I don't care.
MAN: What about your job? [*Silence*] You got to keep your
   job, haven't you? [*Silence*] Haven't you?
WOMAN: I suppose so.
MAN: Well—there you are!
WOMAN: [*Silence—then*] All right—let's go now— You
   got the address?
MAN: Now you're coming to.
   [*They get up and go off. Exit* MAN *and* WOMAN.]

YOUNG WOMAN: [*At Table 3*] A bottle like that? [*She picks
   it up.*]
1ST MAN: Yeah—filled with pebbles.
YOUNG WOMAN: What kind of pebbles?
1ST MAN: Pebbles! Off the ground.
YOUNG WOMAN: Oh.
1ST MAN: Necessity, you know, mother of invention. [*As*
   YOUNG WOMAN *handles the bottle*] Ain't a bad weapon—
   first you got a sledge hammer—then you got a knife.
YOUNG WOMAN: Oh. [*Puts bottle down*]
1ST MAN: Women don't like knives, do they? [*Pours
   drink*]

YOUNG WOMAN: No.

1ST MAN: Don't mind a hammer so much, though, do they?

YOUNG WOMAN: No—

1ST MAN: I didn't like it myself—any of it—but I had to get free, didn't I? Sure I had to get free, didn't I? [*Drinks*] Now I'm damn glad I did.

YOUNG WOMAN: Why?

1ST MAN: You know why. [*He puts his hand over hers.*]

MAN: [*At Table 2*] Let's go to my rooms—and I'll show them to you—I have a first edition of Verlaine that will simply make your mouth water. [*They stand up.*] Here—there's just a sip at the bottom of my glass— [BOY *takes it.*] That last sip that's sweetest—Wasn't it?

BOY: [*Laughs*] And I always thought that was dregs. [*Exit* MAN *followed by* BOY.]

[*At Table 3. The* MAN *is holding her hand across the table.*]

YOUNG WOMAN: When you put your hand over mine! When you just touch me!

1ST MAN: Yeah? [*Pause*] Come on, kid, let's go!

YOUNG WOMAN: Where?

1ST MAN: You haven't been around much, have you, kid?

YOUNG WOMAN: No.

1ST MAN: I could tell that just to look at you.

YOUNG WOMAN: You could?

1ST MAN: Sure I could. What are you running around with a girl like that other one for?

YOUNG WOMAN: I don't know. She seems to have a good time.

1ST MAN: So that's it?

YOUNG WOMAN: Don't she?

1ST MAN: Don't you?

YOUNG WOMAN: No.

1ST MAN: Never?

YOUNG WOMAN: Never.

1ST MAN: What's the matter?

YOUNG WOMAN: Nothing—just me, I guess.

1ST MAN: You're all right.

YOUNG WOMAN: Am I?

1ST MAN: Sure. You just haven't met the right guy—that's all—a girl like you—you got to meet the right guy.

YOUNG WOMAN: I know.

1ST MAN: You're different from girls like that other one—any guy'll do her. You're different.

YOUNG WOMAN: I guess I am.

1ST MAN: You didn't fall for that business gag—did you—when they went off?

YOUNG WOMAN: Well, I thought they wanted to be alone probably, but—

1ST MAN: And how!

YOUNG WOMAN: Oh—so that's it.

1ST MAN: That's it. Come along—let's go—

YOUNG WOMAN: Oh, I couldn't! Like this?

1ST MAN: Don't you like me?

YOUNG WOMAN: Yes.

1ST MAN: Then what's the matter?

YOUNG WOMAN: Do—you—like me?

1ST MAN: Like yuh? You don't know the half of it—listen—you know what you seem like to me?

YOUNG WOMAN: What?

1ST MAN: An angel. Just like an angel.

YOUNG WOMAN: I do?

1ST MAN: That's what I said! Let's go!

YOUNG WOMAN: Where?

1ST MAN: Where do you live?

YOUNG WOMAN: Oh, we can't go to my place.

1ST MAN: Then come to my place.

YOUNG WOMAN: Oh I couldn't—is it far?

1ST MAN: Just a step—come on—

YOUNG WOMAN: Oh I couldn't—what is it—a room?

1ST MAN: No—an apartment—a one-room apartment.

YOUNG WOMAN: That's different.

1ST MAN: On the ground floor—no one will see you—coming or going.

YOUNG WOMAN: [Getting up] I couldn't.

1ST MAN: [Rises] Wait a minute—I got to pay the damage—and I'll get a bottle of something to take along.

YOUNG WOMAN: No—don't.

1ST MAN: Why not?

YOUNG WOMAN: Well—don't bring any pebbles.

1ST MAN: Say—forget that! Will you?

YOUNG WOMAN: I just meant I don't think I'll need any-thing to drink.

1ST MAN: [*Leaning to her eagerly*] You like me—don't you, kid?

YOUNG WOMAN: Do you me?

1ST MAN: Wait!

[*He goes to the bar. She remains, her hands out-stretched on the table staring ahead. Enter a* MAN *and a* GIRL. *They go to one of the empty tables. The* WAITER *goes to them.*]

MAN: [*To* GIRL] What do you want?

GIRL: Same old thing.

MAN: [*To the* WAITER] The usual. [*Makes a sign "2"*]

[*The* 1ST MAN *crosses to* YOUNG WOMAN *with a wrapped bottle under his arm. She rises and starts out with him. As they pass the piano, he stops and puts in a nickel—the music starts as they exit. The scene blacks out.*]

[*The music of the electric piano continues until the lights go up for Episode Six, and the music has become the music of a hand organ, very very faint.*]

EPISODE SIX

Intimate

SCENE:
  a dark room.

SOUNDS:
  a hand organ; footbeats, of passing feet.

CHARACTERS:
  MAN,
  YOUNG WOMAN.

AT RISE:
  Darkness. Nothing can be discerned. From the outside comes the sound of a hand organ, very faint, and the irregular rhythm of passing feet. The hand organ is playing Cielito Lindo, *that Spanish song that has been on every hand organ lately.*

MAN: You're awful still, honey. What you thinking about?
WOMAN: About sea shells. [*The sound of her voice is beautiful.*]
MAN: Sheshells? Gee! I can't say it!
WOMAN: When I was little my grandmother used to have a big pink sea shell on the mantel behind the stove. When we'd go to visit her they'd let me hold it, and listen. That's what I was thinking about now.
MAN: Yeah?
WOMAN: You can hear the sea in 'em, you know.
MAN: Yeah, I know.

WOMAN: I wonder why that is?

MAN: Search me. [*Pause*]

WOMAN: You going?
  [*He has moved.*]

MAN: No. I just want a cigarette.

WOMAN: [*Glad, relieved*] Oh.

MAN: Want one?

WOMAN: No. [*Taking the match*] Let me light it for you.

MAN: You got might pretty hands, honey. [*The match is out.*] This little pig went to market. This little pig stayed home. This little pig went—

WOMAN: [*Laughs*] Diddle diddle dee.
  [*Laughs again*]

MAN: You got awful pretty hands.

WOMAN: I used to have. But I haven't taken much care of them lately. I will now— [*Pause. The music gets clearer.*] What's that?

MAN: What?

WOMAN: That music?

MAN: A dago hand organ. I gave him two bits the first day I got here—so he comes every day.

WOMAN: I mean—what's that he's playing?

MAN: *Cielito Lindo.*

WOMAN: What does that mean?

MAN: Little Heaven.

WOMAN: Little Heaven?

MAN: That's what lovers call each other in Spain.

WOMAN: Spain's where all the castles are, ain't it?

MAN: Yeah.

WOMAN: Little Heaven—sing it!

MAN: [*Singing to the music of the hand organ*] De la sierra morena viene, bajando viene, bajando; un par de ojitos negros—cielito lindo—da contrabando.

WOMAN: What does it mean?

MAN: From the high dark mountains.

WOMAN: From the high dark mountains—?

MAN: Oh it doesn't mean anything. It doesn't make sense. It's love. [*Taking up the song*] Ay-ay-ay-ay.

WOMAN: I know what that means.

MAN: What?

WOMAN: Ay-ay-ay-ay.
  [*They laugh.*]

MAN: [*Taking up the song*] Canta non llores—Sing don't cry—

WOMAN: [*Taking up song*] La-la-la-la-la-la-la-la-la-la—Little Heaven!

MAN: You got a nice voice, honey.

WOMAN: Have I?
[*Laughs—tickles him*]

MAN: You bet you have—hey!

WOMAN: [*Laughing*] You ticklish?

MAN: Sure I am! Hey! [*They laugh.*] Go on, honey, sing something.

WOMAN: I couldn't.

MAN: Go on—you got a fine voice.

WOMAN: [*Laughs and sings*] Hey, diddle, diddle, the cat and the fiddle,
The cow jumped over the moon
The little dog laughed to see the sport
And the dish ran away with the spoon—
[*Both laugh.*] I never thought that had any sense before—now I get it.

MAN: You got me beat.

WOMAN: It's you and me.—La—lalalalalala—lalalalalala—Little Heaven. You're the dish and I'm the spoon.

MAN: You're a little spoon all right.

WOMAN: And I guess I'm the little cow that jumped over the moon. [*A pause*] Do you believe in sorta guardian angels?

MAN: What?

WOMAN: Guardian angels?

MAN: I don't know. Maybe.

WOMAN: I do. [*Taking up the song again*] Lalalalala-lalalalala-lalalala—Little Heaven. [*Talking*] There must be something that looks out for you and brings you your happiness, at last—look at us! How did we both happen to go to that place today if there wasn't something!

MAN: Maybe you're right.

WOMAN: Look at us!

MAN: Everything's us to you, kid—ain't it?

WOMAN: Ain't it?

MAN: All right with me.

WOMAN: We belong together! We belong together! And we're going to stick together, ain't we?

MAN: Sing something else.

WOMAN: I tell you I can't sing!

MAN: Sure you can!

WOMAN: I tell you I hadn't thought of singing since I was a little bit of a girl.

MAN: Well sing anyway.

WOMAN: [*Singing*] And every little wavelet had its night cap on—its night cap on—its night cap on—and every little wave had its night cap on—so very early in the morning. [*Talking*] Did you used to sing that when you were a little kid?

MAN: Nope.

WOMAN: Didn't you? We used to—in the first grade—little kids—we used to go round and round in a ring—and flop our hands up and down—supposed to be the waves. I remember it used to confuse me—because we did just the same thing to be little angels.

MAN: Yeah?

WOMAN: You know why I came here?

MAN: I can make a good guess.

WOMAN: Because you told me I looked like an angel to you! That's why I came.

MAN: Jeez, honey, all women look like angels to me—all white women. I ain't been seeing nothing but Indians, you know, for the last couple a years. Gee, when I got off the boat here the other day—and saw all the women—gee I pretty near went crazy—talk about looking like angels—why—

WOMAN: You've had a lot of women, haven't you?

MAN: No so many—real ones.

WOMAN: Did you—like any of 'em—better than me?

MAN: Nope—there wasn't one of 'em any sweeter than you, honey—not as sweet—no—not as sweet.

WOMAN: I like to hear you say it. Say it again—

MAN: [*Protesting good humoredly*] Oh—

WOMAN: Go on—tell me again!

MAN: Here! [*Kisses her*] Does that tell you?

WOMAN: Yes. [*Pause*] We're going to stick together—always—aren't we?

MAN: [*Honestly*] I'll have to be moving on, kid—some day, you know.

WOMAN: When?

MAN: Quien sabe?

WOMAN: What does that mean?

MAN: Quien sabe? You got to learn that, kid, if you're figuring on coming with me. It's the answer to everything—below the Rio Grande.

WOMAN: What does it mean?

MAN: It means—who knows?

WOMAN: Keen sabe?

MAN: Yep—don't forget it—now.

WOMAN: I'll never forget it!

MAN: Quien sabe?

WOMAN: And I'll never get to use it.

MAN: Quien sabe.

WOMAN: I'll never get—below the Rio Grande—I'll never get out of here.

MAN: Quien sabe.

WOMAN: [*Change of mood*] That's right! Keen sabe? Who knows?

MAN: That's the stuff.

WOMAN: You must like it down there.

MAN: I can't live anywhere else—for long.

WOMAN: Why not?

MAN: Oh—you're free down there! You're free!

[*A street light is lit outside. The outlines of a window take form against this light. There are bars across it, and from outside it, the sidewalk cuts across almost at the top. It is a basement room. The constant going and coming of passing feet, mostly feet of couples, can be dimly seen. Inside, on the ledge, there is a lily blooming in a bowl of rocks and water.*]

WOMAN: What's that?

MAN: Just the street light going on.

WOMAN: Is it as late as that?

MAN: Late as what?

WOMAN: Dark.

MAN: It's been dark for hours—didn't you know that?

WOMAN: No!—I must go! [*Rises*]

MAN: Wait—the moon will be up in a little while—full moon.

WOMAN: It isn't that! I'm late! I must go! [*She comes into the light. She wears a white chemise that might be the*

*tunic of a dancer, and as she comes into the light she
fastens about her waist a little skirt. She really wears
almost exactly the clothes that women wear now, but
the finesse of their cut, and the grace and ease with
which she puts them on, must turn this episode of her
dressing into a personification, an idealization of a
woman clothing herself. All her gestures must be un-
conscious, innocent, relaxed, sure and full of natural
grace. As she sits facing the window pulling on a stock-
ing]* What's that?

MAN: What?

WOMAN: On the window ledge.

MAN: A flower.

WOMAN: Who gave it to you?

MAN: Nobody gave it to me. I bought it.

WOMAN: For yourself?

MAN: Yeah—why not?

WOMAN: I don't know.

MAN: In Chinatown—made me think of Frisco where I
was a kid—so I bought it.

WOMAN: Is that where you were born—Frisco?

MAN: Yep. Twin Peaks.

WOMAN: What's that?

MAN: A couple hills—together.

WOMAN: One for you and one for me.

MAN: I bet you'd like Frisco.

WOMAN: I know a woman went out there once!

MAN: The bay and the hills! Jeez, that's the life! Every
Saturday we used to cross the Bay—get a couple nags
and just ride—over the hills. One would have a blanket
on the saddle—the other, the grub. At night, we'd make
a little fire and eat—and then roll up in the old blanket
and—

WOMAN: Who? Who was with you?

MAN: *[Indifferently]* Anybody. *[Enthusiastically]* Jeez,
that dry old grass out there smells good at night—full
of tar weed—you know—

WOMAN: Is that a good smell?

MAN: Tar weed? Didn't you ever smell it? *[She shakes
her head, "No."]* Sure it's a good smell! The Bay and
the hills. *[She goes to the mirror of the dresser, to*

finish dressing. She has only a dress to put on that is in one piece—with one fastening on the side. Before slipping it on, she stands before the mirror and stretches. Appreciatively but indifferently] You look in good shape, kid. A couple of months riding over the mountains with me, you'd be great.

WOMAN: Can I?

MAN: What?

WOMAN: Some day—ride mountains with you?

MAN: Ride mountains? Ride donkeys!

WOMAN: It's the same thing!—with you!—Can I—some day? The high dark mountains?

MAN: Who knows?

WOMAN: It must be great!

MAN: You ever been off like that, kid?—high up? On top of the world?

WOMAN: Yes.

MAN: When?

WOMAN: Today.

MAN: You're pretty sweet.

WOMAN: I never knew anything like this way! I never knew that I could feel like this! So,—so purified! Don't laugh at me!

MAN: I ain't laughing, honey.

WOMAN: Purified.

MAN: It's a hell of a word—but I know what you mean. That's the way it is—sometimes.

WOMAN: [*She puts on a little hat, then turns to him*] Well—goodbye.

MAN: Aren't you forgetting something? [*Rises*]

WOMAN: [*She looks toward him, then throws her head slowly back, lifts her right arm—this gesture that is in so many statues of women—Volupte. He comes out of the shadow, puts his arm around her, kisses her. Her head and arm go further back,—then she brings her arm around with a wide encircling gesture, her hand closes over his head, her fingers spread. Her fingers are protective, clutching. When he releases her, her eyes are shining with tears. She turns away. She looks back at him—and the room—and her eyes fasten on the lily.*] Can I have that?

MAN: Sure—why not?

[*She takes it—goes. As she opens the door, the music is louder. The scene blacks out.*]

WOMAN: Goodbye. And— [*Hesitates*] And—thank you.

CURTAIN

[*The music continues until the Curtain goes up for Episode Seven. It goes up on silence.*]

EPISODE SEVEN

Domestic

SCENE:
  a sitting room:
  a divan,
  a telephone,
  a window.

CHARACTERS:
  HUSBAND,
  YOUNG WOMAN.

[*They are seated on opposite ends of the divan. They are both reading papers—to themselves.*]

HUSBAND: Record production.

YOUNG WOMAN: Girl turns on gas.

HUSBAND: Sale hits a million—

YOUNG WOMAN: Woman leaves all for love—

HUSBAND: Market trend steady—

YOUNG WOMAN: Young wife disappears—

HUSBAND: Owns a life interest— [*Phone rings.* YOUNG WOMAN *looks toward it.*] That's for me. [*In phone*] Hello—oh hello, A.B. It's all settled?—Everything signed? Good. Good! Tell R.A. to call me up. [*Hangs up phone—to* YOUNG WOMAN] Well, it's all settled. They signed!—aren't you interested? Aren't you going to ask me?

YOUNG WOMAN: [*By rote*] Did you put it over?

HUSBAND: Sure I put it over.

YOUNG WOMAN: Did you swing it?

HUSBAND: Sure I swung it.

YOUNG WOMAN: Did they come through?

HUSBAND: Sure they came through.

YOUNG WOMAN: Did they sign?

HUSBAND: I'll say they signed.

YOUNG WOMAN: On the dotted line?

HUSBAND: On the dotted line.

YOUNG WOMAN: The property's yours?

HUSBAND: The property's mine. I'll put a first mortgage. I'll put a second mortgage and the property's mine. Happy?

YOUNG WOMAN: [*By rote*] Happy.

HUSBAND: [*Going to her*] The property's mine! It's not all that's mine! [*Pinching her cheek—happy and playful*] I got a first mortgage on her—I got a second mortgage on her—and she's mine! [YOUNG WOMAN *pulls away swiftly.*] What's the matter?

YOUNG WOMAN: Nothing—what?

HUSBAND: You flinched when I touched you.

YOUNG WOMAN: No.

HUSBAND: You haven't done that in a long time.

YOUNG WOMAN: Haven't I?

HUSBAND: You used to do it every time I touched you.

YOUNG WOMAN: Did I?

HUSBAND: Didn't know that, did you?

YOUNG WOMAN: [*Unexpectedly*] Yes. Yes, I know it.

HUSBAND: Just purity.

YOUNG WOMAN: No.

HUSBAND: Oh, I liked it. Purity.

YOUNG WOMAN: No.

HUSBAND: You're one of the purest women that ever lived.

YOUNG WOMAN: I'm just like anybody else only—[*Stops*]

HUSBAND: Only what?

YOUNG WOMAN: [*A pause*] Nothing.

HUSBAND: It must be something.

[*Phone rings. She gets up and goes to window.*]

HUSBAND: [*In phone*] Hello—hello, R.A.—well, I put it over—yeah, I swung it—sure they came through—did they sign? On the dotted line! The property's mine. I made the proposition. I sold them the idea. Now watch me. Tell D.D. to call me up. [*Hangs up*] That was R.A. What are you looking at?

YOUNG WOMAN: Nothing.

HUSBAND: You must be looking at something.

YOUNG WOMAN: Nothing—the moon.

HUSBAND: The moon's something, isn't it?

YOUNG WOMAN: Yes.

HUSBAND: What's it doing?

YOUNG WOMAN: Nothing.

HUSBAND: It must be doing something.

YOUNG WOMAN: It's moving—moving— [*She comes down restlessly.*]

HUSBAND: Pull down the shade, my dear.

YOUNG WOMAN: Why?

HUSBAND: People can look in. [*Phone rings.*] Hello— hello D.D.—Yes—I put it over—they came across—I put it over on them—yep—yep—yep—I'll say I am— yep—on the dotted line— Now you watch me—yep. Yep, yep. Tell B.M. to phone me. [*Hangs up*] That was D.D. [*To* YOUNG WOMAN *who has come down to davenport and picked up a paper*] Aren't you listening?

YOUNG WOMAN: I'm reading.

HUSBAND: What are you reading?

YOUNG WOMAN: Nothing.

HUSBAND: Must be something. [*He sits and picks up his paper.*]

YOUNG WOMAN: [*Reading*] Prisoner escapes—lifer breaks jail—shoots way to freedom—

HUSBAND: Don't read that stuff—listen—here's a first rate editorial. I agree with this. I agree absolutely. Are you listening?

YOUNG WOMAN: I'm listening.

HUSBAND: [*Importantly*] All men are born free and entitled to the pursuit of happiness. [YOUNG WOMAN *gets up.*] My, you're nervous tonight.

YOUNG WOMAN: I try not to be.

HUSBAND: You inherit that from your mother. She was in the office today.

YOUNG WOMAN: Was she?

HUSBAND: To get her allowance.

YOUNG WOMAN: Oh—

HUSBAND: Don't you know it's the *first*.

YOUNG WOMAN: Poor Ma.

HUSBAND: What would she do without me?

YOUNG WOMAN: I know. You're very good.

HUSBAND: One thing—she's grateful.

YOUNG WOMAN: Poor Ma—poor Ma.

HUSBAND: She's got to have care.

YOUNG WOMAN: Yes. She's got to have care.

HUSBAND: A mother's a very precious thing—a good mother.

YOUNG WOMAN: [*Excitedly*] I try to be a good mother.

HUSBAND: Of course you're a good mother.

YOUNG WOMAN: I try! I try!

HUSBAND: A mother's a very precious thing— [*Resuming his paper*] And a child's a very precious thing. Precious jewels.

YOUNG WOMAN: [*Reading*] Sale of jewels and precious stones. [YOUNG WOMAN *puts her hand to throat.*]

HUSBAND: What's the matter?

YOUNG WOMAN: I feel as though I were drowning.

HUSBAND: Drowning?

YOUNG WOMAN: With stones around my neck.

HUSBAND: You just imagine that.

YOUNG WOMAN: Stifling.

HUSBAND: You don't breathe deep enough—breathe now—look at me. [*He breathes.*] Breath is life. Life is breath.

YOUNG WOMAN: [*Suddenly*] And what is death?

HUSBAND: [*Smartly*] Just—no breath!

YOUNG WOMAN: [*To herself*] Just no breath. [*Takes up paper*]

HUSBAND: All right?

YOUNG WOMAN: All right.

HUSBAND: [*Reads as she stares at her paper. Looks up after a pause*] I feel cold air, my dear.

YOUNG WOMAN: Cold air?

HUSBAND: Close the window, will you?

YOUNG WOMAN: It isn't open.

HUSBAND: Don't you feel cold air?

YOUNG WOMAN: No—you just imagine it.

HUSBAND: I never imagine anything. [YOUNG WOMAN *is staring at the paper.*] What are you reading?

YOUNG WOMAN: Nothing.

HUSBAND: You must be reading something.

YOUNG WOMAN: Woman finds husband dead.

HUSBAND: [*Uninterested*] Oh. [*Interested*] Here's a man says "I owe my success to a yeast cake a day—my digestion is good—I sleep very well—and— [*His wife gets up, goes toward door.*] Where are you going?

YOUNG WOMAN: No place.

HUSBAND: You must be going some place.

YOUNG WOMAN: Just—to bed.

HUSBAND: It isn't eleven yet. Wait.

YOUNG WOMAN: Wait?

HUSBAND: It's only ten-forty-six—wait! [*Holds out his arms to her*] Come here!

YOUNG WOMAN: [*Takes a step toward him—recoils*] Oh—— I want to go away!

HUSBAND: Away? Where?

YOUNG WOMAN: Anywhere—away.

HUSBAND: Why, what's the matter?

YOUNG WOMAN: I'm scared.

HUSBAND: What of?

YOUNG WOMAN: I can't sleep—I haven't slept.

HUSBAND: That's nothing.

YOUNG WOMAN: And the moon—when it's a full moon.

HUSBAND: That's nothing.

YOUNG WOMAN: I can't sleep.

HUSBAND: Of course not. It's the light.

YOUNG WOMAN: I don't see it! I feel it! I'm afraid.

HUSBAND: [*Kindly*] Nonsense—come here.

YOUNG WOMAN: I want to go away.

HUSBAND: But I can't get away now.

YOUNG WOMAN: Alone!

HUSBAND: You've never been away alone.

YOUNG WOMAN: I know.

HUSBAND: What would you do?

YOUNG WOMAN: Maybe I'd sleep.

HUSBAND: Now you wait.

YOUNG WOMAN: [*Desperately*] Wait?

HUSBAND: We'll take a trip—we'll go to Europe—I'll get my watch—I'll get my Swiss watch—I've always wanted a Swiss watch that I bought right there—isn't that funny? Wait—wait. [YOUNG WOMAN *comes down to davenport—sits.* HUSBAND *resumes his paper.*] Another revolution below the Rio Grande.

YOUNG WOMAN: Below the Rio Grande?

HUSBAND: Yes—another—

YOUNG WOMAN: Anyone—hurt?

HUSBAND: No.

YOUNG WOMAN: Any prisoners?

HUSBAND: No.

YOUNG WOMAN: All free?

HUSBAND: All free.

[*He resumes his paper.* YOUNG WOMAN *sits, staring ahead of her—The music of the hand-organ sounds off very dimly, playing* Cielito Lindo. *Voices begin to sing it—'Ay-ay-ay-ay'—and then the words—the music and voices get louder.*]

THE VOICE OF HER LOVER: They were a bunch of bandidos—bandits you know—holding me there—what was I to do—I had to get free—didn't I? I had to get free—

VOICES: Free—free—free—

LOVER: I filled an empty bottle with small stones—

VOICES: Stones—stones—precious stones—millstones—stones—stones—millstones—

LOVER: Just a bottle with small stones.

VOICES: Stones—stones—small stones—

LOVER: You only need a bottle with small stones.

VOICES: Stones—stones—small stones—

VOICE OF A HUCKSTER: Stones for sale—stones—stones—small stones—precious stones—

VOICES: Stones—stones—precious stones—

LOVER: Had to get free, didn't I? Free?

VOICES: Free? Free?

LOVER: Quien sabe? Who knows? Who knows?

VOICES: Who'd know? Who'd know? Who'd know?

HUCKSTER: Stones—stones—small stones—big stones—millstones—cold stones—head stones—

VOICES: Head stones—head stones—head stones.

[*The music—the voices—mingle—increase—the* YOUNG WOMAN *flies from her chair and cries out in terror.*]

YOUNG WOMAN: Oh! Oh!

[*The scene blacks out—the music and the dim voices,* "Stones—stones—stones," *continue until the scene lights for Episode Eight:*]

EPISODE EIGHT

The Law

SCENE:
   courtroom.

SOUNDS:
   clicking of telegraph instruments offstage.

CHARACTERS:
   JUDGE,
   JURY,
   LAWYERS,
   SPECTATORS,
   REPORTERS,
   MESSENGER BOYS,
   LAW CLERKS,
   BAILIFF,
   COURT REPORTER,
   YOUNG WOMAN.

The words and movements of all these people except the YOUNG WOMAN *are routine—mechanical. Each is going through the motions of his own game.*

AT RISE:
   all assembled, except JUDGE.

   [*Enter* JUDGE.]
BAILIFF: [*Mumbling*] Hear ye—hear ye—hear ye!
   [*All rise.* JUDGE *sits. All sit.* LAWYER FOR DEFENSE *gets to his feet—He is the verbose, "eloquent"—typical crim-*

inal defense lawyer. JUDGE *signs to him to wait—turns to* LAW CLERKS, *grouped at foot of the bench*]

1ST CLERK: [*Handing up a paper—routine voice*] State versus Kling—stay of execution.

JUDGE: *Denied.*

[1ST CLERK *goes.*]

2ND CLERK: Bing vs. Ding—demurrer.

[JUDGE *signs.* 2ND CLERK *goes.*]

3RD CLERK: Case of John King—habeas corpus.

[JUDGE *signs.* 3RD CLERK *goes.* JUDGE *signs to* BAILIFF.]

BAILIFF: [*Mumbling*] People of the State of——versus Helen Jones.

JUDGE: [*To* LAWYER FOR THE DEFENSE] Defense ready to proceed?

LAWYER FOR DEFENSE: We're ready, your Honor.

JUDGE: Proceed.

LAWYER FOR DEFENSE: Helen Jones.

BAILIFF: HELEN JONES!

[YOUNG WOMAN *rises.*]

LAWYER FOR DEFENSE: Mrs. Jones, will you take the stand?

[YOUNG WOMAN *goes to witness stand.*]

1ST REPORTER: [*Writing rapidly*] The defense sprang a surprise at the opening of court this morning by putting the accused woman on the stand. The prosecution was swept off its feet by this daring defense strategy and— [*Instruments get louder.*]

2ND REPORTER: Trembling and scarcely able to stand, Helen Jones, accused murderess, had to be almost carried to the witness stand this morning when her lawyer—

BAILIFF: [*Mumbling—with Bible*] Do you swear to tell the truth, the whole truth and nothing but the truth—so help you God?

YOUNG WOMAN: I do.

JUDGE: You may sit.

[*She sits in witness chair.*]

COURT REPORTER: What is your name?

YOUNG WOMAN: Helen Jones.

COURT REPORTER: Your age?

YOUNG WOMAN: [*Hesitates—then*] Twenty-nine.

COURT REPORTER: Where do you live?

YOUNG WOMAN: In prison.

LAWYER FOR DEFENSE. This is my client's legal address. [*Hands a scrap of paper.*]

LAWYER FOR PROSECUTION: [*Jumping to his feet*] I object to this insinuation on the part of counsel on any illegality in the holding of this defendant in jail when the law—

LAWYER FOR DEFENSE: I made no such insinuation.

LAWYER FOR PROSECUTION: You implied it—

LAWYER FOR DEFENSE: I did not!

LAWYER FOR PROSECUTION: You're a—

JUDGE: Order!

BAILIFF: Order!

LAWYER FOR DEFENSE: Your Honor, I object to counsel's constant attempt to—

LAWYER FOR PROSECUTION: I protest—I—

JUDGE: Order!

BAILIFF: Order!

JUDGE: Proceed with the witness.

LAWYER FOR DEFENSE: Mrs. Jones, you are the widow of the late George H. Jones, are you not?

YOUNG WOMAN: Yes.

LAWYER FOR DEFENSE: How long were you married to the late George H. Jones before his demise?

YOUNG WOMAN: Six years.

LAWYER FOR DEFENSE: Six years! And it was a happy marriage, was it not? [YOUNG WOMAN *hesitates.*] Did you quarrel?

YOUNG WOMAN: No, sir.

LAWYER FOR DEFENSE: Then it was a happy marriage, wasn't it?

YOUNG WOMAN: Yes, sir.

LAWYER FOR DEFENSE: In those six years of married life with your late husband, the late George H. Jones, did you EVER have a quarrel?

YOUNG WOMAN: No, sir.

LAWYER FOR DEFENSE: Never one quarrel?

LAWYER FOR PROSECUTION: The witness has said—

LAWYER FOR DEFENSE: Six years without one quarrel! Six years! Gentlemen of the jury, I ask you to consider this fact! Six years of married life without a quarrel.

[*The* JURY *grins.*] I ask you to consider it seriously! Very seriously! Who of us—and this is not intended as any reflection on the sacred institution of marriage—no—but!

JUDGE: Proceed with your witness.

LAWYER FOR DEFENSE: You have one child—have you not, Mrs. Jones?

YOUNG WOMAN: Yes, sir.

LAWYER FOR DEFENSE: A little girl, is it not?

YOUNG WOMAN: Yes, sir.

LAWYER FOR DEFENSE: How old is she?

YOUNG WOMAN: She's five—past five.

LAWYER FOR DEFENSE: A little girl of past five. Since the demise of the late Mr. Jones you are the only parent she has living, are you not?

YOUNG WOMAN: Yes, sir.

LAWYER FOR DEFENSE: Before your marriage to the late Mr. Jones, you worked and supported your mother, did you not?

LAWYER FOR PROSECUTION: I object, your honor! Irrelevant—immaterial—and—

JUDGE: Objection sustained!

LAWYER FOR DEFENSE: In order to support your mother and yourself as a girl, you worked, did you not?

YOUNG WOMAN: Yes, sir.

LAWYER FOR DEFENSE: What did you do?

YOUNG WOMAN: I was a stenographer.

LAWYER FOR DEFENSE: And since your marriage you have continued as her sole support, have you not?

YOUNG WOMAN: Yes, sir.

LAWYER FOR DEFENSE: A devoted daughter, gentlemen of the jury! As well as a devoted wife and a devoted mother!

LAWYER FOR PROSECUTION: Your honor!

LAWYER FOR DEFENSE: [*Quickly*] And now, Mrs. Jones, I will ask you—the law expects me to ask you—it demands that I ask you—did you—or did you not—on the night of June 2nd last or the morning of June 3rd last—kill your husband, the late George H. Jones—did you, or did you not?

YOUNG WOMAN: I did not.

LAWYER FOR DEFENSE: You did not?

YOUNG WOMAN: I did not.

LAWYER FOR DEFENSE: Now, Mrs. Jones, you have heard the witnesses for the State—They were not many—and they did not have much to say—

LAWYER FOR PROSECUTION: I object.

JUDGE: Sustained.

LAWYER FOR DEFENSE: You have heard some police and you have heard some doctors. None of whom was present! The prosecution could not furnish any witness to the crime—not one witness!

LAWYER FOR PROSECUTION: Your Honor!

LAWYER FOR DEFENSE: Nor one motive.

LAWYER FOR PROSECUTION: Your Honor—I protest! I—

JUDGE: Sustained.

LAWYER FOR DEFENSE: But such as these witnesses were, you have heard them try to accuse you of deliberately murdering your own husband, this husband with whom, by your own statement, you had never had a quarrel— not one quarrel in six years of married life, murdering him, I say, or rather they say, while he slept, by brutally hitting him over the head with a bottle—a bottle filled with small stones—Did you, I repeat this, or did you not?

YOUNG WOMAN: I did not.

LAWYER FOR DEFENSE: You did not! Of course you did not! [*Quickly*] Now, Mrs. Jones, will you tell the jury in your own words exactly what happened on the night of June 2nd or the morning of June 3rd last, at the time your husband was killed.

YOUNG WOMAN: I was awakened by hearing somebody— something—in the room, and I saw two men standing by my husband's bed.

LAWYER FOR DEFENSE: Your husband's bed—that was also your bed, was it not, Mrs. Jones?

YOUNG WOMAN: Yes.

LAWYER FOR DEFENSE: You hadn't the modern idea of separate beds, had you, Mrs. Jones?

YOUNG WOMAN: Mr. Jones objected.

LAWYER FOR DEFENSE: I mean you slept in the same bed, did you not?

YOUNG WOMAN: Yes.

LAWYER FOR DEFENSE: Then explain just what you meant by saying "my husband's bed."

YOUNG WOMAN: Well—I—

LAWYER FOR DEFENSE: You meant his side of the bed, didn't you?

YOUNG WOMAN: Yes. His side.

LAWYER FOR DEFENSE: That is what I thought, but I wanted the jury to be clear on that point. [*To the* JURY] Mr. and Mrs. Jones slept in the same bed. [*To her*] Go on, Mrs. Jones. [*As she is silent*] You heard a noise and—

YOUNG WOMAN: I heard a noise and I awoke and saw two men standing beside my husband's side of the bed.

LAWYER FOR DEFENSE: Two men?

YOUNG WOMAN: Yes.

LAWYER FOR DEFENSE: Can you describe them?

YOUNG WOMAN: Not very well—I couldn't see them very well.

LAWYER FOR DEFENSE: Could you say whether they were big or small—light or dark, thin or—

YOUNG WOMAN: They were big dark looking men.

LAWYER FOR DEFENSE: Big dark looking men?

YOUNG WOMAN: Yes.

LAWYER FOR DEFENSE: And what did you do, Mrs. Jones, when you suddenly awoke and saw two big dark looking men standing beside your bed?

YOUNG WOMAN: I didn't do anything!

LAWYER FOR DEFENSE: You didn't have time to do anything—did you?

YOUNG WOMAN: No. Before I could do anything—one of them raised—something in his hand and struck Mr. Jones over the head with it.

LAWYER FOR DEFENSE: And what did Mr. Jones do?

[SPECTATORS *laugh*.]

JUDGE: Silence.

BAILIFF: Silence.

LAWYER FOR DEFENSE: What did Mr. Jones do, Mrs. Jones?

YOUNG WOMAN: He gave a sort of groan and tried to raise up.

LAWYER FOR DEFENSE: Tried to raise up!

YOUNG WOMAN: Yes!

LAWYER FOR DEFENSE: And then what happened?

YOUNG WOMAN: The man struck him again and he fell back.

LAWYER FOR DEFENSE: I see. What did the men do then? The big dark looking men.

YOUNG WOMAN: They turned and ran out of the room.

LAWYER FOR DEFENSE: I see. What did you do then, Mrs. Jones?

YOUNG WOMAN: I saw Mr. Jones was bleeding from the temple. I got towels and tried to stop it, and then I realized he had—passed away—

LAWYER FOR DEFENSE: I see. What did you do then?

YOUNG WOMAN: I didn't know what to do. But I thought I'd better call the police. So I went to the telephone and called the police.

LAWYER FOR DEFENSE: What happened then?

YOUNG WOMAN: Nothing. Nothing happened.

LAWYER FOR DEFENSE: The police came, didn't they?

YOUNG WOMAN: Yes—they came.

LAWYER FOR DEFENSE: [*Quickly*] And that is all you know concerning the death of your husband in the late hours of June 2nd or the early hours of June 3rd last, isn't it?

YOUNG WOMAN: Yes sir.

LAWYER FOR DEFENSE: All?

YOUNG WOMAN: Yes sir.

LAWYER FOR DEFENSE: [*To* LAWYER FOR PROSECUTION] Take the witness.

1ST REPORTER [*Writing*] The accused woman told a straightforward story of—

2ND REPORTER: The accused woman told a rambling, disconnected story of—

LAWYER FOR PROSECUTION: You made no effort to cry out, Mrs. Jones, did you, when you saw those two big dark men standing over your helpless husband, did you?

YOUNG WOMAN: No sir. I didn't, I—

LAWYER FOR PROSECUTION: And when they turned and ran out of the room, you made no effort to follow them or cry out after them, did you?

YOUNG WOMAN: No sir.

LAWYER FOR PROSECUTION: Why didn't you?

YOUNG WOMAN: I saw Mr. Jones was hurt.

LAWYER FOR PROSECUTION: Ah! You saw Mr. Jones was hurt! You saw this—how did you see it?

YOUNG WOMAN: I just saw it.

LAWYER FOR PROSECUTION: Then there was a light in the room?

YOUNG WOMAN: A sort of light.

LAWYER FOR PROSECUTION: What do you mean—a sort of light? A bed light?

YOUNG WOMAN: No. No, there was no light on.

LAWYER FOR PROSECUTION: Then where did it come from—this sort of light?

YOUNG WOMAN: I don't know.

LAWYER FOR PROSECUTION: Perhaps—from the window.

YOUNG WOMAN: Yes—from the window.

LAWYER FOR PROSECUTION: Oh, the shade was up!

YOUNG WOMAN: No—no, the shade was down.

LAWYER FOR PROSECUTION: You're sure of that?

YOUNG WOMAN: Yes. Mr. Jones always wanted the shade down.

LAWYER FOR PROSECUTION: The shade was down—there was no light in the room—but the room was light—how do you explain this?

YOUNG WOMAN: I don't know.

LAWYER FOR PROSECUTION: You don't know!

YOUNG WOMAN: I think where the window was open—under the shade—light came in—

LAWYER FOR PROSECUTION: There is a street light there?

YOUNG WOMAN: No—there's no street light.

LAWYER FOR PROSECUTION: Then where did this light come from—that came in under the shade?

YOUNG WOMAN: [*Desperately*] From the moon!

LAWYER FOR PROSECUTION: The moon!

YOUNG WOMAN: Yes! It was bright moon!

LAWYER FOR PROSECUTION: It was bright moon—you are sure of that!

YOUNG WOMAN: Yes.

LAWYER FOR PROSECUTION: How are you sure?

YOUNG WOMAN: I couldn't sleep—I never can sleep in the bright moon. I never can.

LAWYER FOR PROSECUTION: It was bright moon. Yet you

could not see two big dark looking men—but you could see your husband bleeding from the temple.

YOUNG WOMAN: Yes sir.

LAWYER FOR PROSECUTION: And did you call a doctor?

YOUNG WOMAN: No.

LAWYER FOR PROSECUTION: Why didn't you?

YOUNG WOMAN: The police did.

LAWYER FOR PROSECUTION: But you didn't?

YOUNG WOMAN: No.

LAWYER FOR PROSECUTION: Why didn't you? [*No answer*] Why didn't you?

YOUNG WOMAN: [*Whispers*] I saw it was—useless.

LAWYER FOR PROSECUTION: Ah! You saw that! You saw that—very clearly.

YOUNG WOMAN: Yes.

LAWYER FOR PROSECUTION: And you didn't call a doctor.

YOUNG WOMAN: It was—useless.

LAWYER FOR PROSECUTION: What did you do?

YOUNG WOMAN: It was useless—there was no use of anything.

LAWYER FOR PROSECUTION: I asked you what you did?

YOUNG WOMAN: Nothing.

LAWYER FOR PROSECUTION: Nothing!

YOUNG WOMAN: I just sat there.

LAWYER FOR PROSECUTION: You sat there! A long while, didn't you?

YOUNG WOMAN: I don't know.

LAWYER FOR PROSECUTION: You don't know? [*Showing her the neck of a broken bottle*] Mrs. Jones, did you ever see this before?

YOUNG WOMAN: I think so.

LAWYER FOR PROSECUTION: You think so.

YOUNG WOMAN: Yes.

LAWYER FOR PROSECUTION: What do you think it is?

YOUNG WOMAN: I think it's the bottle that was used against Mr. Jones.

LAWYER FOR PROSECUTION: Used against him—yes— that's right. You've guessed right. This neck and these broken pieces and these pebbles were found on the floor and scattered over the bed. There were no fingerprints, Mrs. Jones, on this bottle. None at all. Doesn't that seem strange to you?

YOUNG WOMAN: No.

LAWYER FOR PROSECUTION: It doesn't seem strange to you that this bottle held in the big dark hand of one of those big dark men left no mark! No print! That doesn't seem strange to you?

YOUNG WOMAN: No.

LAWYER FOR PROSECUTION: You are in the habit of wearing rubber gloves at night, Mrs. Jones—are you not? To protect—to soften your hands—are you not?

YOUNG WOMAN: I used to.

LAWYER FOR PROSECUTION: Used to—when was that?

YOUNG WOMAN: Before I was married.

LAWYER FOR PROSECUTION: And after your marriage you gave it up?

YOUNG WOMAN: Yes.

LAWYER FOR PROSECUTION: Why?

YOUNG WOMAN: Mr. Jones did not like the feeling of them.

LAWYER FOR PROSECUTION: You always did everything Mr. Jones wanted?

YOUNG WOMAN: I tried to—Anyway I didn't care any more—so much—about my hands.

LAWYER FOR PROSECUTION: I see—so after your marriage you never wore gloves at night any more?

YOUNG WOMAN: No.

LAWYER FOR PROSECUTION: Mrs. Jones, isn't it true that you began wearing your rubber gloves again—in spite of your husband's expressed dislike—about a year ago—a year ago this spring?

YOUNG WOMAN: No.

LAWYER FOR PROSECUTION: You did not suddenly begin to care particularly for your hands again—about a year ago this spring?

YOUNG WOMAN: No.

LAWYER FOR PROSECUTION: You're quite sure of that?

YOUNG WOMAN: Yes.

LAWYER FOR PROSECUTION: Quite sure?

YOUNG WOMAN: Yes.

LAWYER FOR PROSECUTION: Then you did not have in your possession, on the night of June 2nd last, a pair of rubber gloves?

YOUNG WOMAN: [*Shakes her head*] No.

LAWYER FOR PROSECUTION: [*To* JUDGE] I'd like to introduce these gloves as evidence at this time, your Honor.

JUDGE: Exhibit 24.

LAWYER FOR PROSECUTION: I'll return to them later—now, Mrs. Jones—this nightgown—you recognize it, don't you?

YOUNG WOMAN: Yes.

LAWYER FOR PROSECUTION: Yours, is it not?

YOUNG WOMAN: Yes.

LAWYER FOR PROSECUTION: The one you were wearing the night your husband was murdered, isn't it?

YOUNG WOMAN: The night he died—yes.

LAWYER FOR PROSECUTION: Not the one you wore under your peignoir—I believe that is what you call it, isn't it? A peignoir? When you received the police—but the one you wore before that—isn't it?

YOUNG WOMAN: Yes.

LAWYER FOR PROSECUTION: This was found—not where the gloves were found—no—but at the bottom of the soiled clothes hamper in the bathroom—rolled up and wet—why was it wet, Mrs. Jones?

YOUNG WOMAN: I had tried to wash it.

LAWYER FOR PROSECUTION: Wash it? I thought you had just sat?

YOUNG WOMAN: First—I tried to make things clean.

LAWYER FOR PROSECUTION: Why did you want to make this—clean—as you say?

YOUNG WOMAN: There was blood on it.

LAWYER FOR PROSECUTION: Spattered on it?

YOUNG WOMAN: Yes.

LAWYER FOR PROSECUTION: How did that happen?

YOUNG WOMAN: The bottle broke—and the sharp edge cut!

LAWYER FOR PROSECUTION: Oh, the bottle broke and the sharp edge cut!

YOUNG WOMAN: Yes. That's what they told me afterwards.

LAWYER FOR PROSECUTION: Who told you?

YOUNG WOMAN: The police—that's what they say happened.

LAWYER FOR PROSECUTION: Mrs. Jones, why did you try so desperately to wash that blood away—before you called the police?

LAWYER FOR DEFENSE: I object!

JUDGE: Objection overruled.

LAWYER FOR PROSECUTION: Why, Mrs. Jones?

YOUNG WOMAN: I don't know. It's what anyone would have done, wouldn't they?

LAWYER FOR PROSECUTION: That depends, doesn't it? [*Suddenly taking up bottle*] Mrs. Jones—when did you first see this?

YOUNG WOMAN: The night my husband was—done away with.

LAWYER FOR PROSECUTION: Done away! You mean killed?

YOUNG WOMAN: Yes.

LAWYER FOR PROSECUTION: Why don't you say killed?

YOUNG WOMAN: It sounds so brutal.

LAWYER FOR PROSECUTION: And you never saw this before then?

YOUNG WOMAN: No sir.

LAWYER FOR PROSECUTION: You're quite sure of that?

YOUNG WOMAN: Yes.

LAWYER FOR PROSECUTION: And these stones—when did you first see them?

YOUNG WOMAN: The night my husband was done away with.

LAWYER FOR PROSECUTION: Before that night your husband was murdered—you never saw them? Never before then?

YOUNG WOMAN: No sir.

LAWYER FOR PROSECUTION: You are quite sure of that!

YOUNG WOMAN: Yes.

LAWYER FOR PROSECUTION: Mrs. Jones, do you remember about a year ago, a year ago this spring, bringing home to your house—a lily, a Chinese water lily?

YOUNG WOMAN: No—I don't think I do.

LAWYER FOR PROSECUTION: You don't think you remember bringing home a water lily growing in a bowl filled with small stones?

YOUNG WOMAN: No—No I don't.

LAWYER FOR PROSECUTION: I'll show you this bowl, Mrs. Jones. Does that refresh your memory?

YOUNG WOMAN: I remember the bowl—but I don't remember—the lily.

LAWYER FOR PROSECUTION: It is yours, isn't it?

YOUNG WOMAN: It was in my house—yes.

LAWYER FOR PROSECUTION: How did it come there?

YOUNG WOMAN: How did it come there?

LAWYER FOR PROSECUTION: Yes—where did you get it?

YOUNG WOMAN: I don't remember.

LAWYER FOR PROSECUTION: You don't remember?

YOUNG WOMAN: No.

LAWYER FOR PROSECUTION: You don't remember about a year ago bringing this bowl into your bedroom filled with small stones and some water and a lily? You don't remember tending very carefully that lily till it died? And when it died you don't remember hiding the bowl full of little stones away on the top shelf of your closet— and keeping it there until—you don't remember?

YOUNG WOMAN: No, I don't remember.

LAWYER FOR PROSECUTION: You may have done so?

YOUNG WOMAN: No—no—I didn't! I didn't! I don't know anything about all that.

LAWYER FOR PROSECUTION: But you do remember the bowl?

YOUNG WOMAN: Yes. It was in my house—you found it in my house.

LAWYER FOR PROSECUTION: But you don't remember the lily or the stones?

YOUNG WOMAN: No—No I don't!

[LAWYER FOR PROSECUTION *turns to look among his papers in a brief case.*]

1ST REPORTER [*Writing*] Under the heavy artillery fire of the State's attorney's brilliant cross-questioning, the accused woman's defense was badly riddled. Pale and trembling she—

2ND REPORTER [*Writing*] Undaunted by the Prosecution's machine-gun attack, the defendant was able to maintain her position of innocence in the face of rapid-fire questioning that threatened, but never seriously menaced her defense. Flushed but calm she—

LAWYER FOR PROSECUTION: [*Producing paper*] Your Honor, I'd like to introduce this paper in evidence at this time.

JUDGE: What is it?

LAWYER FOR PROSECUTION: It is an affidavit taken in the State of Guanajuato, Mexico.

LAWYER FOR DEFENSE: Mexico? Your Honor, I protest. A Mexican affidavit! Is this the United States of America or isn't it?

LAWYER FOR PROSECUTION: It's properly executed—sworn to before a notary—and certified to by an American Consul.

LAWYER FOR DEFENSE: Your Honor! I protest! In the name of this great United States of America—I protest—are we to permit our sacred institutions to be thus—

JUDGE What is the purpose of this document—who signed it?

LAWYER FOR PROSECUTION: It is signed by one Richard Roe, and its purpose is to refresh the memory of the witness on the point at issue—and incidentally supply a motive for this murder—this brutal and cold-blooded murder of a sleeping man by—

LAWYER FOR DEFENSE: I protest, your Honor! I object!

JUDGE: Objection sustained. Let me see the document. [*Takes paper which is handed up to him—looks at it.*] Perfectly regular. Do you offer this affidavit as evidence at this time for the purpose of refreshing the memory of the witness at this time?

LAWYER FOR PROSECUTION: Yes, your Honor.

JUDGE: You may introduce the evidence.

LAWYER FOR DEFENSE: I object! I object to the introduction of this evidence at this time as irrelevant, immaterial, illegal, biased, prejudicial, and—

JUDGE: Objection overruled.

LAWYER FOR DEFENSE: Exception.

JUDGE: Exception noted. Proceed.

LAWYER FOR PROSECUTION: I wish to read the evidence to the jury at this time.

JUDGE: Proceed.

LAWYER FOR DEFENSE: I object.

JUDGE: Objection overruled.

LAWYER FOR DEFENSE: Exception.

JUDGE: Noted.

LAWYER FOR DEFENSE: Why is this witness himself not brought into court—so he can be cross-questioned?

LAWYER FOR PROSECUTION: The witness is a resident of the Republic of Mexico and as such not subject to subpoena as a witness to this court.

LAWYER FOR DEFENSE: If he was out of the jurisdiction of this court how did you get this affidavit out of him?

LAWYER FOR PROSECUTION: This affidavit was made voluntarily by the deponent in the furtherance of justice.

LAWYER FOR DEFENSE: I suppose you didn't threaten him with extradition on some other trumped-up charge so that—

JUDGE: Order!

BAILIFF: Order!

JUDGE: Proceed with the evidence.

LAWYER FOR PROSECUTION: [*Reading*] In the matter of the State of——vs. Helen Jones, I Richard Roe, being of sound mind, do herein depose and state that I know the accused, Helen Jones, and have known her for a period of over one year immediately preceding the date of the signature on this affidavit. That I first met the said Helen Jones in a so-called speakeasy somewhere in the West 40s in New York City. That on the day I met her, she went with me to my room, also somewhere in the West 40s in New York City, where we had intimate relations—

YOUNG WOMAN: [*Moans*] Oh!

LAWYER FOR PROSECUTION: [*Continues reading*] —and where I gave her a blue bowl filled with pebbles, also containing a flowering lily. That from the first day we met until I departed for Mexico in the fall, the said Helen Jones was an almost daily visitor to my room where we continued to—

YOUNG WOMAN: No! No!

[*Moans*]

LAWYER FOR PROSECUTION: What is it, Mrs. Jones—what is it?

YOUNG WOMAN: Don't read any more! No more!

LAWYER FOR PROSECUTION: Why not?

YOUNG WOMAN: I did it! I did it! I did it!

LAWYER FOR PROSECUTION: You confess?

YOUNG WOMAN: Yes—I did it!

LAWYER FOR DEFENSE: I object, your Honor.

JUDGE: You confess you killed your husband?

YOUNG WOMAN: I put him out of the way—yes.

JUDGE: Why?

YOUNG WOMAN: To be free.

JUDGE: To be free? Is that the only reason?

YOUNG WOMAN: Yes.

JUDGE: If you just wanted to be free—why didn't you divorce him?

YOUNG WOMAN: Oh I couldn't do that!! I couldn't hurt him like that!

[*Burst of laughter from all in the court. The* YOUNG WOMAN *stares out at them, and then seems to go rigid.*]

JUDGE: Silence!

BAILIFF: Silence!

[*There is a gradual silence.*]

JUDGE: Mrs. Jones, why— [YOUNG WOMAN *begins to moan—suddenly—as though the realization of the enormity of her isolation had just come upon her. It is a sound of desolation, of agony, of human woe. It continues until the end of the scene.*] Why—?

[YOUNG WOMAN *cannot speak.*]

LAWYER FOR DEFENSE: Your Honor, I ask a recess to—

JUDGE: Court's adjourned.

[SPECTATORS *begin to file out. The* YOUNG WOMAN *continues in the witness box, unseeing, unheeding.*]

1ST REPORTER: Murderess confesses.

2ND REPORTER: Paramour brings confession.

3RD REPORTER: I did it! Woman cries!

[*There is a great burst of speed from the telegraphic instruments. They keep up a constant accompaniment to the* WOMAN's *moans. The scene blacks out as the courtroom empties and two policemen go to stand by the woman. The sound of the telegraph instruments continues until the scene lights into Episode Nine— and the prayers of the* PRIEST.]

EPISODE NINE

A Machine

SCENE:
a prison room. The front bars face the audience. They are set back far enough to permit a clear passageway across the stage.

SOUNDS:
the voice of a NEGRO singing; the whir of an aeroplane flying.

CHARACTERS:
YOUNG WOMAN,
A PRIEST,
A JAILER,
TWO BARBERS,
A MATRON,
MOTHER,
TWO GUARDS.

AT RISE:
in front of the bars, at one side, sits a MAN; at the opposite side, a WOMAN—the JAILER and the MATRON.

Inside the bars, a MAN and a WOMAN—the YOUNG WOMAN and a PRIEST. The YOUNG WOMAN sits still with folded hands. The PRIEST is praying.

PRIEST: Hear, oh Lord, my prayer; and let my cry come to Thee. Turn not away Thy face from me; in the day when I am in trouble, incline Thy ear to me. In what

day soever I shall call upon Thee, hear me speedily.
For my days are vanished like smoke; and my bones
are grown dry, like fuel for the fire. I am smitten as
grass, and my heart is withered; because I forgot to eat
my bread. Through the voice of my groaning, my bone
hath cleaved to my flesh. I am become like to a pelican
of the wilderness. I am like a night raven in the house.
I have watched and become as a sparrow all alone on
the housetop. All the day long my enemies reproach
me; and they that praised me did swear against me. My
days have declined like a shadow, and I am withered
like grass. But Thou, oh Lord, end rest forever. Thou
shalt arise and have mercy, for it is time to have mercy.
The time is come.

[*Voice of* NEGRO *offstage—Begins to sing a Negro spiritual*]

PRIEST: The Lord hath looked upon the earth, that He
might hear the groans of them that are in fetters, that
He might release the children of—

[*Voice of* NEGRO *grown louder.*]

JAILER: Stop that nigger yelling.

YOUNG WOMAN: No, let him sing. He helps me.

MATRON: You can't hear the Father.

YOUNG WOMAN: He helps me.

PRIEST: Don't I help you, daughter?

YOUNG WOMAN: I understand him. He is condemned. I
understand him.

[*The voice of the* NEGRO *goes on louder, drowning out
the voice of the* PRIEST.]

PRIEST: [*Chanting in Latin*] Gratiam tuum, quaesumus,
Domine, metibus nostris infunde, ut qui, angelo nuntiante, Christifilii tui incarnationem cognovimus, per
passionem eius et crucem ad ressurectionis gloriam
perducamus. Per eudem Christum Dominum nostrum.

[*Enter* TWO BARBERS. *There is a rattling of keys.*]

1ST BARBER: How is she?

MATRON: Calm.

JAILER: Quiet.

YOUNG WOMAN: [*Rising*] I am ready.

1ST BARBER: Then sit down.

YOUNG WOMAN: [*In a steady voice*] Aren't you the death
guard come to take me?

1ST BARBER: No, we ain't the death guard. We're the barbers.

YOUNG WOMAN: The barbers.

MATRON: Your hair must be cut.

JAILER: Must be shaved.

BARBER: Just a patch. [*The* BARBERS *draw near her.*]

YOUNG WOMAN: No!

PRIEST: Daughter, you're ready. You know you are ready.

YOUNG WOMAN: [*Crying out*] Not for this! Not for this!

MATRON: The rule.

JAILER: Regulations.

BARBER: Routine. [*The* BARBERS *take her by the arms.*]

YOUNG WOMAN: No! No! Don't touch me—touch me! [*They take her and put her down in the chair, cut a patch from her hair.*] I will not be submitted—this indignity! No! I will not be submitted!—Leave me alone! Oh my God am I never to be let alone! Always to have to submit—to submit! No more—not now—I'm going to die—I won't submit! Not now!

BARBER: [*Finishing cutting a patch from her hair*] You'll submit, my lady. Right to the end, you'll submit! There, and a neat job too.

JAILER: Very neat.

MATRON: Very neat.

[*Exit* BARBERS.]

YOUNG WOMAN: [*Her calm shattered*] Father, Father! Why was I born?

PRIEST: I came forth from the Father and have come into the world—I leave the world and go into the Father.

YOUNG WOMAN: [*Weeping*] Submit! Submit! Is nothing mine? The hair on my head! The very hair on my head—

PRIEST: Praise God.

YOUNG WOMAN: Am I never to be let alone! Never to have peace! When I'm dead, won't I have peace?

PRIEST: Ye shall indeed drink of my cup.

YOUNG WOMAN: Won't I have peace tomorrow?

PRIEST: I shall raise Him up at the last day.

YOUNG WOMAN: Tomorrow! Father! Where shall I be tomorrow?

PRIEST: Behold the hour cometh. Yea, is now come. Ye shall be scattered every man to his own.

YOUNG WOMAN: In Hell! Father! Will I be in Hell?

PRIEST: I am the Resurrection and the Life.

YOUNG WOMAN: Life has been Hell to me, Father!

PRIEST: Life has been Hell to you, daughter, because you never knew God! Gloria in excelsis Deo.

YOUNG WOMAN: How could I know Him, Father? He never was around me.

PRIEST: You didn't seek Him, daughter. Seek and ye shall find.

YOUNG WOMAN: I sought something—I was always seeking something.

PRIEST: What? What were you seeking?

YOUNG WOMAN: Peace. Rest and peace. Will I find it tonight, Father? Will I find it?

PRIEST: Trust in God.

[*A shadow falls across the passage in the front of the stage—and there is a shirring sound.*]

YOUNG WOMAN: What is that? Father! Jailer! What is that?

JAILER: An aeroplane.

MATRON: Aeroplane.

PRIEST: God in His Heaven.

YOUNG WOMAN: Look, Father! A man flying! He has wings! But he is not an angel!

JAILER: Hear his engine.

MATRON: Hear the engine.

YOUNG WOMAN: He has wings—but he isn't free! I've been free, Father! For one moment—down here on earth—I have been free! When I did what I did I was free! Free and not afraid! How is that, Father? How can that be? A great sin—a mortal sin—for which I must die and go to Hell—but it made me free! One moment I was free! How is that, Father? Tell me that?

PRIEST: Your sins are forgiven.

YOUNG WOMAN: And that other sin—that other sin—that sin of love—That's all I ever knew of Heaven—Heaven on earth! How is that, Father? How can that be—a sin— a mortal sin—all I know of Heaven?

PRIEST: Confess to Almighty God.

YOUNG WOMAN: Oh, Father, pray for me—a prayer—that I can understand!

PRIEST: I will pray for you, daughter, the prayer of desire.
Behind the King of Heaven, behold Thy Redeemer and
God, Who is even now coming; prepare thyself to receive Him with love, invite Him with the ardor of thy
desire; come, oh my Jesus, come to thy soul which desires Thee! Before Thou givest Thyself to me, I desire
to give Thee my miserable heart. Do Thou accept it,
and come quickly to take possession of it! Come my
God, hasten! Delay no longer! My only and Infinite
Good, my Treasure, my Life, my Paradise, my Love,
my all, my wish is to receive Thee with the love with
which—

[*Enter the* MOTHER. *She comes along the passageway
and stops before the bars.*]

YOUNG WOMAN: [*Recoiling*] Who's that woman?

JAILER: Your mother.

MATRON: Your mother.

YOUNG WOMAN: She's a stranger—take her away—she's
a stranger.

JAILER: She's come to say goodbye to you—

MATRON: To say goodbye.

YOUNG WOMAN: But she's never known me—never known
me—ever— [*To the* MOTHER] Go away! You're a
stranger! Stranger! Stranger! [MOTHER *turns and starts
away. Reaching out her hands to her.*] Oh Mother!
Mother!

[*They embrace through the bars. Enter two* GUARDS.]

PRIEST: Come, daughter.

1ST GUARD: It's time.

2ND GUARD: Time.

YOUNG WOMAN: Wait! Mother, my child; my little strange
child! I never knew her! She'll never know me! Let her
live, Mother. Let her live! Live! Tell her—

PRIEST: Come, daughter.

YOUNG WOMAN: Wait! wait! Tell her—

[*The* JAILER *takes the* MOTHER *away.*]

1st GUARD: It's time.

YOUNG WOMAN: Wait! Wait! Tell her! Wait! Just a minute
more! There's so much I want to tell her—Wait—

[*The* JAILER *takes the* MOTHER *off. The two* GUARDS
take the YOUNG WOMAN *by the arms, and start through
the door in the bars and down the passage, across stage*

and off. The PRIEST *follows; the* MATRON *follows the*
PRIEST; the PRIEST *is praying. The scene blacks out.*
The voice of the PRIEST *gets dimmer and*
dimmer.]

PRIEST: Lord have mercy—Christ have mercy—Lord
have mercy—Christ hear us! God the Father of Heaven!
God the Son, Redeemer of the World, God the Holy
Ghost—Holy Trinity one God—Holy Mary—Holy
Mother of God—Holy Virgin of Virgins—St. Michael—
St. Gabriel—St. Raphael—

[*His voice dies out. Out of the darkness come the*
voices of REPORTERS.]

1ST REPORTER: What time is it now?

2ND REPORTER: Time now.

3RD REPORTER: Hush.

1ST REPORTER: Here they come.

3RD REPORTER: Hush.

PRIEST: [*His voice sounds dimly—gets louder—continues*
until the end.] St. Peter pray for us—St. Paul pray for
us—St. James pray for us—St. John pray for us—all ye
holy Angels and Archangels—all ye blessed orders of
holy spirits—St. Joseph—St. John the Baptist—St.
Thomas—

1ST REPORTER: Here they are!

2ND REPORTER: How little she looks! She's gotten smaller.

3RD REPORTER: Hush.

PRIEST: St. Phillip pray for us. All ye Holy Patriarchs and
prophets—St. Phillip—St. Matthew—St. Simon—St.
Thaddeus—All ye holy apostles—all ye holy disci-
ples—all ye holy innocents—Pray for us—Pray for us—
Pray for us—

1ST REPORTER: Suppose the machine shouldn't work!

2ND REPORTER: It'll work!—It always works!—

3RD REPORTER: Hush!

PRIEST: Saints of God make intercession for us—Be merciful—Spare us, oh Lord—be merciful—

1ST REPORTER: Her lips are moving—what is she saying?

2ND REPORTER: Nothing.

3RD REPORTER: Hush!

PRIEST: Oh Lord deliver us from all evil—from all sin—
from Thy wrath—from the snares of the devil—from
anger and hatred and every evil will—from—

1ST REPORTER: Did you see that? She fixed her hair under the cap—pulled her hair out under the cap.

3RD REPORTER: Hush!

PRIEST: —Beseech Thee—hear us—that Thou would'st
spare us—that Thou would'st pardon us—Holy Mary—
pray for us—

2ND REPORTER: There—

YOUNG WOMAN: [*Calling out*] Somebody! Somebod—
[*Her voice is cut off.*]

PRIEST: Christ have mercy—Lord have mercy—Christ
have mercy—

CURTAIN

Selected Bibliography

Abrahamson, Irving. "The Career of Rachel Crothers in the American Drama." Dissertation, University of Chicago, 1956.

Akins, Zoë. *Déclassée: Daddy's Gone A-Hunting:* and *Greatness—A Comedy*. New York: Boni and Liveright, 1923.

———. *The Old Maid*. New York: Appleton-Century, 1935.

Anthony, Katharine. *First Lady of the Revolution: The Life of Mercy Otis Warren*. Garden City, New York: Doubleday, 1958.

Barnes, Eric Wollencott. *The Lady of Fashion: The Life and the Theatre of Anna Cora Mowatt*. New York: Scribner's, 1954.

Brown, Alice. *Children of Earth*. New York: Macmillan, 1915.

———. *Mercy Warren*. New York: Scribner's, 1896.

———. *One Act Plays*. New York: Macmillan, 1921.

Cook, George Cram, and Frank Shay, eds. *The Provincetown Plays*. Cincinnati: Stewart Kidd, 1921.

Cordell, Kathryn Coe, and William H. Cordell, eds. *The Pulitzer Prize Plays 1918–1934*. New York: Random House, 1935.

Crothers, Rachel. *As Husbands Go*. New York: Samuel French, 1931.

———. *He and She*. In *Representative American Plays*. Edited by Arthur Hobson Quinn. 6th ed., rev. New York: Appleton-Century, 1938, pp. 891–928.

———. *Mary the Third*. In *Modern American and British Plays*. Edited by S. Marion Tucker. New York: Harper, 1931, pp. 503–39.

———. *Nice People*. In *Representative American Dramas*. Edited by Montrose J. Moses. Boston: Little, Brown, 1925, pp. 447–88.

———. *Six One-Act Plays*. Boston: Baker, 1925.

———. *Susan and God*. New York: Random House, 1938.

———. *When Ladies Meet*. New York: Samuel French, 1932.

Derleth, August. *Still Small Voice: The Biography of Zona Gale*. New York: Appleton-Century, 1940.

Deutsch, Helen, and Stella Hanau. *The Provincetown*. New York: Farrar & Rinehart, 1931.

Eaton, Walter Prichard. *At the New Theatre and Others*. Boston: Small, Maynard, 1910.

Ferguson, Phyllis Marschall. "Women Dramatists in the American Theatre, 1901–1940." Dissertation, University of Pittsburgh, 1957.

Flexner, Anne Crawford. *The Marriage Game*. New York: Huebsch, 1916.

Frame, Virginia. "Women Who Have Written Successful Plays." *Theatre Magazine*, 6 (October 1906), 264–7, ix–x.

France, Rachel, ed. *A Century of Plays by American Women*. New York: Richards Rosen, 1979.

Gale, Zona. *Birth*. New York: Macmillan, 1918.

———. *Faint Perfume*. New York: Appleton, 1923. [novel]

———. *Faint Perfume*. New York: Samuel French, 1934. [play]

———. *Mister Pitt*. New York: Appleton, 1925.

Gerstenberg, Alice. *Ten One-Act Plays*. New York: Brentano's, 1921.

Glaspell, Susan. *Alison's House*. In *The Pulitzer Prize Plays 1918–1934*. Edited by Kathryn Coe Cordell and William H. Cordell. New York: Random House, 1935, pp. 649–91.

———. *Inheritors*. Boston: Small, Maynard, 1921.

———. *Plays*. Boston: Small, Maynard, 1920.

———. *The Road to the Temple*. New York: Frederick A. Stokes, 1927.

———. *The Verge*. Boston: Small, Maynard, 1922.

Gottlieb, Lois C. *Rachel Crothers*. Boston: Twayne, 1979.

Harrison, James A., ed. *Complete Works of Edgar Allan Poe*. Vol. 12. New York: Fred de Fau, 1902.

Howard, Sidney. *The Silver Cord*. In *Representative American Plays*. Edited by Arthur Hobson Quinn. 6th ed., rev. New York: Appleton-Century, 1938, pp. 1011–58.

Kelly, George. *Craig's Wife*. In *The Pulitzer Prize Plays 1918–1934*. Edited by Kathryn Coe Cordell and William H. Cordell. New York: Random House, 1935, pp. 317–79.

Kummer, Clare. *Good Gracious, Annabelle*. New York: Samuel French, 1922.

Mersand, Joseph. *When Ladies Write Plays*. New York: The Modern Chapbooks, 1937.

Millay, Edna St. Vincent. "Aria da Capo." In *Twenty-Five Best Plays of the Modern American Theatre: Early Series*. Edited by John Gassner. New York: Crown, 1949, pp. 712–20.

———. *The Princess Marries the Page*. New York: Harper, 1932.

Moore, Honor, ed. *The New Women's Theatre*. New York: Random House, 1977.

Morton, Martha. *A Bachelor's Romance*. New York: Samuel French, 1912.

Mowatt, Anna Cora. *Autobiography of an Actress*. Boston: Ticknor, Reed, & Fields, 1854.

Nichols, Anne. *Abie's Irish Rose*. New York: Samuel French, 1924.

Peabody, Josephine Preston. *The Piper*. Boston: Houghton Mifflin, 1909.

Pierce, Lucy France. "Women Who Write Plays." *The World To-day*, 15 (June 1908), 725–31.

Quinn, Arthur Hobson. *A History of the American Drama from the Beginning to the Civil War*. 2nd ed. New York: Appleton-Century-Crofts, 1943.

———. *A History of the American Drama from the Civil War to the Present Day*. Rev. ed. New York: Appleton-Century-Crofts, 1936.

Rice, Elmer. *The Adding Machine*. In *Three Plays*. New York: Hill and Wang, 1965.

Rich, Adrienne. "The Problem With Lorraine Hansberry." *Freedomways*, 19 (1979), 247–55.

Rowson, Susanna. *Slaves in Algiers*. Philadelphia: Wrigley & Berriman, 1794.

Simonson, Harold P. *Zona Gale*. New York: Twayne, 1962.

Sullivan, Victoria, and James Hatch, eds. *Plays By and About Women*. New York: Random House, 1973.

Sutherland, Cynthia. "American Women Playwrights as Mediators of the 'Woman Problem.'" *Modern Drama*, 21(September 1978), 319–36.

Thomas, Augustus. *As a Man Thinks*. In *Modern American Plays*. Edited by George P. Baker. New York: Harcourt Brace, 1920, pp. 1–100.

Treadwell, Sophie. *Hope for a Harvest*. New York: Samuel French, 1942.

Warren, Mercy Otis. *The Group* (1779). Ann Arbor: William L. Clements Library, University of Michigan, 1953.

Waterman, Arthur E. *Susan Glaspell*. New York: Twayne, 1966.

Watkins, Maurine. *Chicago*. New York: Knopf, 1927.

Weales, Gerald. "The Quality of Mercy, or Mrs. Warren's Profession." *The Georgia Review*, 33 (Winter 1979), 881–94.

Weil, Dorothy. *In Defense of Women: Susanna Rowson (1762–1824)*. University Park: Pennsylvania State University Press, 1976.

"Where Are the Women Playwrights?" *New York Times*, May 20, 1973, Sec. 2, pp. 1 & 3.

The Theatre Research Collection of the New York Public Library at Lincoln Center has extensive clipping files on *A Man's World*, *Miss Lulu Bett*, and *Machinal*.

◢ BARD BOOKS
DISTINGUISHED DRAMA

AVON Paperback

BDD 1-81